Drug Treatment: What Works?

Britain, like almost everywhere else, has a burgeoning drug problem. Finding ways of dealing with this problem is a major platform of government policy and a great deal has been made of the impact of treatment on drug users. *Drug Treatment: What Works?* Is a cutting-edge survey of the latest developments in these treatments, and it sets out to ask some of the crucial questions in the treatment of drug abusers; including:

- Which treatments work with what sorts of abusers?
- What are the key indicators of likely success?
- Does coercion work or must treatment be freely entered into?
- Is drug testing an essential backup for successful treatment?

Featuring contributions from some the leading figures in this field, *Drug Treatment: What Works?* will be essential reading for students, academics and professionals studying drug treatment in the areas of criminology, social policy and medicine.

Philip Bean is (Emeritus) Professor of Criminology and formerly Director of the Midland Centre for Criminology and Criminal Justice at Loughborough University.

Teresa Nemitz was formerly a Research Fellow and Part-time lecturer at Loughborough University.

Drug Treatment:
What Works?

**Edited by Philip Bean
and Teresa Nemitz**

Routledge
Taylor & Francis Group

LONDON AND NEW YORK

First published 2004 by Routledge
2 Park Square, Milton Park, Abingdon, Oxon, OX14 4RN

Simultaneously published in the USA and Canada
by Routledge
29 West 35th Street, New York, NY 10001

Routledge is an imprint of the Taylor & Francis Group

© 2004 Philip Bean and Teresa Nemitz

Typeset in by Garamond by Taylor & Francis Books Ltd

Printed and bound in Great Britain by TJ International Ltd,
Padstow, Cornwall

British Library Cataloguing in Publication Data

A catalogue record for this book is available from the British Library

Library of Congress Cataloging in Publication Data (to follow)

ISBN 0–415–26816–8 (hbk)
ISBN 0–415–26817–6 (pbk)

Contents

List of illustrations

Contributors

Tammy L. Anderson received her PhD in sociology: justice at the American University in December 1991. She is currently an Assistant Professor and Ethnographer in the Department of Sociology and Criminal Justice at the University of Delaware. Her research interests focus on substance abuse aetiology, drug-related identity change and career pathways, social welfare programmes and substance abuse, HIV risk among older injectors, health issues among substance abusers, and race and gender differences in the drugs experience. She has published more than twenty papers on these topics. Dr Anderson's research has been funded by the National Science Foundation, the National Institute on Drug Abuse, the Robert Wood Johnson Foundation and the National Institute on Aging.

Philip Bean is Professor of Criminology (Emeritus) and was formerly Director of the Midlands Centre for Criminology at the University of Loughborough (1990–2003). He is the author/editor of a number of books and papers published in learned journals, mainly concentrating on drugs and crime and mental disorder and crime. His most recent publications are *Drugs and Crime* (2nd edition, Willan Publishing, 2004) and *Crime; Critical Concepts* (ed., four vols, Routledge, 2003). A forthcoming book entitled *Madness, Crime and Compulsion* is to be published by Willan Publishing in 2005. He has held Visiting Professorships in Canada, the USA and Australia. From 1996 to 1999 he was President of the British Society of Criminology. He is currently an Associate of the General Medical Council.

Helen Bourne is a Research Psychologist in north Nottinghamshire. She holds a degree in applied social studies from Sheffield Hallam University. Her research interests include the comorbidity of substance misuse and mental health disorders, and the management and treatment of patients in the community with personality disorder. She is currently working with staff at Leicester University to help coordinate a major study of a treatment for personality disorder in the Trent region that includes a multi-site, randomised controlled trial.

Colin Brewer qualified in medicine at St Bartholomew's Hospital, London, in 1963 and after a short period in general practice and as a ship's surgeon, specialised in psychiatry. From the early 1970s he developed a special interest in addiction treatment. He was successively lecturer and research fellow at Birmingham University and director of the alcoholism service at Westminster Hospital 1980–6. In 1987 he founded the Stapleford Centre, a private, research-based, mainly outpatient treatment centre in London. He now concentrates on research and writing and his interests include rapid opiate detoxification techniques, oral and implanted naltrexone, disulfiram, methadone maintenance, hair testing for drugs of abuse and probation-linked treatments for offenders who abuse alcohol and other drugs.

John A. Carver's career has been devoted to public administration and justice system improvement. After graduating from Georgetown University Law Center, he served as Deputy Director then Director of the District of Columbia Pretrial Services Agency, an organisation nationally recognised as a pioneer in bail reform. In 1984 the Pretrial Services Agency became the first in the United States to establish comprehensive on-site pretrial drug testing of all arrestees, a programme that was expanded to the juvenile justice system two years later. In 1994 the Agency and the DC Superior Court launched a drug court demonstration project with an experimental evaluation design to measure the impact of drug treatment, drug testing and immediate sanctions. In 1997 Jay Carver was appointed by the Attorney General to lead the consolidation and reorganisation of the District of Columbia's pretrial, probation and parole systems. As head of the Court Services and Offender Supervision Agency, he directed a massive revitalisation of the offender supervision infrastructure, with particular emphasis on the expansion of the Agency's on-site drug testing capabilities.

Joris Casselman studied medicine, psychiatry, psychology, sexology and obtained a PhD in criminology at the Catholic University of Leuven (Belgium). He followed a postgraduate course in community psychiatry at Dingleton Hospital, Melrose (Scotland), and a postgraduate course in substance-related problems and forensic psychiatry at the University of Geneva (Switzerland). He is currently Associate Professor in forensic mental health care at the Faculty of Medicine (Department of Psychiatry) and at the Faculty of Law (Department of Criminology) of the Catholic University of Leuven (Belgium). His publications and research are situated within the interface between the mental health system and the administration of justice, with a special interest in alcohol- and other drug-related problems.

Ken Checinski is Senior Lecturer in Addictive Behaviour, St George's Hospital Medical School, London. He trained in Cambridge and London and has published and lectured widely on addiction treatment issues, specialising in dual diagnosis. He is a consultant for NHS substance misuse services in Surrey and has developed and implemented a number of innovative therapeutic approaches.

David Farabee is Associate Research Psychologist and Director of the Juvenile Justice Research Group at UCLA Integrated Substance Abuse Programs. He previously served as lead analyst for criminal justice research at the Texas Commission on Alcohol and Drug Abuse (1992–5) and as Assistant Professor of Psychiatry and Research Scientist at the University of Kentucky Center on Drug and Alcohol Research (1995–7). He is currently leading studies of substance abuse, medication adherence and criminality among mentally ill parolees; and a statewide programme to transition mentally ill inmates back into the community. He also is a member of the Advisory Committee on HIV and STD Prevention for the US Centers for Disease Control and Prevention. His research interests include substance abuse, crime, HIV/AIDS and offender treatment. He is co-editor of *Treatment of Drug Offenders* (2002) and *The Offender Substance Abuse Report*, a bimonthly report published by the Civic Research Institute.

Hamid Ghodse studied at St Bartholomew's Medical School for his PhD and undertook further specialist training at the Institute of Psychiatry, University of London. He is Professor of Psychiatry and Director of the International Centre for Drug Policy at St George's Hospital Medical School, University of London. He is author of numerous scientific papers in learned and professional journals. His definitive textbook *Drugs and Addictive Behaviour: A Guide to Treatment* (3rd edn), his textbook/reference book on legal aspects of drugs and criminal justice (also in its third edition), as well as his book on the rational use of controlled drugs, which has been translated into eight languages, are all widely used.

Michael Gossop is a professor and Head of Research in the Addictions Directorate at the Maudsley Hospital in London, and a leading researcher in the National Addiction Centre at the London University Institute of Psychiatry. He is the Director of NTORS, the National Treatment Outcome Research Study. He is the founding editor of *Addiction Abstracts*, and his publications include seven books and more than 300 articles.

Lana Harrison received her PhD in sociology from the University of Michigan in 1988. She is the Associate Director of the Center for Drug and Alcohol Studies at the University of Delaware, overseeing a staff of about thirty research professionals, and an Associate Professor in the Department of Sociology and Criminal Justice. She is currently the Principal Investigator of two National Institutes of Health (NIH) studies and Co-Principal Investigator on another. Previously, Dr Harrison was employed at the National Institute on Drug Abuse and the National Institute of Justice, and has worked on three of the nation's largest epidemiological drug studies.

Her research interests centre on drug epidemiology, treatment alternatives, improving survey methodology, comparative international research, and drug policy. She has authored or coauthored over fifty publications in these areas.

Paul Hayes has been Chief Executive of the National Treatment Agency (NTA) since its creation in 2001. As Chief Executive Paul advises ministers and senior officials in the Department of Health and Home Office about all issues to do with the provision of drug treatment in England. He is the lead adviser to the NTA Board, which is responsible for shaping the NTA's strategic direction, and leads the Senior Management Team in implementing the agency's work programme. Prior to joining the NTA Paul worked for the Probation Service for over twenty years.

Muhammad Z. Iqbal qualified in medicine from the University of the Punjab in Lahore, Pakistan, and after initially working in that country undertook further training at Guy's Hospital in London and in Sheffield. He is now a Consultant Psychiatrist in Dudley, West Midlands, with a particular remit for providing dual diagnosis services. He has investigated comorbidities along with his coauthors in this book in a project under the auspices of Imperial College, University of London, and has also undertaken a series of studies of methadone pharmacokinetics.

Douglas Longshore is Principal Investigator and Associate Director at the UCLA Integrated Substance Abuse Programs (UCLA–ISAP) and Adjunct Senior Behavioral Scientist at RAND. He has published extensively in the field of motivation for drug abuse treatment and recovery, ethnic/cultural factors in drug abuse and culturally appropriate intervention. He has led numerous evaluations of community-based interventions for drug-using offenders. His research team designed and conducted a randomised field trial of a culture-based motivational intervention targeting African-American heroin and cocaine users in South Central Los Angeles. The intervention was successful in raising motivation for drug abstinence at post-test and curbing drug use, as indicated by self-report and urine testing, at a one-year follow-up.

Joy Mott worked for the Home Office from January 1962 until she retired in 1994. For most of this time she was responsible for carrying out research on the social and criminal characteristics of drug misusers, for commissioning external research on these topics, and for providing advice on research findings to administrators and working groups of the Advisory Council on the Misuse of Drugs. She has published numerous papers on drug misuse and crime and reported the findings of the 1992 British Crime Survey, which provided the first national estimates of drug misuse in England and Wales. Since her retirement she has prepared the report of a working group of the Mental Health Foundation on street drinkers and later acted as the research secretary to the Police Foundation's independent enquiry into the Misuse of Drugs Act 1971, published as 'Drugs and the Law' in 2000. She then edited H. B. Spear's book *Heroin Care and Control: the British System 1916 to 1984* (2002). She is presently a Honorary Senior Research Fellow at Imperial College, assisting on a project on heroin prescribing to addicts.

Teresa Nemitz was formerly a Research Fellow and Part Time Lecturer in Criminology at Loughborough University. She retired in September 2003. She lectured mainly on Women and Crime but her research interests were wider, centring around mental disorder and crime, particularly concerning the use of the appropriate adult and informers. She has published widely; her recent publications include *Informers, Police Policy and Practice* (ed., with Philip Bean and Roger Billingsley). She was Secretary and later Chair of the Midlands Branch of the British Society of Criminology over a ten-year period, and national administrator from 1996 to 2001.

Michael L. Prendergast is Director of the Criminal Justice Research Group at UCLA Integrated Substance Abuse Programs. He has been involved in various aspects of substance abuse research for over twenty years. He has been director or principal investigator of studies of drug treatment strategies in the criminal justice system, including a process and outcome evaluation of the Forever Free Treatment Program at the California Institution for Women. He now leads a study of sixteen treatment programmes within the California prison system, five of which involve twelve-month follow-ups with treatment and matched comparison groups. He is conducting a five-year longitudinal follow-up study of inmates who participated in the evaluation of the Amity Treatment Program at the R. J. Donovan Correctional Facility and a randomised trial of the use of vouchers within a drug court treatment programme to promote abstinence and prosocial behaviours. He is Principal Investigator of one of the seven research centres of NIDA's Criminal Justice Drug Abuse Treatment System. He is also Co-Principal Investigator of the statewide evaluation of California's Substance Abuse and Crime Prevention Act (Proposition 36). He has published meta-analyses of the effectiveness of drug abuse treatment. His research interests include treatment effectiveness, research syntheses, treatment policy, issues in coerced treatment, and treatment for drug-abusing offenders.

Andrew Ravenscroft is a Consultant Anaesthetist at Nottingham City Hospital, where he is the Lead Clinician for Multi-Pain Management directing the hospital pain clinic, which treats over 1,000 patients per year. He is a Clinical Teacher for Nottingham University and a Member of the British Pain Society. His current research interests are in various chronic pain syndromes, including the use of opiates in chronic malignant pain.

Nicholas Seivewright is Consultant Psychiatrist in Substance Misuse at Sheffield Care NHS Trust, and was previously Senior Lecturer in Drug Dependence at the University of Manchester Department of Psychiatry. His psychiatric training was in Nottingham, where he gained a doctorate from the University of Nottingham in the field of personality disorders. He now combines full-time clinical duties in addictions with various research interests, including those in pharmacological treatments, benzodiazepine misuse and dual diagnosis.

Preface

In spite of claims that 'Treatment Works' — a view adopted by the British government and numerous treatment agencies, there is little research evidence to confirm that assertion. This in spite of a burgeoning drug problem in Britain and a Government wanting to increase treatment facilities. Throughout this book we have adopted a bias towards treatment, and have wanted to strike an optimistic note, although not so optimistic as to ignore the obvious limitations. We do so knowing that this optimism is fragile and easily overturned. For example, we do not know how treatment works, with whom it works, or whether some treatment modalities work better than others. What we offer is a popular belief that it does work, and this view is supported by a number of chapters in this volume (see Chapters 2, 3, 4 and 5). Like governments, we too have accepted it readily because it provides the only sure way of dealing with the problem; it provides a life-raft and gives hope against an otherwise relentless increase in drug use.

That claim, or rather the assumption that underlies the theme of this book, is that treatment does work. Our aim has been to pull together some of the more interesting features of the treatment of substance abuse, hoping to place it at the centre of the drugs debate. We have tried also to cover areas which we think will be of interest to academics and practitioners alike. We cannot claim to have covered more than a small part of a largely uncharted area, but sufficient, we hope, to raise awareness.

A recurring theme throughout is the lamentable shortage of British research on treatment. It is little short of a disgrace that funding has not been forthcoming. If this book promotes more research, then all to the good. Perhaps then we shall begin to answer some basic questions, such as how and in what way treatment works, or what the effects of treatment practices are. Research is long overdue, although the establishment of a National Treatment Agency (NTA) provides hints of a better future, but the NTA cannot expect to be the sole research provider.

We wish to thank all those who have helped produce this book, whether as contributors or colleagues, and especially those in the Midlands Centre for Criminology and the Department of Social Sciences,

University of Loughborough. Errors such as remain are, of course, the responsibility of the editors. We hope that this book will move things forward, whether by research or informed debate.

Philip Bean and Teresa Nemitz, January 2004

1 Introduction

Drug treatment; what works?
An overview

Philip Bean and Teresa Nemitz

From the mid-1990s onwards British governments have increasingly allocated funds for the treatment of substance abusers – they recognise that treatment offers one of their few remaining options. Throughout this book we have wanted to look at the nature of treatment and consider why it should be given this priority. Treatment is defined widely; the definition given by the Royal College of Psychiatrists is used here; that is, as the prevention and reduction of harm resulting from the use of drugs (Royal College of Psychiatrists 2000: 155). Treatments taking place inside the criminal justice system are included, as well as the more traditional settings associated with and by reference to that provided by the National Health Service (NHS) or voluntary services. 'Treatment' is a ubiquitous term and we see no reason to restrict its use – at least until there is agreement generally about its nature and effects.

Treatment has been thrust into prominence for a number of reasons. One is the growing belief that treatment works, although as we say throughout this is more in the nature of a slogan than anything else; second, it is thought treatment helps reduce crime as there is a strong belief that drug taking causes crime. Overwhelmed by the increase in drug use and the apparent criminality it produced ('apparent' because the links with crime are more tenuous than they at first appear; see Bean 2001), the Government's response has been to seek an ever-increasing number of treatment programmes. These, it is thought, provide relief from the revolving door whereby drug users move effortlessly in and out of the various systems, including the criminal justice system. A user whose addiction is out of control probably seeks treatment a number of times before treatment is successful (Gebelein 2000: 2).

This book deals with the nature of treatment, and some of the problems associated with providing treatment for substance misusers, as well as concentrating on criminal justice. Drug users are heavily concentrated in criminal justice populations. Studies in Britain also show that many arrested offenders tested positive for a range of drugs and were committing crime under the influence of numerous substances (Bennett 1998). A street heroin addict probably commits over 80 serious property crimes per year, alongside numerous other offences. High-frequency drug users tend to be high-rate offenders, yet periods in treatment produce dramatic reductions in criminality. The point is that drug use and criminality are inextricably bound together – and in saying this nothing is implied about whether one leads to the other. We believe that about 60 per cent of all referrals to treatment providers come from criminal justice, although no data are available, and we suspect that the figure could increase were more facilities available. These high-risk/high-need populations place considerable strain on existing services, as well as being excessively demanding in time and resources. They may not always be the most rewarding as patients – they are what has been described in another context as the unloved and unlovable – but they will continue to require treatment, and in ever-increasing numbers. Questions about the types of services provided and entry into those services require attention.

An overview and background to the belief that treatment works

In 1995 *Tackling Drugs Together: A Strategy for England 1995–8* was produced for England; that for Wales and Scotland followed soon afterwards (HM Government 1995; Welsh Office 1998). *Tackling Drugs Together* committed the Government 'to take effective action by vigorous law enforcement, accessible treatment and a new emphasis in education and prevention' (HM Government 1995: 1). There were no details of the treatment programme in these Strategies, but promises were made that these would be provided in a later Task Force Report. The emphasis in *Tackling Drugs Together* was on reorganising local services, more often than not replacing them with Drug Action Teams (DATs).

In 1998 a second Drug Strategy was introduced by the newly appointed Anti-Drugs Co-ordinator, entitled *Tackling Drugs to Build a Better Britain; The Government's 10 Year Strategy for Tackling Drug Misuse* (HM Government 1998). This largely reiterated the themes of the 1995 document, whilst adding performance targets for drug reduction for the next decade. Finally, in 1999 Guidelines on the clinical management of drug users (Department of Health 1999) gave advice to the medical profession about how best to implement the Drug Strategy (see Chapter 2 of this volume).

All these Government initiatives emphasised the need for treatment. It was to operate alongside law enforcement, prevention, and control – the latter mainly through the criminal justice system. Treatment was endorsed as a desirable platform in the Government's strategy, which inevitably concentrated on Class A drugs controlled by the 1971 Prevention of Misuse Act, i.e. usually heroin and cocaine. In this, the Government called on the substantial evidence from America, but now transformed into British thinking, which shows that 'Treatment Works' – a slogan particularly favourable to Britain, which nationally has one of the most developed and widespread treatment services.

In April 2001 the National Treatment Agency (NTA), a Special Health Authority within the NHS was launched (see Chapter 7 of this volume). The NTA covers England; other arrangements are in place for Scotland, Wales and Northern Ireland. This statement of purpose is in line with the Government's strategy '[t]o increase participation of problem drug misusers including prisoners in drug treatment programmes which have a positive impact on health and crime by 66% by 2005 and by 100% by 2008' (ibid.) In February 2002 the NTA produced *Models of Care for Substance Misuse Treatment*, aimed at providing a framework 'intended to achieve equity, parity and consistency in the commissioning and provision of substance misuse treatment and care in the UK' (Department of Health 2002: 2).

The report sets out, or, rather, provides a consensus about the essential components of specialist substance misuse services and stresses the importance of links with other health, social care and criminal justice agencies (ibid.: 3). Its weakness is that there is little on criminal justice, where most of the problems lie and where a great deal of treatment should be directed. As a result the report places too much emphasis on medical matters such as blood-borne diseases, reflecting the strong medical membership of the project team responsible for the report.

Yet behind the slogan that 'Treatment Works' lie a range of difficult questions, many are rarely asked and most produce no easy answers. First, there is a group of empirical questions, such as: with whom does treatment work? Can successful treatments be given over a single period, or do they require subsequent treatments even if the first was successful? Is a single type of treatment appropriate to all patients? Then there are questions about the principles of treatment: what are the aims of treatment? What should be the remit, and to whom should it be given? Finally there are questions about outcomes: does treatment need to be voluntarily undertaken to be effective (see Chapters 9, 10 and 11 of this volume)? And what outcome measures should be used, abstinence or controlled use?

In Britain we rarely ask these questions, largely because we have not needed to, or, if we have, then we have preferred not to wait for the answers, for they bring to light matters we prefer to keep hidden. They demand evaluations about the way the treatment agencies operate. By implication they introduce pertinent questions about the distribution and location of services, and demand an examination of current practices. In short, they furnish a revolution, or if not quite that then something close to it. We hope that some of these questions will be asked throughout this book, and, if not, then hopefully later.

Looking through the British research cupboard we have to say it is fairly bare. One of the best and earliest pieces of research, by Hartnoll *et al.* (1980), involved a random allocation of patients to receive injectable heroin or oral methadone. The results showed that those who were given injectable heroin tended to remain in treatment, but, whilst fewer remained in treatment when on oral methadone, overall they had a better outcome. From this study in 1980 there was very little until the National Treatment Outcome Research Study (NTORS) in 1995 (see also Chapter 3 in this volume), prompted by the Department of Health Task Force Report (Department of Health 1996). The lack of research in Britain on drug treatment is little short of a disgrace and an indictment of the way research is viewed at Government level and beyond. The NTORS study provides the exception to an otherwise bleak picture. Local treatment centres have also been remiss, often failing to evaluate their programmes.

The nature of treatment

What do we know of treatment and how does it work? We have to say that little is written about it, but the literature, such as there is, suggests that the treatment of substance abuse involves a mixture of traditional medical interventions together with a range of therapies – the latter used more than the former. For a patient in the early stages of treatment the focus tends to be narrow, but broadens later to include different aspects of the drug takers' lives (see Chapter 2 of this volume). The Royal College of Psychiatrists' version of treatment, defined as being the prevention and reduction of harm resulting from the use of drugs, includes social, psychological or physical harm, and may involve medical, social or educational interventions, including prevention and harm reduction (Royal College of Psychiatrists 2000: 155).

This is an inclusive definition. It also sets out the treatment aims, which tend to be avoided in most definitions elsewhere. Textbooks on treatment usually begin with a description of the nature of drugs and addiction, then move to the process of treatment, i.e. to questions of assessment. Invariably this is followed by an examination of measures of intervention – usually including a discussion on the range of treatments provided and the special types of problems encountered – concluding with a section on follow-up and outcome. Central questions about aims and justification are neatly bypassed. In contrast, the Royal College has produced a more workable definition which provides a framework for treatment and defines the boundaries of the subject matter.

Treatment in whatever form, and for whatever group, deviant or otherwise, is derived from a theory of morals. It is aimed at producing an acceptable change in the patient's behaviour – in this case reducing the use of drugs and preventing future use. Treatment is often presented as if it were solely a medical matter, whether conceptually or by the actions of the treatment personnel, but, as the Royal College definition suggests, this is not so. For whilst the language of medicine may dominate (as if treatment was aimed at curing an illness, the illness being addiction or substance misuse and being diagnosed after eliciting the signs and symptoms of the patient's condition), in practice only a small part of the overall package may involve medicine, and then this is likely to be confined to the initial period of detoxification or withdrawal. The remainder is more about encouraging the patient to stay in the programme, resisting further temptation to take drugs, and leading a productive and useful life – as aptly described by the Royal College of Psychiatrists in their definition. Paradoxically a full-blown disease model is more likely to be found in Alcoholics Anonymous (AA) or Narcotics Anonymous (NA) in their '12-Step' programmes – we say paradoxically, because the AA/NA model eschews the direct use of medicine in its treatment.

The stages of treatment invariably follow a set pattern, although an ever-widening range of treatments is available. Basically there are four, possibly five major treatment modalities: detoxification, outpatient drug-free programmes, methadone maintenance (or other maintenance programmes which might involve heroin prescribing) and therapeutic communities, the latter coming in various forms, whether religious or secular.

Anglin and Hser say these four types accounted for over 90 per cent of all patients in treatment in the USA in 1987 (Anglin and Hser 1990: 397). In Britain some patients are also treated by their general practitioner (GP), so that might perhaps reduce the American figure to about 80 per cent. Medical detoxification is usually the first stage. This itself does little to change long-term drug use but it safely manages the acute physical symptoms of withdrawal. Of the four modalities, detoxification is less concerned with producing therapeutic endeavours, and is more to provide symptomatic relief from the opioid abstinence syndrome while physical dependence on the drugs is being eliminated (ibid.: 423). Detoxification provides a gateway to treatment, encouraging users to avoid what they often fear most, the withdrawal symptoms of opioid use. For those unable or unwilling to withdraw maintenance medications are available, of which the most widely used is methadone – in Britain heroin/morphine is still prescribed by some licensed physicians; the number of patients receiving maintenance heroin is not known but is thought to be about 500 (Home Office, personal communication with the authors).

Once off drugs, i.e. once through the detoxification programme, other treatments are available, whether as an inpatient or outpatient, usually given as therapies such as Motivational Enhancement Therapy, Behavioural Therapy and Relapse Prevention Therapy, etc. The aims, however, are the same: to return the drug user to productive functioning in the family, workplace and community (see Chapter 4 of this volume). The best, or rather the most comprehensive programmes provide a combination of these therapies.

Nowadays treatment providers increasingly have patients with two or more comorbidities – i.e. suffering from the so-called dual diagnosis condition, which often means substance abuse and mental disorder, but could equally involve HIV/AIDS. These patients place additional burdens on the treatment services. Diagnosis is difficult as the conditions mimic and mask each other. For example, the hallucinations produced by some of the drugs (e.g. LSD) are the same in form and content as those in schizophrenia. The presence of one condition may mask the other – as where cocaine use covers up an endogenous depression or heroin use covers up phobic anxieties. Then there are questions about treatment: which condition to treat first? That which occurred first or that which is the most severe? And is treatment to be the same for both conditions? Many psychiatrists are uncomfortable treating substance misusers, who are invariably disruptive and take up a dispropor-tionate amount of time and effort. Similarly, many treatment providers are ill equipped to treat mental disorders. Dual diagnosis patients simply add to existing difficulties for patients and staff (see Chapter 5 of this volume).

We have little data on the treatment personnel. Anglin and Hser say that the philosophies and policies of providers of treatment services are more diverse than the programme modalities, components and approaches, but even in the USA these are the least quantifiable and least studied features of treatment programmes (ibid.: 441). However, some programme staff provide individual and unique interpretations of the programme, often with consider-able success. Anglin and Hser cite American research evidence which shows that some programmes are more successful than others even though the philosophy and patient group are similar. Differences in outcomes are related to the quality of staff as much as the quality of the programme, although the more flexible the programme the better the success rate (ibid.: 441).

Little is known about the cost-effectiveness of individual treatments – few long-term studies are available. The American National Institute on Drug Abuse (NIDA) reports that treatment is less expensive than non-treatment, as the latter often involves incarcerating the drug users in prison. According to other estimates, in drug court, for example, for every \$1 spent on treatment \$7 is saved – the costings are complicated and include savings on health care, as well as from policing, etc. (NIDA, quoted in Bean 2003). NIDA adds that 'major savings to the individual and society also come from signif-icant drops in interpersonal conflicts, improvements in workplace productivity, and reductions in drug related accidents' (ibid.; see also Chapter 11 of this volume). In Britain NTORS, which followed the progress of 1,075 clients in treatment, the majority of whom have been opiate depen-dent for many years, calculated a return of more than £3 for every £1 spent on treatment, this saving coming mainly from the criminal justice system (see Chapter 3 of this volume).

Governments wanting further justification for expanding treatment services have seized upon this data, especially when backed by statements such as the following: 'It is an inescapable conclusion that treatment lowers crime and health costs as well as associated social and criminal justice costs' (Lipton 1995: 520). However, some critics dispute these figures, arguing that the criminal justice system benefits little from treatment programmes, for the amount saved by a small reduction in the prison population is negli-gible, and immediately offset by an enormous cost involved in expanding existing treatment services. To offset these there may be savings in other parts of the health system, and in social terms treatment may produce a reduction in criminality. Even so, savings are difficult to calculate; for example, how to measure the cost of a reduction in the fear of crime? The ease with which these figures have been accepted suggests they provide information that is welcomed.

Until recently the data, such as there was, came from the Regional Drugs Misuse Databases (RDMD). In 2001 a census was carried out of all drug misusers in treatment during April to September 2000, taken with routine RDMD data. These databases routinely collected data on users presenting for treatment for the first time, or for the first time in six months. These databases were later replaced by the National Drugs Treatment Monitoring System (NDTMS), introduced on 1 April 2001, which improves the quality of data by including more information on those in treatment. Results show that in England during the year 2001:

- The number of users reported as being in treatment with drug misuse agencies and GPs was around 118,500.
- This compares with around 33,100 who presented for treatment for the first time, or for the first time in six months or more, during the six-month period ending 30 September 2000.
- About one-third (32 per cent) of users in treatment were under the age of 25 years.
- The great majority of users reported as being in treatment (87 per cent) were attending community specialist services – these were thought to include community-based drugs services, hospital outpatient and drug dependency unit outpatient services.

(Department of Health 2001)

These results are not surprising, especially those that show only 32 per cent in treatment under the age of 25 years, even though most drug users are under 25 years. There is an enormous gap between those receiving treatment and those needing it or who would benefit from treatment were it available. The size of that gap is difficult to determine but it probably understates demand by a factor of 10. Add to this another group called therapeutic addicts, whose addiction comes from medical over-prescribing. These people are almost always disregarded when we talk of substance misuse yet they take huge quantities of prescribed drugs (see Chapter 6 in this volume). They are often over the age of 45, antecedently non-delinquent, and rarely see them-selves as addicts yet might freely admit they have a drug problem. They eschew notions of addiction yet exhibit all the features of the street junkie when they seek the drug of their choice on demand. Assuming that every GP in the country has between eight and 10 of these patients, the numbers nationally must be huge. Bringing this group into treatment is another mammoth task.

The data in Britain is simply not available to determine with any degree of certainty that treatment works. Long-term studies are nonexistent; nor are there many which have evaluated the programmes. Looking back over the last decade or so we need to ask why so little research was undertaken. The opportunities were there but were missed and chances overlooked. At a basic level advances could have been made had programmes been evaluated, evaluations being the *sine qua non* of all treatment programmes. Sadly, this was rarely done. And we need to ask why? There may be many reasons; lack of funding is the most obvious, but so too is a lack of a research tradition which sees research as important. Too often there remains the view that research is a luxury which programmes can ill afford, or, worse, that it is unnecessary. We are paying heavily for that omission.

That which we have is not entirely complimentary, especially where it is concerned with the structure and delivery of services. A review of treatment services in Britain by the Audit Commission began by saying that 'the complex nature of drug misuse means that many drug misusers require varying combinations of services during the course of their treatment and need to be supported along a treatment pathway' (Audit Commission 2002: 4). It recognised that services must be matched according to patients' needs and it emphasised that drug misuse is a chronic relapsing condition and recovery is all too often followed by a recurrence of misuse. Accordingly, it accepted that most patients require several episodes of treatment (ibid.: 4). Yet 'while some areas had developed effective and innovative approaches to supporting drug misusers widespread problems common to many areas reduced the scope and quality of care for individual services' (ibid.: 5).

The list of failings was extensive. First, in many areas drug misusers experienced considerable difficulty accessing appropriate drug treatment services because of limited treatment options, reflecting the piecemeal and unplanned development of the treatment sector. Second, the Audit Commission found the median waiting time for prescribing services was 35 days, though in some areas it was over 100 days. 'In one area where clients routinely waited 5 months for an appointment at the CDT (community drug teams) only 1 in every 3 clients ever attended' (ibid.: 5). Third, many drug users, especially the more chaotic heroin users, were sometimes put off by the way the treatment services operated, so that they failed to attract and retain those who needed treatment the most. Fourth, there was poor management and co-ordination within the treatment services, with a failure to provide a care plan in half the cases examined, with poorly developed links with other treatment providers. Finally, there were poor links with primary care services such as GPs – not, incidentally, always created by the treatment providers, as many GPs were unable to offer the levels of assistance required by their drug-misusing patients (ibid.: 7).

Some of the failings were thought to be related to low levels of training and staff expertise:

> Many staff in the drug treatment sector are well qualified, but their training is not always relevant to the job they are doing. Many receive

little or no training relevant to their needs. Recruiting and retaining suitable staff is also a problem, exacerbated by the rapid growth of the treatment sector.

(Audit Commission 2002: 6)

Others were more endemic, involving lengthy waiting times, a common recurring problem. For example, in our own research back in 1995 in Leicester drug offenders complained of intolerable waiting times – three months was usual – and by the time their appointment was due many had committed further offences, including completing another prison sentence. Almost all remained on drugs. One of the key assumptions behind American drug courts is that the drug user is at his/her most vulnerable, and therefore more susceptible to treatment, when he/she has just been 'busted'. Miss this opportunity and the key moment has gone – three months' wait misses that moment by a long way (Bean 2001).

The Audit Commission made a number of recommendations, including establishing clear arrangements for joint commissioning of drug treatment services within the DAT area, promoting effective links between DATs and key local partnerships, developing more effective assessment procedures and identifying the needs and profile of all problem drug misusers in their areas. All in their way need attention but it requires more than an exhortation from the Audit Commission to realise them. However, the latter, which requires DATs to know the extent and nature of their problem would seem a necessary prerequisite for planning and future action. This is very rarely undertaken – almost never, from our experience. It is not just a DAT problem – although, as is shown in Chapter 10, one wonders if it was wise for the Government to make DATs the focus of treatment provisions. The police have a similar problem about the collection and use of data. Mayor Guiliani in a visit to Britain in 2002 said he required the New York City Police Department to review daily the arrests for drug traffickers and users in each precinct and commanders were required to defend the manner in which they deployed their officers. No such daily briefings exist in Britain; the Metropolitan police produce their statistics three months in arrears, other police areas not at all, and up-to-date information is simply not available. Yet if treatment services and police operations are to be data led, as they ought to be, good data provide the necessary baseline from which to measure change.

The Audit Commission was critical too of the processes surrounding treatment provisions; i.e. the way treatment services operate. The Commission did not comment on treatment programmes within the criminal justice system, which were outside their brief, or on the likely impact of the large sums of money given to the DATs. Had they done so it might have confirmed their criticism about the lack of a shared vision or common understanding. Sadly, the picture the Commission painted was of a service struggling to cope with the demands being placed on it.

Measures of outcome

In terms of outcomes, apart from the NTORS study there is little other data available in Britain. We might speculate or hope treatment works, but that is not supported by a great deal of hard evidence. Assuming, however, that treatment does work, what then? An obvious outcome is that treatment services will have a higher profile and a greater public recognition than hitherto. That could lead to an increase in funding accompanied by higher status and accord for treatment personnel. Presumably that will lead to innovative practices accompanied by higher levels of professionalism, which will also produce an upward developing spiral of achievement. Yet with these new ways of working some cherished beliefs and practices may need to be shed. Weaknesses otherwise left uncovered may be exposed, not just of those working in the treatment services but also of those in attendant occupations. New services may cream off the better patients, leaving the less deserving untreated alongside those who create most trouble in the wards or elsewhere.

The simplest research evaluation is to take the period prior to treatment and compare it to the period after treatment in terms of the agreed outcome variables. Anglin and Hser say that this type of design is now recognised as having serious methodological flaws: 'Because the pre-treatment period was almost invariably characterised by abnormally high levels of drug use, crime or both, improvement might be no more than regression to the mean in a later period particularly when the pre-treatment period was short' (1990: 407). They suggest a longer pre-treatment period extending at least three to five years prior to treatment. That may well be a recipe for sound research methodologies, but, again, how to get valid and reliable data over that time span.

The most obvious outcome measurement is subsequent use of drugs: a reduction in use from the pre-treatment period is seen as a success. However, presumably more than this is required; a reduction in criminality, and improved social and psychological performances would also be included. There is little point in treating an addicted unemployed thief to see him become a non-addicted unemployed thief. Indeed, Anglin and Hser say that it is important that outcome measures encompass a variety of behaviours measured at determined time intervals to see if the patient has changed for the better (ibid.: 409). Measuring these outcomes is difficult enough, but follow-up data is particularly difficult to obtain, especially where the user has relapsed, and we need to identify the results as being due to treatment. We cannot assume that therapeutic interventions come only from the treatment programme; friends, family or others also provide assistance.

Anglin and Hser show there are serious methodological problems in simply examining a pre-and post-treatment period. The presence of a control group would help overcome some of the difficulties, one of which is that treatment is itself often a self-selecting process, for 'in the absence of a control group it is difficult to determine whether unanticipated bias occurred in selecting the subjects for study' (ibid.: 408). The best and most appropriate design involves randomly allocating patients to various treatment modalities, with some patients given a placebo or no treatment at all. The ethical difficulties are immense, not least because they involve a group of patients who are not given treatment.

In spite of these constraints, sound and effective evaluations are possible, and effective evaluations are necessary if we are to make progress. We need to determine the overall effectiveness of all treatment regimes and modalities – the latter even more complicated than the former – and need also to determine these in relation to the client population. Differences in outcome may be related to differences in gender or ethnicity, alongside age, social class, etc., and these need to be identified. Above all we need to know if treatment really works or if this is just another slogan.

The emphasis in this volume

This introductory chapter has provided an overview of some of the matters to be discussed throughout. The aim has been to draw attention to questions about current issues, especially surrounding the lack of research. This is a recurrent theme, but at the risk of being repetitive it needs emphasis. The chapters described below reflect the aim of the book, which is not to provide a text dealing with the nature of treatment, though that is important, but to examine the philosophy of treatment and show how treatment can be improved. If that means altering existing structures, then so be it, and if it involves new ways of working, then all to the good. Treatment cannot be seen as the sole province of those undertaking the programmes; it has wider sociological implications which require consideration.

Joy Mott in Chapter 2 examines the 'Guidelines on the clinical management of opioid dependence in the UK'. The first set of Guidelines goes back to the Rolleston Committee in 1926; they have been updated regularly since then, the latest revision taking place in 1999. They provide authoritative advice and set standards on the good practice of treatment, but more than this they are 'dictats'. For physicians whose standards fall short of good practice there remains the threat of the General Medical Council, which will use those Guidelines as a yardstick when considering matters of serious professional misconduct.

The Guidelines themselves, as Joy Mott points out, have gone through various stages of development, the 1999 version being more comprehensive and detailed than those in 1984 and 1991. One major difference is that the emphasis in 1999 is more on long-term prescribing and the use of oral methadone in selected medical settings. Another is the distinction made between the generalist, the specialist generalist and the specialist doctor, distinguished by the extent of their training and experience and their clinical contact with drug users and the role of each in shared care. These Guidelines do not have the force of law, but they represent a standard of good-quality care appropriate to good medical practice. Joy Mott says the most acute shortcoming in the 1999 Guidelines is the lack of attention given to diamorphine maintenance prescribing. It is almost as if prescribing did not exist. The British system established by Rolleston in 1926 is not quite finished; about 500 addicts in Britain still receive heroin on prescription.

Chapter 3, entitled 'Types of treatment for types of patients', by Ken Checinski and Hamid Ghodse, provides an overview of treatment. The authors begin with what they call the 'key dimensions that help the conceptualisation of the link between individuals with drug problems, treatments for these problems and measurable outcomes', i.e. factors concerning the patients' treatment, as well as expectations for outcome. The central part of the chapter concerns assessment, which includes a section on how to undertake an assessment and the factors to be considered. There is a final section on treatment modalities. This chapter is geared to the practitioner but it provides a summary of much that follows in later chapters.

Chapter 4, by Michael Gossop, follows on from this. It focuses on clinical practice within UK treatment services and examines areas where there have been changes in the identification of clinical problems and in the delivery of treatment. The chapter covers a wide range of issues, many of which are also picked up and dealt with elsewhere; for example, coerced treatment is examined in Chapter 10. The section in Chapter 2 on 'Treatment outcomes' draws heavily on NTORS, incidentally one of the few comprehensive research studies on treatment carried out in Britain, and shows how treatment can have an impact on a wide variety of morbidities. NTORS shows that treatment can effect a significant reduction in heroin use, as well as the practise of injecting and the sharing of injecting equipment. Moreover, for those in treatment there was a reduction in acquisitive crime, especially among the most criminally active drug users. However, there were variations in the success rates of agencies, for, as Michael Gossop says, '[t]he results at one year show a huge variation in the behavioural changes of clients from different agencies,...some agencies, for whatever reason, were not achieving satisfactory client outcomes'. It is not clear why this was so. This and the problem of identifying the impact of treatment process variables are regarded by Michael Gossop as the next steps to be taken.

Whilst Chapters 3 and 4 provide a comprehensive overview of many of the key questions and make suggestions for the future, the chapter by Colin Brewer, Chapter 5, is more contentious, highlighting issues associated with treatment programmes. These include misconceptions about the use of the medical model, the continued, and what Colin Brewer regards as the inappropriate, use of psychoanalytical concepts (where it is considered more important to attack the underlying problems than the alcohol or heroin use), ignorance of the literature by many treatment providers, and professional rivalries that emerge, etc. He reserves his most telling criticism for what he refers to as 'the placebo effect', or what he later refers to as the 'therapeutic delusion', i.e. 'the natural tendency for those involved in therapeutic activity to believe what they do is useful' when they may have little impact at all. Colin Brewer's interests are not in these therapeutic areas; he is much more inclined towards physiological treatments which act as antagonists, especially antibuse (disulfiram), whether for alcohol or cocaine. He champions the cause of naltrexone, a long-acting oral opiate antagonist, which he says has useful effects in alcohol abuse. He also champions the cause of methadone maintenance programmes. This is a hard-hitting chapter, to some extent polemical but no less worthy for that.

In Chapter 6 Douglas Longshore, Michael L. Prendergast and David Farabee, examine one of the means by which offenders/patients enter treatment. They call their chapter 'Coerced treatment for drug-using criminal offenders'. Coerced treatment is not a popular concept in the UK, for there is still the belief that for treatment to be effective it must be based on a willingness of the patient to enter the programme freely. Coercion appears to violate that principle. Yet, as is often the case, matters are not that simple. The authors show that 'coercion' is not the other side of 'choice', or 'freedom'; that is, patients who are not coerced are not always free. A number of different people can coerce patients into treatment through a number of different routes and in a number of different ways. Coercion can take many forms and operate at a number of different levels; it is not the sole prerogative of the criminal justice system, as some would believe. Coercion can be by family, friends, therapists and the like, and involve threats as well as promises of rewards. Yet the moment or point in time when offenders are arrested includes the period when they are most likely to consider treatment as an option; miss this opportunity and it might not come again.

That apart, there are outcomes to be considered. The authors point to the research literature, which shows that the reasons for entering treatment are not related to outcomes; the length of stay in treatment is a better predictor of outcome than the reason for entering treatment. That is to say, the longer the person stays in the programme the greater the chances of success. The trick, of course, is to find ways of keeping the patient interested.

Hopefully this chapter will encourage a greater appreciation of the complexities of treatment and encourage a more informed debate. Slogans about the dangers of coercion are inappropriate in their way. The authors make the point that the field must move beyond this oversimplified binary question; coercion, they say, is a multidimensional phenomenon. They suggest three areas for further research. The first is to determine to what extent the patient's perception of coercion differs from that of the criminal justice agencies; that is, to what extent does the patient's internal motivation for treatment correspond to the objective external forces? Second, research is needed on the factors that may moderate the outcomes of coerced treatment; that is, on programme structures, provision of aftercare, etc. Finally, research is required on the manner in which external coercion is internalised as an acceptable phenomenon. Clearly, it is not necessary for drug users to 'hit bottom' before being accepted into treatment; as the authors say, 'reliance on coercion presupposes that treatment can be effective with persons who perceive the adverse consequences of their drug use to be minimal or acceptable'.

The so-called dual diagnosis patient is the subject of Chapter 7, by Nicholas Seivewright, Muhammad Z. Iqbal and Helen Bourne. Dual diagnosis is an unfortunate term, implying that the patient has been given two diagnoses when in fact dual diagnosis means something quite different. It can refer to those patients with at least two morbidities, usually, and for these purposes, that means substance abuse and mental disorder, but it is likely to include HIV/AIDS as well as hepatitis C. The diagnosis and treatment of such patients requires skills over and above those required in treatment settings since one condition can mimic or mask the other; that is, drug psychoses have many features of schizophrenia, and the depressed patient can mask his/her depression by the use of cocaine.

Moreover, as the authors say, 'prognosis has been found to be worsened by the additional presence of substance misuse in psychotic patients in aspects including frequency of relapses and severity of psychiatric symptoms'. Dual diagnosis patients are more likely to relapse, are more disruptive in the wards as an inpatient and are more demanding of staff time. How, then, to treat them? Psychiatrists traditionally concerned with or specialising in mental disorders with little or no experience of substance misuse shy away from them, whilst drug specialists tend not to be able to treat mental disorders. What the authors call 'service issues', which means treatments for dual diagnosis patients, are given special attention in this chapter, and this means finding ways in which drug treatment services and psychiatric services can work together.

Jay Carver opens Chapter 8, on 'Drug testing', with the following comment:

> [D]rug testing is quick. It is accurate. It is becoming cheaper. It quickly cuts through the denial associated with addiction. And it has great potential to change behaviours when used within the context of accountability, with immediate consequences for drug use. Yet as part of a comprehensive national strategy, drug testing has yet to achieve anything close to its real potential.

If this is what he thinks of America, what would he think of Britain! Here drug testing is used rarely, and when it is, then often without attention to the necessary details. That means there remains the possibility of giving false readings, where little or no attention is given to the ways in which the tests can be sabotaged, and rarely is consideration given to providing a cheaper yet more efficient product. In a striking criticism of the present system Jay Carver says this:

Some supervision programs test only infrequently, and then on regularly scheduled reporting days. Some drug testing programs have so few internal controls that offenders find it easy to avoid detection through any number of techniques. Even if a probationer tests positive, the most likely response will be nothing but a warning from the probation officer at the next reporting date, which could be a month after the test was taken. If the violation does come before the judge, the hearing is likely to be months after the fact....If one set out to design a system to produce failure, it is hard to imagine a better one.

But why? Jay Carver gives the following reasons: first, a failure to invest in community corrections, leaving a structural imbalance in corrections spending where the prison system swallows up a disproportionate amount of resources; second (and this is also a point made below in the chapter by one of the editors (Philip Bean, Chapter 9), poor communication between the criminal justice system and the treatment agencies, where, as Jay Carver says, 'the two professions often regarded each other with deep-seated mistrust or even hostility'; third, a remaining mistaken belief that nothing works in rehabilitation programmes. He says there are two pervading myths: that drug testing is useless without treatment, when it can itself serve as a way of tracking offenders who use drugs; and that coerced treatment does not work (also the subject of Chapter 6 of this volume). Jay Carver is clear: drug testing is a necessary prerequisite for the effective treatment of drug users, although to achieve optimal effectiveness it is just one element in a comprehensive strategy.

The major classification of drug misusers by the Home Office from 1926 up to about 1960 was according to their perceived aetiology. One group, non-therapeutic addicts, it was said, started taking drugs for non-medical reasons, or, as the 1926 Rolleston Committee said, as a form of vicious indulgence. The second group, therapeutic addicts, became addicted as a result of being prescribed addictive drugs for their medical condition, including relief of medical symptoms. Up to about 1960 the latter outnumbered the former, but after 1960 the numbers of non-therapeutic addicts increased alarmingly. Terms like 'therapeutic' and 'non-therapeutic' are not used nowadays, but the conditions to which they refer remain. In Britain still, some 50 years later, there are thought to be large numbers of so-called non-therapeutic addicts. They can be found in almost every GP's caseload. They take huge quantities of narcotic drugs and whilst they may eschew all attempts to call them addicts they display many of the symptoms of the 'junkie': they seek their drug of choice on demand.

In Chapter 9 Philip Bean and Andrew Ravenscroft look more closely at this group. Their conclusion is that these therapeutic addicts are addicts, albeit with differences. They will probably have remained addicted longer than the non-therapeutic group but take an equally wide range of drugs; they take painkillers, sleeping pills, anti-depressants, etc. They are, however, older, not antecedently delinquent and rarely take substances illegally. The authors suggest that the problem stems from an inherent contradiction within medical practice, the desire on behalf of the physician to relieve pain – hence the addictive painkillers – and the demand to be restrictive. They say the model to treat pain is not the same as treating addiction; one is permissive, the other restrictive. Clearly the problem is a huge one, largely unrecognised and unreported.

In Chapter 10 Tammy L. Anderson and Lana Harrison describe a treatment programme for prisoners. They begin by saying that programmes promoting effective treatments involving re-entry of prisoners into the outside world are critically important for criminal justice policy. Without intervention drug offenders may repeat the same types of behaviours that led them to prison in the first place. The authors argue that of the interventions recently emerging to cultivate improved outcomes among drug offenders the therapeutic community (or TC) is the best. TC, which begins with the offender in prison and continues on discharge, requires the offender to go through the various roles and steps within the programme as part of the main aim, which is to give the offender a sense of his own responsibility. Although TCs use a variety of techniques (group counselling, cognitive and emotional therapies, etc.), the distinguishing features are the deliberate use of their peers in prison and on discharge, linked to the way offenders are connected to their communities outside prison. Clearly TC is an extensive and expensive approach, which the authors claim is 'unparalleled in other correctional programs'. The British equivalent would be in Grendon Underwood Prison, where intensive peer-directed therapy occurs. Unfortunately it does not continue on the prisoners' release.

Paul Hayes, the first chief executive of the newly formed NTA, describes in Chapter 11 the background, role and progress of the Agency since it was established in 2001. It has specific targets, such as doubling the number in effective well-managed treatment from 100,000 in 1998 to 200,000 in 2008. To meet these targets the NTA works in partnership with other agencies, focusing on improving the commissioning of drug treatment services, promoting evidence-based and co-ordinated practice and improving the performance of DATs and treatment providers. DATs are central to the Government's strategy; Paul Hayes describes them as 'consortiums responsible for local delivery of the national drugs strategy – including the planning and commissioning of drug treatment'. There are 149 of these throughout England, and all must look to the NTA for approval, as the NTA is responsible for scrutinising all DATs' draft treatment plans. If the DATs fail to produce the goods the NTA will be seen to fail likewise. Thus far, however, Paul Hayes is upbeat, listing an impressive set of achievements, including improving the numbers in treatment and reducing waiting times. Hopefully he will meet the full target for 2008.

The chapter by one of the editors (Philip Bean, Chapter 12) is concerned to bring together these two services involved in treatment, the treatment providers usually working within the NHS or with voluntary bodies, and those in the criminal justice system. At present they talk past each other or are frankly hostile. Suspicion is based on a number of factors, the main one being ideological: from the treatment providers in the NHS, etc. that the criminal justice system is 'punitive' and 'authoritarian' whereas treatment services are 'medical' and therefore somehow more humanistic; and from the criminal justice personnel that the others do not understand offenders. Successful programmes, such as those in Australia, have integrated their services to the point where ideological differences have been removed. This has not been easy, requiring a short- and long-term strategy with a commitment to integrate at all levels in the organisations.

The aim in Chapter 12 has been to produce a model which centres on the integration of those systems, where those in treatment are supported by supervision assisted by the use of drug testing facilities. This model has been used effectively elsewhere, albeit with small populations, but the time is right to use it more extensively. This chapter takes on the theme of the book: that we can do something about the drug problem and that treatment works. Or, rather, it works if we get the other bits right.

Finally, Chapter 13, by Joris Casselman, a practising psychiatrist from Belgium, sets out the practical difficulties alongside the need to motivate clients/patients from the criminal justice system into treatment. Joris Casselman stresses the point, made often throughout this book, that treatment services and criminal justice system operate in different worlds with different objectives. How to bring them together is a matter of some importance, and the subject of this chapter. He starts from the basic premise that if the clients/patients are not motivated for treatment, then the task of the treatment professional is not to send them away but to enhance their motivation. Motivational enhancement can be developed in a number of ways, and, similarly, reduced or removed altogether by a series of ill-considered comments or actions by the treatment provider, for example by arguing with the patient. Joris Casselman goes through the various stages of treatment, or, rather, the motivation for treatment, which the patient and treatment provider are likely to experience, but always with the idea that keeping the patient in treatment is the task in hand. This is a practitioner's chapter written by an experienced professional.

References

Anglin, M. D. and Hser, Y. (1990) 'Treatment of Drug Abuse', in M. Tonry and J. Q. Wilson (eds) *Drugs and Crime*, Chicago: University of Chicago Press.

Audit Commission (2002) *Changing Habits. The Commissioning and Management of Drug Services for Adults*, Audit Commission.

Bean, P. T. (2001) *Drugs and Crime*, Cullompton, Devon: Willan Publishing.

Bean, P. T. (2003) *Drugs and Crime*, report to the EMCDDA (mimeo).

Bennett, T. (1998) *Drugs and Crime. The Results of Research, Drug Testing and Interviewing Arrestees*, Home Office Research Study 193, London: Home Office.

Department of Health (1996) *Task Force to Review Services for Drug Misusers. Report of an Independent Review of Drug Treatment Services in England*, London: Department of Health.

Department of Health (1999) *Drug Misuse and Dependence. Guidelines on Clinical Management*, London: HMSO.

Department of Health (2001) *Statistical Press Release. Statistics from the Regional Drug Misuse Databases on Drug Misusers in Treatment in England. 2000/1* (11 October), London: Department of Health.

Department of Health (2002) *Models of Care for Substance Misuse Treatment* (Draft Report) (mimeo), London: Department of Health.

Gebelein, R. S. (2000) *The Rebirth of Rehabilitation; Promises and Perils of Drug Court*, Washington, DC: National Institute of Justice.

Hartnoll,R., Mitcheson, M., Battersby, A., Brown, G., Ellis, M., Fleming, P. and Hedley, N. (1980) 'Evaluation of Heroin Maintenance in a Controlled Trial', *Archives of General Psychiatry* 37: 877–84.

HM Government (1998) *Tackling Drugs to Build a Better Britain; the Government's 10 Year Strategy for Tackling Drug Misuse*, Cm. 3945, London: The Stationery Office.

Lipton, D. S. (1995) *The Effectiveness of Treatment for Drug Abusers under Criminal Justice Supervision*, Washington, DC: National Institute of Justice.

Welsh Office (1998) *Forward Together, a Strategy to Combat Drugs and Alcohol Abuse in Wales*, Cardiff: HMSO.

2 What should work

Guidelines on the clinical
management of opioid dependence in
the United Kingdom

Joy Mott

Introduction

Advice was first given to doctors on the treatment of morphine and heroin users in 1926 by the Departmental Committee on Morphine and Heroin Addiction (Ministry of Health 1926) (the Rolleston Committee), convened by the Ministry of Health. In 1982 the Advisory Council on the Misuse of Drugs noted that 'in spite of the fact that there has always been a broad consensus as to good and effective treatment of problem drug takers, it has not been widely known or widely applied' (1982: para. 7.21) and recommended that 'guidelines should be prepared on good medical practice in the treatment of problem drug takers' (para. 7.21). The Council considered that 'an authoritative statement of good practice...is required urgently' (para. 7.24). Guidelines prepared by a medical working group convened by the Department of Health were published in 1984, with revised versions in 1991 and 1999 (Medical Working Group 1984; Department of Health *et al.* 1991, 1999). (The guidelines also offer advice on the treatment and management of misusers of sedatives, benzodiazepines, alcohol, stimulants and some other misused substances.)

The advice of the Rolleston Committee and the later three sets of guidelines is described in terms of their sources of advice, the aims of treatment, methods of treatment and management, and the effectiveness of treatment.

Sources of advice

The Rolleston Committee relied on the clinical experience of its members (all were practising doctors) and of its medical witnesses. The 1984 guidelines were prepared by a medical working group made up of members nominated by 'representative medical bodies and individuals with expertise' (Medical Working Group 1984: para. 1). The 1991 guidelines were also prepared by a medical working group of doctors with experience in treating drug misusers, including psychiatrists, a consultant with experience in treating HIV-positive patients, two general practitioners (GP) and a prison medical officer. The membership of the working group which prepared the 1999 guidelines, while mainly medical, reflected the involvement of other professionals in the management of drug dependence by including a professor of nursing, a pharmacist, a representative of the non-statutory agencies and a representative of the General Medical Council. The 1999 guidelines were described as 'evidence-based', using 'evidence from expert committee reports and the clinical experience of respected authorities' as well as 'all significant published evidence' since 1996 (Department of Health 1999: xiv).

The aims of treatment

The Rolleston Committee described the aim of treatment as 'to free the patient from his addiction' (para. 44) from morphine or heroin, noting:

> Success in enabling the patient...to become (for the time being) independent of the drug must be regarded as the completion of the first stage of treatment. For permanent cure a prolonged period of aftercare is necessary, in order to educate the patient's willpower and to change his mental outlook. Attention must also be paid to the possibility of improvement in the patient's social conditions.
> (Department Committee on Morphine and Heroin Addiction 1926: para. 6(f))

The 1984 guidelines described the aim of treatment as 'to help the individual to deal with problems causing as well as caused by his drug use, and eventually to achieve a drug-free life' (Medical Working Group 1984: para. 7).

The 1991 guidelines listed five aims for clinical management as helping the patient:

- to deal with the problems related to drug use;
- to reduce the damage during drug use, particularly the risk of HIV (e.g. from injecting and sharing);
- to reduce the chance of further relapse into drug use;
- to reduce the duration of episodes of current drug use and of relapses;
- to remain healthy until, with appropriate care, he can achieve a drug-free life.

(Department of Health 1991: para. 3.2.2)

The 1999 guidelines added five further aims:

- to reduce the use of illicit or non-prescribed drugs by the individual;

- to reduce the need for criminal activity to finance drug misuse;
- to reduce the risk of prescribed drugs being diverted on to the illegal drug market;
- to stabilise the patient where appropriate on a substitute medication to alleviate withdrawal symptoms;
- to improve overall personal, social and family functioning.

(Department of Health 1999: para. 1)

Advice on treatment and management

The Rolleston Committee

The methods of treatment described by the Rolleston Committee were: abrupt rapid withdrawal, rapid withdrawal in the course of a few days, gradual withdrawal 'on a systematic plan' (described in some detail in paragraph 38 of the report). The Committee had been particularly asked to examine the abrupt rapid withdrawal method because 'some eminent physicians, especially in the United States' (para. 6) considered that an addict 'could always be cured by sudden withdrawal under proper precautions'.

The Committee found there was 'a distinct conflict of opinion as to the merits and demerits of the various methods' (para. 41) of treatment, with prison medical officers most in favour of abrupt withdrawal. The Committee considered that abrupt or rapid withdrawal should only carried out 'in a well-appointed institution and with the aid of skilled nursing and constant medical supervision' and then only for 'young healthy adults in whom the addiction is of recent date and only moderate doses are being taken'.

On the whole medical opinion was found to be:

> strongly in favour of the gradual withdrawal method to be more generally suitable and free from risk than either the abrupt or rapid withdrawal methods. It entails less stress and distress upon the patient, is unattended by collapse and other withdrawal symptoms may by large measure be prevented by its adoption.
>
> (Ministry of Health 1926: para. 000)

Several witnesses who gave evidence to the Committee were insistent 'that the actual withdrawal of the drug of addiction must be looked upon merely as the first stage of treatment, if a complete and permanent cure is looked for' (para. 42).

The Committee concluded that:

There are two groups of persons suffering from addiction to whom administration of morphine or heroin may be regarded as legitimate medical treatment, namely:-

(a)   Those who are undergoing treatment for cure fo the addiction by the gradual withdrawal method;

(b)   Persons for whom, after every effort has been made for the cure of the addiction, the drug cannot be safely withdrawn, either because:-

(i)   Complete withdrawal produces serious symptoms which cannot be satisfactorily treated under the ordinary conditions of private practice;

or

(ii)   The patient while capable of leading a useful and fairly normal life so long ashe takes a certain non-progressive quantity, usually small, of the drug of addiction, ceases to be able to do so when the regular allowance is withdrawn.

(Ministry of Health 1926: conclusion para. 8)

With regard to these groups of patients, the Committee made the following provison:

It should not be too lightly assumed in any case, however unpromising it may appear to be at first sight, that an irreducible minimum of the drug has been reached which cannot be withdrawn and which, therefore, must be continued indefinitely.

(Ministry of Health 1926: para. 49)

The 1984 guidelines

The medical working group was 'concerned that treatment has become synonymous with prescribing the drug of dependence or a substitute...treatment is much more than this' (Medical Working Group 1984: para. 6). The importance of support services, including family and friends, in helping with problems of accommodation, employment and personal relationships was emphasised.

Four groups of drug misusers were distinguished:

•   those, often adolescents, who were experimenting with drugs or taking them intermittently, and who might not be physically dependent and have no major problems but who were at risk of increasing the frequency of their drug use;

•   dependent misusers whose lives were centred on drugs and usually had many drug-related problems;

•   stable drug users who were psychologically and/or physically dependent on opioids or other drugs which had originally been prescribed to treat physical disorders;

•   long-term drug users who had led stable social and working lives but with anticipated or current legal problems.

These guidelines offered general guidance to all doctors with specific guidance for GPs, psychiatrists, casualty officers, other hospital-based staff, police surgeons and prison medical officers. Appendices provided detailed advice on managing withdrawal symptoms and detoxification from opioids for inpatients and by GPs, including oral methadone equivalents for the most commonly misused opioids.

GPs were encouraged to treat drug misusers and 'and to help them in every possible way' (para. 1) and psychiatrists were encouraged to share the care of stable users. The most detailed guidance was provided for GPs, including, for example, on the conduct of the diagnostic interview, the physical examination, urine testing and screening for hepatitis B. They were advised that 'only in exceptional circumstances should controlled drugs be prescribed initially' (para. 20) and that for the 'young intermittent drug misuser counselling about drug misuse and personal and family problems may be the most effective response' (para. 12). If opioid drugs were later prescribed, they should beoctors were 'strongly recommended' to avoid prescribing tablets or suppositories because they could be crushed or melted and injected.

When undertaking detoxification, the doctor was advised to establish a mutually agreed contract with the patient before detoxification, 'otherwise a maintenance regime might be established or an overall increase in the drug dosage' (para. 22). GPs were advised not to attempt detoxification of pregnant women, high-dose heroin users or those with marked physical and psychiatric pathology or those who were 'socially chaotic and unco-operative' (para. 14). Such patients should be referred for specialist treatment.

GPs were also advised not to undertake long-term prescription of opioids unless in consultation and in conjunction with a specialist in drug treatment experienced in using this approach.

The 1991 guidelines

These guidelines offered advice on 'clinical management' and were particularly concerned with reducing the spread of HIV and other blood-borne infections among injecting drug users. The concept of harm minimisation was discussed and it was emphasised that 'skilful clinical management will reduce the harm to the patient from drug misuse' (Department of Health 1991: para. 3.5.1), for example by not prescribing drugs which could be used by injection such as temazepam capsules or methadone tablets and which could be sold on the black market. Advice was provided on the provision of condoms, and of sterile injecting equipment to reduce sharing, as well as on cleaning used syringes with household bleach.

The advice for doctors working in different settings differed little from that offered in 1984. The only substantial addition was advice to doctors working in the independent sector to consult with local National Health Service (NHS) colleagues, to limit their practice to patients living 'within easy reach', and warning them of the need to obtain evidence of the patients' ability to pay fees and prescription charges by legitimate means.

As in the 1984 guidelines, no advice was offered on maintenance prescribing because 'it is a specialised form of treatment best provided by, or in consultation with, a specialist drug misuse service' (para. 3.5.3).

The appendix on managing withdrawal was more detailed than in 1984, with an added emphasis on the importance of psychological support and a suggestion that cognitive therapy 'may be of value'.

The 1999 guidelines

These guidelines are more comprehensive and very much more detailed than those published in 1984 and 1991. They take into account changes in NHS policy for the delivery of health care by giving a greater emphasis to shared care and multidisciplinary working. Instead of offering guidance to doctors working in particular settings, a distinction is made between the 'generalist', 'the specialised generalist' and the 'specialist', distinguished by the extent of their training and experience of clinical contact with drug misusers, and the role of each in shared care (Department of Health 1999: 5, 6).

There are still only two treatments available, gradual withdrawal or detoxification and maintenance prescribing, although there is research on opioid blocking drugs and anti-craving agents as well as some psychological methods of treatment. The guidelines emphasise the importance of assessing the motivation of the patient to stop or change his or her pattern of drug use and/or lifestyle in selecting the type of treatment or management. It is noted that some misusers are able to withdraw from their drugs with general support and encouragement and make changes in their lifestyle and environment without substitute drugs being prescribed.

Withdrawal prescribing regimens

The advice on withdrawal prescribing regimes refers to the range of substitute opioid (methadone mixture, codeine-based drugs and buprenorphine) and non-opioid drugs (lofexidine, clonidine) that can be prescribed.

It is noted that 'withdrawal and detoxification regimes have a high failure rate unless linked to long-term rehabilitation' (para. 1) and that compliance with the whole treatment programme is critical to prevent relapse. Naltrexone may be prescribed to block the effects of opioids by specialised generalists and specialists to assist in relapse prevention in patients who have achieved abstinence. The likelihood of relapse can be reduced by behavioural techniques, and attendance at self-help groups such as Narcotics Anonymous can be helpful. Such psychosocial interventions are considered to be crucial in helping patients to achieve and maintain abstinence.

Oral methadone maintenance prescribing

The major difference between the 1999 guidelines and those published in 1984 and 1991 is the emphasis given to long-term prescribing and maintenance with oral methadone in primary care settings when the doctor has had appropriate training. Oral methadone maintenance is described as 'increasingly recognized to be an effective management strategy' (para. 4(a)), although it is not advised for young people aged under 18. International evidence from controlled trials is quoted as showing that, when delivered in a structured programme, it has been found to be 'vastly superior to control conditions' (para. 4(b)) in reducing injecting behaviour, illicit opioid use, criminal activity and costs to society. A daily dosing regime of between 60 mg and 120 mg of oral methadone is recommended, while larger doses may be required for patients with a high tolerance.

Another oral drug, buprenorphine, also licensed for the management of drug dependence, may be used for maintenance 'in the context of high quality, well supervised and well organised treatment services' (para. 5(b)).

Generalist doctors are recommended to seek advice from a specialised generalist or specialist before embarking on any form of maintenance prescribing. It should not be considered until other treatment options have been tried and should be reviewed at least quarterly and accompanied by social and psychological support.

Maintenance prescribing of injectable drugs

Maintenance prescribing of injectable drugs is described as 'a controversial area where further research is required to guide rational prescribing practice' (para. 6(a)). (No injectable preparation is licensed for the management of drug dependence.) There is said to be 'a very limited clinical place for prescribing injectable methadone' (para. 6(b)) and even less for diamorphine (heroin). Only specialists with a Home Office licence may prescribe diamorphine.

Repeated failure to respond to other forms of treatment is said to be the most usual reason given for undertaking such treatment. It is recommended that it should only be considered when the patient has 'a long and persistent history of injecting drug use, and in all cases there should be clear goals that can be assessed at defined intervals' (para. 6(a)). The greater dangers and the cost of such prescribing, as well as the likelihood that it will become a long-term commitment, are emphasised.

Treatment compliance

Doctors are reminded of the consequences of patients' non-compliance with any prescribing regimen, including the risk of overdose and death and sale of the drug on the illicit market. Recommendations for improving compliance include regular assessment to ensure that the patient is being prescribed a sufficient dose of the substitute drug and the provision of sterile needles and syringes if they continue to inject illegally obtained drugs. Other recommendations include supervised consumption, random urine testing, requiring patients to collect their dose each day and instalment prescriptions.

Prescribing safeguards

The Rolleston Committee emphasised the importance of the doctor keeping close control of the amount of morphine or heroin being prescribed, whether the addict was being treated by the gradual with-drawal method or by 'continuous administration of the drug indefinitely' (para. 54). The subsequent guidelines also warn against over-prescribing and advise against the prescribing of injectable formulations and of oral preparations that can be used for injecting. The 1999 guidelines specify which drugs are licensed for the treatment of opioid dependence (methadone mix BNF 1 mg/ml, buprenorphine).

Treatment outcomes

The Rolleston Committee was given estimates of the proportion of 'complete cures' of cases of addiction ranging from 15–20 per cent to 60–70 per cent, with doctors who had treated patients in prisons or nursing homes by the abrupt withdrawal method claiming the highest rates. It must be remembered that the Committee was advised that a considerable proportion, possibly ranging from one-quarter to half, of morphine or heroin addicts at the time were therapeutic addicts who had been introduced to the drugs during the course of medical treatment for the relief of pain.

By the mid-1960s the great majority of known addicts were of non-therapeutic origin and the later guidelines were less optimistic about the outcome of treatment or management. The 1984 guidelines note only that there was an 'emerging consensus and recognition that many drug users respond positively to appropriate treatment and rehabilitation' and 'research suggests that in time many will achieve increased stability in their lives and ultimate abstinence' (Medical Working Group 1984: paras 10, 2).

The 1991 guidelines comment:

> Drug misuse is at least as responsive to treatment as familiar medical conditions such as diabetes or rheumatoid arthritis. Outcome studies show that, with effective care, about 30–40% of opioid misusers will become abstinent and many of the others will be using less heavily or

less dangerously. In general, a shorter history of drug misuse carries a better prognosis.

(Department of Health 1991: para. 3.2)

The expectations of the 1999 guidelines are more qualified:

In a substantial proportion of patients drug misuse tends to improve with age, particularly when specific treatment and rehabilitation techniques are used.

(Department of Health 1999: para. 7)

Legal status of the guidelines

The guidelines do not have the force of law. The Misuse of Drugs Act 1971 allows any doctor to prescribe any controlled drug to an addict (except heroin, cocaine or dipipanone unless he is licensed to do so) in whatever form and quantity his or her clinical judgement dictates so long as it does not appear to be 'irresponsible'. The Home Secretary has powers under the Act to convene a medical tribunal to consider evidence that a doctor has been prescribing controlled drugs 'irresponsibly'. The Advisory Council on the Misuse of Drugs suggested that guidelines of good clinical practice would help to identify such cases but that prescribing controlled drugs privately or not following a course of treatment recommended by the guidelines for the treatment of addicts is not *prima facie* evidence of 'irresponsibility'.

The foreword to the 1999 guidelines (p. xv) describes them as providing a standard of quality of care and 'appropriate' treatment for drug misusers and representing 'a consensus view of good clinical practice'. In noting that the recommendations in the guidelines 'will be a significant reference point in assisting the General Medical Council' to consider whether to take action when a doctor's professional performance is alleged to be seriously deficient and possibly putting patients at risk, there is an implicit threat that deviation from them could result in disciplinary action. Similarly, the recommendations will also 'be taken into account' by the NHS bodies which monitor the quality of local clinical services in England and Wales.

Discussion

The four sets of guidelines, all sponsored by the government department responsible for health matters, provided authoritative advice for their time on good practice for doctors in the treatment and management of opioid dependence. By 1999 the fundamental aims and principles of medical treatment recommended by the Rolleston Committee in 1926 had not changed; nor has its emphasis after withdrawl from their drugs on the importance of 'a prolonged period of aftercare' (Ministry of Health 1926: para. 6(f)).

The most significant change has been that drugs not available at the time, particularly oral methadone, are now preferred to injectable morphine or heroin for withdrawal and maintenance prescribing.

Reflecting current concern about the extent of drug-related crime, the 1999 guidelines include the reduction of the need for criminal activity to finance drug misuse and the risk of prescribed drugs being diverted on to the illegal drug market among the aims of treatment and management of drug dependence.

The 1999 guidelines were generally welcomed as providing a standard for the treatment of opioid dependence and for the emphasis on the right of drug users to treatment by the NHS and for the recognition of the importance of shared care (Keen 1999). Criticisms include the lack of advice on the criteria for offering maintenance prescribing (Malinowski 1999) and the recommendations for supervised consumption because it may deter some users from seeking medical help (Carmichael 1999). The most serious criticism is that, unlike the 1984 and 1991 guidelines, which 'offered flexible guidance' and were 'suggestions, not instructions', these guidelines are 'dictats', and there are fears that 'rigid application may stultify future progress' (Waller 1999: 7) as well as representing 'dogmatic interference with clinical judgement on prescribing and dispensing' (Hewitt 1999: 7).

The most controversial aspect of the 1999 guidelines is the short shrift given to diamorphine maintenance prescribing, which appears to fly in the face of research findings available from Switzerland at the time, and more recently from the Netherlands, of its effectiveness. In the 2002 report of the House of Commons Home Affairs Committee a Home Office minister is quoted as saying:

> The current guidance has led us to be a little too restrictive as to where we are prepared to offer heroin as a form of treatment...people are not being allowed access to that treatment where it might well be appropriate.
>
> (House of Commons Home Affairs Committee 2002: para. 182)

Opponents of prescribing diamorphine argued to the Committee that it would mean 'colluding and creating life long addicts' (para. 188), a risk which surely also applies to maintenance prescribing of oral methadone.

As further revisions of the guidelines will be evidence based, the recommendations by the Home Affairs Committee for a series of pilot studies on prescribing diamorphine should be welcomed and funded.

In May 2003 the National Treatment Agency considerably amplified the advice given to doctors in the 1999 clinical guidelines on injectable opioid substitution treatment.'Initial guidance' was provided on 'the potential role of injectable heroin and injectable methadone substitute maintenance prescribing' for the minority of opioid users thought likely to benefit from such treatment (National Treatment Agency for Substance Misuse 2003: para 1.1). The guidance was based on expert reviews of the evidence from the UK, the Netherlands and Switzerland, as well as advice from an expert group of doctors, nurses, researchers, service providers, policy advisers, pharmacists and representatives from the Royal Colleges of Psychiatrists and General Practitioners.

It is recommended that maintenance prescribing of injectable heroin or methadone should only be undertaken in accordance with certain principles including:

- ensuring such substitute prescribing is part of 'an integrated package of care' (p. 4) tailored to the needs of the individual patient;
- patients who do not respond to oral methadone maintenance treatment should be offered other options, in steps starting with 'optimised higher dose oral methadone or buprenorphine maintenance treatment, then injectable methadone or injectable heroin maintenance (perhaps in combination with oral preparations)'.

(National Treatment Agency for Substance Misuse 2003: 4)

It was generally agreed by the expert group that, when considering prescribing injectable preparations, account should be taken of the age of the patient; duration of drug use; willingness to comply with supervision and monitoring and the care options offered; avoidance of some risky behaviours and of diverting prescribed drugs to the illicit market; and persistence of poor outcomes while on an optimised oral treatment programme.

Six outcome measures were suggested: retention in treatment; reduction in hazardous injecting; improvements in physical and mental health; improved social stability; and reduced criminal activity.

References

Advisory Council on the Misuse of Drugs (1982) *Treatment and Rehabilitation*, London: HMSO.

Carmichael, P. (1999) *Druglink* 14: 6.

Department of Health, Scottish Home and Health Department, Welsh Office (1991) *Drug Misuse and Dependence – Guidelines on Clinical Management*, London: HMSO.

Department of Health, Scottish Office Department of Health, Welsh Office, Department of Health and Social Services (1999) *Drug Misuse and Dependence – Guidelines on Clinical Management*, London: The Stationery Office.

Ministry of Health (1926) *Departmental Committee on Morphine and Heroin Addiction: Report* (the Rolleston Report), London: HMSO.

Hewitt, L. (1999) *Druglink* 14: 7.

House of Commons Home Affairs Committee (2002) *The Government's Drug Policy: Is It Working?*, London: The Stationary Office Limited.

Keen, J. (1999) 'Managing Drug Misuse in General Practice', *British Medical Journal* 318: 1,503–4.

Malinowski, A. (1999) *Druglink* 14: 7.

Medical Working Group (1984) *Guidelines of Good Clinical Practice in the Treatment of Drug Misuse*, London: Department of Health and Social Security.

National Treatment Agency for Substance Misuse (2003) *Injectable Heroin (and Injectable Methadone). Potential Roles in Drug Treatment. Full Guidance Report*, London: National Treatment Agency.

Waller, T. (1999) *Druglink* 14: 7.

3   Types of treatment for types of patients

Ken Checinski and Hamid Ghodse

Introduction

People use drugs for a wide variety of reasons, some of which are easily understandable and some covert and obscure. It is no surprise that heterogeneity in the treatment of drug misusers has developed for many reasons. When considering it, there are a number of key dimensions that help the conceptualisation of the link between individuals with drug problems, treatments for these problems and measurable outcomes. These are patient factors, chronological factors, treatment factors and outcome factors.

Dimension one: patient factors

An overview is important. Holistic approaches to achieve this involve biological, psychological and social aspects. Biologically, the drugs misused, their liability to cause psychological and physical dependence, and their associated complications (e.g. communicable diseases) should be considered. Additionally, psychological factors include the presence of maladaptive personality traits (and their amplification by drug-misusing behaviour), the level of willingness to consider and be involved in their drug misuse ('motivation'), and associated co-morbid psychiatric illness are important. Individuals with drug problems do not exist within a vacuum: Relevant social aspects will include basic needs such as housing and food, educational/vocational issues and their legal/forensic status. These factors should be taken together to provide a comprehensive picture.

Dimension two: chronological factors

Behaviours, their stressors and their consequences change over time. It is important to consider past events, including hereditary, family and developmental factors, that might lead to vulnerability. Moving to the present, more recent precipitating factors, including physical illness, contact with the criminal justice system and family disruption and schism, are of more immediate importance. Continuing stressors may act as maintaining factors:

...uld include the presence of a formal dependence syndrome, living ...a drug-misusing partner and identifying with a drugs subculture. The ...imeline can often illuminate the reasons when and why individuals decide to take action about their drug problems.

Dimension three: treatment factors

The term 'treatment' includes a range of biological, psychological and social interventions. No single area is a panacea. Pharmacological stabilisation and detoxification are valid only if substitution is available. This is primarily for opioid and sedative-hypnotic physical dependence. In addition, pharmacological agents may be useful as adjunctive treatments to assist in relapse prevention, although these are only widely available and used for opioid misuse. Many of the major advances in the treatment of drug misuse have come in the form of psychological interventions. Such treatments include motivational interviewing and relapse prevention. However, they depend on a degree of stability so that patients can adhere to a programme (e.g. that patients attend their appointments). Some interventions are delivered individually but others are delivered better in groups (e.g. Twelve-Step approaches and psychodynamic interventions). Some of these may require inpatient or residential phases of treatment to manage the crises and risks that can occur within an active treatment phase. Of course, social intervention underpins all treatment and may define where treatment occurs (e.g. residential or custodial venues compared to community locations). It is very important to ensure that treatment is commensurate with the type of problem, relevant aetiological factors and patient preference.

Progress is being made in the development of medication specific to addictions. Treatment services are placing increasing emphasis on anti-craving agents and the greater recognition of their role in relapse prevention.

Dimension four: outcome factors

Given that drug misuse is such a complex phenomenon, it is not surprising that multiple systems are involved. These include: the individual; the treating agencies; the peer group; the family; the local community; and society at large (including the legal context of the individual and his/her drug misuse). It is very important to recognise that different systems will have different expectations for positive outcomes, and indeed negative outcomes too. These expectations will change over time. For instance, a chaotic heroin user may see avoidance of withdrawal symptoms as positive; the family may prioritise the person's personal safety. Additionally, in this case, society may emphasise the community's safety from drug-related crime. Understandably, sometimes these outcome expectations will appear divergent, though a global view of the individual in society should show a convergence of expectation over time. Somehow, the unrealistic expectation of perfect outcomes should be challenged by therapeutic realism and prag-matism (e.g. harm minimisation as a recognised positive outcome). The therapeutic timeline should reflect the natural history of the patient's drug problem and recognise the complexities of addressing aetiological main-taining factors.

In this way, it is important to recognise both the divergence and comple-mentarity of considering a wide range of outcome factors.

Assessment

Assessment (Ghodse 2002) comprises much more than information gathering. It is the time when the individual engages in, or is engaged in, treatment. Most patients, whatever their problem, find this a difficult situation, and when the problem is one of drug misuse or dependence the patient is likely to be very anxious indeed. It takes great courage to admit to a drug problem and to ask for help, especially if there have been previous attempts at dealing with it and previous failures. Anxiety may be disguised by hostile or aggressive behaviour; some patients, having taken drugs to give them courage to attend, may be intoxicated. Nevertheless, their seeking help is the all-important first step, which they alone can take and which should be (must be) rewarded by positive responses from all involved in the assessment procedure.

For many drug misusers, and especially those with long and complex drug problems, the assessment procedure itself may be a therapeutic process. The telling of the 'life history' – some of it spontaneously, some in answer to direct questions – helps the patient, perhaps for the first time, to see his/her drug-taking in some sort of perspective. The account of the present social circumstances clearly identifies current problems and needs. This clarifica-tion to an outsider is, or can be, a clarification to the drug misuser too, and what needs to be done, the way forward, becomes apparent to both.

Assessment is not an end in itself. There is no point in defining the problem, understanding the antecedent circumstances and merely observing and recording the adverse consequences. The aim of assessment is to offer the patient an appropriate treatment programme. This will involve the drug of misuse certainly, but many other areas of the patient's life are likely to be affected too. Assessment should make apparent to both parties what changes are necessary, in which areas of the patient's life, and what the realistic expectations of such change are (although the drug misuser and professional may not always agree). The skill of the helping professional lies in the accu-rate assessment of the problem and the accurate matching of the patient to a treatment option.

The substance itself

The identification of the psychoactive substance used may be made on the basis of self-report data, objective analysis of specimens of urine, blood, saliva or other evidence (presence of drug samples in the patient's possession, clinical signs and symptoms, or reports from informed third parties, as described earlier). Objective analysis provides the most compelling evidence of present or recent use, although this information is of limited value in relation to past use. Whenever possible, it is always advisable to seek corroboration from more than one source of evidence.

The nature of the substances misused determines the therapeutic expectations of patient and assessor alike. Opioid dependence is associated with pharmacological substitution (e.g. with methadone or buprenorphine), whereas cocaine misuse cannot be tackled in this way because there is no appropriate substitute. Many patients approach treatment in terms of symptom relief and may be frightened of examining their past histories and feelings. Treatment services should explore these issues at the time of assessment and intervene where it is relevant to the recovery process. For example, a history of experiencing sexual abuse in childhood may be interesting to the therapist but, whilst acknowledged, usually should not dominate initial treatment phases, certainly until the patient is generally more stable and able to cope with the potential distress of the experience.

Risk assessment and management

Hitherto implicit, risk assessment must be a clear aspect of the assessment of any drug misuser. Risk can be split into risks to self and to others. Personal risks include suicidal ideation and behaviour, acute and longer-term risks of chaotic injecting behaviour and accidental overdose. Risks to others include violence, driving whilst intoxicated or in withdrawal, and abuse of children where the individual has parental responsibility. Identified risks must be addressed in the treatment plan with the aim of minimising them, whilst acknowledging that they cannot be completely removed. The link with identifiable psychiatric disorders must be made at this stage.

Summarising the assessment

This is extremely important, doubly so when carried out by more than one person. The biopsychosocial model is cross-referenced with the timeline, generating a formulation matrix (see Table 3.1). This allows therapeutic interventions to be mapped according to the individual needs of the patient. It supports the identification of realistic, demonstrable outcomes

Comprehensive assessment

Holistic assessment of the individual can take a number of forms. A comprehensive outline is given below, indicating key information to give a full picture of the person and their problem.

Table 3.1: Formulation matrix

	Predisposing	Precipitating	Maintaining
Physical	A	B	C
Psychological	a	β	γ
Social	x	y	z

Outline of a drug history scheme (Ghodse 2002)

It is very important to assess the chronological development of drug use, including types of drug, mode of administration and complications. A suggested list of key points is given below.

Reason for referral
Type of help sought.

First exposure
Age
Which drug
Mode of administration
Circumstances:
Where?
Who/how initiated
Source of drug
Reaction to drug

Subsequent use
Which drug(s)
    Dose
    Frequency of administration
    Route
    Date and age of becoming a regular user
Preferred drug(s)
Periods of abstinence:
Voluntary
Enforced
Reasons for relapse

Recent use (last four to six weeks)
Drug(s):
Dose
Frequency

    Periods of heavy use
    Maximum regular amount taken
    Effects of drug
Reasons for continuation
Circumstances of drug-taking: solitary/with friends
Preferred drug(s)
Periods of abstinence:
    Voluntary
    Enforced
    Reasons for relapse

Recent use (last four to six weeks)
Drug(s):
    Dose
    Frequency
    Route
Any withdrawal symptoms
Evidence of increasing tolerance: escalating dose
Source of supply
Price paid
Continued use despite evidence of harm

History of self-injecting

Age first injected
Duration of injecting
Frequency
Route: subcutaneous/intramuscular/intravenous
Site
HIV risk behaviour:
Source of injection equipment
Sharing of injection equipment:

-     Last time shared
-     Number of others shared with

Knowledge about sterilisation procedures
Knowledge about sources of clean equipment
Heterosexual/homosexual risk behaviour
Use of condoms
Sexual behaviour when intoxicated
Knowledge of HIV issues and transmission

Consequences and complications of drug use

Physical illness: malnutrition; hepatitis; jaundice; abscesses; septicaemia;

deep vein thrombosis; overdose; road traffic and other accidents; symptoms of abstinence syndrome.

Mental illness: episodes of drug-induced psychosis; intoxication leading to drowsiness and confusion; dementia.

Social problems: associated with drug use; amount spent weekly on drugs; source of that money; time spent on drug taking; neglect of other activities.

Occupational problems: difficulties at work; suspensions; jobs lost.

Legal problems: drug-related criminal record; any pending court cases.

Contact with other treatment agencies or sources of help

This includes Addiction Treatment Units, doctors, probation services, local authorities, voluntary agencies, religious organisations and self-help groups.

Outline of a life history scheme

Personal developmental, family and legal information places the drug problem in context and suggests contributory factors that have to be considered in helping the individual tackle the problem. A suggested list of key points is given below.

Family history

Age and occupation of parents and siblings (if deceased: date and cause of death, together with patient's age at the time)

Description of parents' personality and their past and present attitudes towards patient

History of illness or delinquency in family members

Drug use (including alcohol, tobacco) by other family members

Knowledge of patient's drug use by other family members, and their attitude towards it

Relationship between various members of family.

Early history

Birth history

Early development, including time of milestones

Childhood neurotic traits (e.g. bedwetting, sleep walking, tantrums) and periods of separation from parents

Childhood illnesses

Home life and atmosphere

School

Schools attended
Educational attainments
Relationships with staff and peers
Truancy
Further education
Vocational training

Employment

Age of starting work
Jobs held:
    Dates
    Duration
    Wage
    Job satisfaction
    Reason for change

Marital and psychosexual history

Date of marriage; spouse's name, age and occupation
Children: names and ages
General marital adjustment; any periods of permanent or temporary separation
The same information should be collected for any further marriages or cohabitations
Partner's drug taking and knowledge of, and attitude to, patient's drug taking
Sexual inclinations and practices: masturbation; sexual fantasies; homosexuality; heterosexual experiences; contraception; sterilisation

Menstrual history

Age when periods started
Length of cycle
Dysmenorrhoea
Pre-menstrual tension
Periods of amenorrhoea
Date of last menstrual period
Climacteric symptoms

Previous illnesses

Physical:
   Major illnesses and accidents
   Dates of admission to hospital
   Accidental overdoses

Psychiatric:
   All psychiatric admissions and treatments
   Attendance at psychiatric clinics
   Suicide attempts; deliberate self-poisoning

Home circumstances

Address; whom is patient living with
Present income; its source
Financial or domestic problems

Legal history

Number of arrests, court appearances, convictions
Periods in detention centre, approved school, Borstal, prison
Periods of probation
Nature of offences
Outstanding court cases
Disqualification from driving

Previous personality – before drug use

Interests, hobbies
Social relations – family, friends
Mood; mood swings
Character; obsessionality, ambitions, future plans
Religious beliefs and observances
Evidence of personality disorders

Outline of a social work history scheme

Current drug use must be considered in the context of current social functioning. The success of most treatment approaches depends on addressing significant social problems. A suggested list of key points is given below.

Accommodation

Locality
Tenure
Condition
Whom the patient is living with

Employment

Work experience and capabilities
Need for vocational guidance and training
Attitude towards work

Finances

Income
Benefits
Debts

Social functioning

How the day is spent

Social networks

Friends and family
Agencies
Involvement with drug sub-culture
Extent of loneliness and isolation

Strengths and weaknesses of different therapeutic modalities

The formulation matrix lends itself to linkage with therapeutic approaches, broadly defined as motivational enhancement, harm minimisation and relapse prevention. Each of these terms encompasses a range of physical, psychological and social interventions (Figure 3.1).

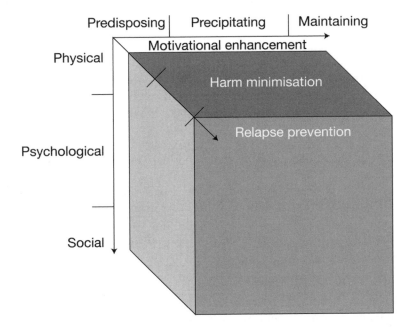

Figure 3.1: Therapeutic mapping dimensions

Specific interventions

Brief interventions

Early interventions are of proven effectiveness for a significant proportion of patients consuming excessive alcohol (Drummond *et al.* 1990). In the primary care setting heavy drinkers consult more frequently, lending them to opportunistic intervention. Results show a 25–35 per cent reduction in drinking at six to twelve months with only five to ten minutes' advice. Follow-up enhances maintenance of the improvement.

However, the evidence for the effectiveness of such interventions with drug misusers is less clear.

Common elements of effective brief interventions are summarised by the acronym FRAMES:

1 Give FEEDBACK of personal risk or impairment.
2 Place emphasis on personal RESPONSIBILITY for change.
3 Offer clear ADVICE to change.
4 Present a MENU of alternative change options.

5   Show therapeutic EMPATHY as a counselling style.
6   Encourage the enhancement of patient SELF-EFFICACY or optimism.

(Bien *et al.* 1993)

Stages of change

Modern treatment of substance misuse is based on a non-linear paradigm, recognising that it is a relapsing and remitting condition, like other serious disruptions to health and to social well-being. Whilst acknowledging that relapse is neither inevitable nor desirable, therapeutic plans should include contingencies and sanctions to support iterative, heuristic recovery processes.

Assessment and enhancement of the individual's motivation and readiness to change are key objectives and increase adherence to treatment and the achievement of positive outcomes. Both motivation and readiness are dynamic factors and can be assessed using instruments such as SOCRATES (Miller and Tonigan 1996). It may be helpful to distinguish readiness to change and readiness for treatment, in that subtly different therapeutic approaches are applied (De Leon 1995). Thus, an appropriate typology for motivation/readiness is:

- Motivation: an internal pressure to change.
- Readiness to change: a willingness to take action.
- Readiness for treatment: a perception that treatment is necessary to achieve self-change.

It is clear that external factors have a major bearing on motivation and that the expression of readiness for treatment is affected by the availability of appropriate and acceptable treatments. External motivating factors must be internalised in order to generate internal pressure to change and consequent readiness. Examples of this dynamic process include the action taken by a person who might lose his/her job and family if drug use continues and the participation in a Drug Treatment and Testing Order programme by an otherwise unengaged drug misuser who faces the aversive prospect of a custodial sentence for drug-related offences. In both examples, unless the effect of these factors is internalised it is likely that cognitive dissonance will lead to relapse into drug use. The relief that an individual is engaged in treatment should not lead to therapeutic complacency in either the drug misuser or the therapist. The use of treatment contracts is widespread where there is substitute prescribing (e.g. methadone for opioid dependence). Whilst there should be common elements, they should be individualised, realistic and bilateral: the responsibilities of the patient must be complemented by those of the treatment agency, otherwise contracts can infantilise patients and create obstacles to progress. The development of Integrated Care Pathways (ICPs) (Department of Health 2002) will ensure that treatment planning is more explicit and less ambiguous for everyone involved.

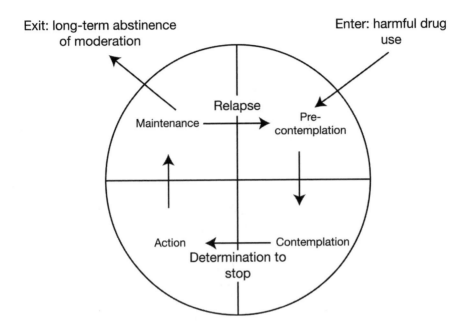

Figure 3.2: Prochaska and DiClemente (1986) stages of change

Supportive treatment that is not based on agreed and systematic protocols, although widely used, is not effective in treating addictions or in
retaining people in treatment. However, relearning, which normally
includes behavioural techniques and interventions targeted at the addictive
behaviour, and dynamic psychotherapies are effective. They are particularly
useful in keeping patients in treatment. It is very important that the therapist has a working knowledge of addictions to establish a sound therapeutic
relationship with the patient.

Cognitive approaches

Motivational interviewing (Miller 1983) is the main tool for maximising
determination, action and maintenance of remission (see Figure 3.2). It is
based on cognitive behavioural principles, but is influenced by a wide range
of counselling and psychotherapeutic techniques. Key elements are:

- listening effectively, allowing the patient to speak and not needlessly
  interrupting;

- using open-ended questions;
- using reflections instead of directing conversation;
- working collaboratively with the patient to set goals;
- reinforcing the patient's personal choice;
- communicating at the patient's level of understanding;
- clarifying important misconceptions;
- soliciting the patient's feedback;
- consistently providing reinforcement to the patient;
- establishing rapport;
- reinforcing the patient for all positive intentions, thoughts and behaviours;
- using summarising statements;
- eliciting self-motivating statements;
- appropriately handling resistance;
- avoiding advice-giving.

Another important cognitive behavioural approach is based on the model of relapse (Marlatt and Gordon 1985). It includes a number of key elements (relapse prevention):

- identification of high-risk relapse factors;
- understanding relapse as both a process and as an event;
- dealing with substance cues as well as with craving;
- dealing with social pressures to use drugs;
- development of supportive networks;
- coping with negative emotional states;
- development of plans to interrupt a lapse or relapse.

Cue exposure (Drummond and Glautier 1994) is a behavioural technique that utilises classical conditioning for relapse prevention by desensitisation of the response to drinking cues. Evidence for efficacy in drug misuse is unclear.

Treatment matching

Project MATCH (Project MATCH Research Group 1998) is the largest ever study of psychological interventions for alcohol misuse. At a cost of over US$30 million, 17,326 patients were randomly allocated into one of three abstinence-based outpatient treatments, on ten different sites in the USA. The treatments were:

- four sessions of motivational intervention/enhancement therapy (MET);
- twelve sessions of cognitive behavioural therapy (CBT);
- twelve sessions of Twelve-Step facilitation therapy (TSF).

All treatment sessions were on a once-weekly, outpatient basis following an intensive assessment. All three treatments were described in carefully written manuals, and therapists were required to follow each session as described. Sessions were videotaped and analysed, and feedback was given to therapists where appropriate in order to standardise sessions and prevent therapist 'drift' and other confounding factors.

The results indicate broadly that all treatments work in some cases. More work is needed to see how patients should be allocated to particular interventions. Clinical judgement is paramount in this matter. This work is yet to be replicated in drug misusers.

Harm minimisation

Injecting drug misusers are at high risk of contracting and spreading blood-borne viruses (e.g. HIV, hepatitis B and hepatitis C) through sharing injecting paraphernalia and engaging in unsafe sexual practices. Many factors are associated with high-risk injecting practices: misusing heroin; misusing cocaine (including crack cocaine); frequent misuse of amphetamines; misusing benzodiazepines; time in prison; having poor accommodation or being homeless; having a sexual partner who injects drugs; and not being in treatment (Donoghoe *et al.* 1992; Baker *et al.* 1995). To a certain extent, all treatment interventions aim to minimise harm. However, recognising that many drug misusers have difficulty achieving and maintaining abstinence, specific techniques are used that do not contribute directly to stopping drug use. Substitute prescribing is one of the most important examples and is discussed in detail below (pp. 46–7). Needle and syringe exchange services have led to lower levels of sharing injecting equipment, fewer sharing partners and less frequent sharing (Marsden *et al.* 2000).

Early intervention

Primary Health Care Teams have a crucial role in the earlier detection and treatment of drug misusers. This should be done with suitable training and support from the specialist drug services (Department of Health 1999). Specialist primary care addiction practitioners yield a high level of satisfaction from general practitioners and their teams (Ghodse *et al.* 1997).

Opioid misuse

Stabilisation

If a person is physically dependent on opioids, pharmacological treatment is required to prevent the development of withdrawal symptoms. Substitution with oral methadone (a synthetic opioid) is effective (Welch and Strang 1999) and leads to:

- reduced illicit drug use
- reduced injecting

- reduced criminal activity
- improved physical health
- improved social well-being.

Methadone has a long half-life (the time taken for the body to deactivate half the amount of the drug available in the body) and can be administered once a day, but LAAM (L-alpha-acetyl methadol) lasts two to three days, making supervised consumption easier to provide. However, it has been withdrawn because of toxicity. The benefits of prescribing injectable opioids are unclear, but any programmes including this aspect of treatment should be carefully managed in order to prevent adverse consequences such as diversion of prescribed medication on to the illicit market or overdose.

Buprenorphine is a partial agonist suitable for stable outpatients. However, it is liable to abuse, especially as there is a risk of injecting, though it may be safer in overdose than methadone (Ling *et al.* 1998). The development of a buprenorphine–naltrexone combination medication will reduce the risk of self-injection (R. E. Johnson *et al.* 2000)

Assisted withdrawal

Opioid-dependent individuals may be safely withdrawn from their dependent state by reduction in the dose of medication prescribed once stabilisation has been achieved. Psychosocial intervention is required to offer support because of craving, psychological response to stress and changes in social behaviour. For instance, an individual must deal with psychological pressure without turning to illicit drugs, and with the peer pressure of members of his/her drug-misusing social network. Reduction in dosage can be achieved over periods of from ten days to many months.

Some people prefer not to take prescribed opioids at all. A group of non-opioid medications known as alpha-2-adrenergic agonists probably work at a site in the brain known as the locus coeruleus (the noradrenergic system is involved in producing symptoms of opioid withdrawal syndrome). Currently, clonidine and lofexidine are used in this way. Side-effects include hypotension on initiation, sedation and rebound hypertension on cessation. In some patients, lofexidine appears to be at least as effective as methadone in inpatient opioid detoxification (Bearn *et al.* 1996). Using naltrexone in combination with clonidine or buprenorphine can shorten the withdrawal period, although not all patients accept it.

Inpatient opioid detoxification is more expensive than outpatient detoxification but cost-effectiveness is equal because inpatient treatment is more successful (Gossop and Strang 2000). Rapid and ultrarapid detoxification involves the use of opioid antagonists such as naloxone or naltrexone, with the addition of heavy sedation or general anaesthesia in the ultrapid variant. Typically, individuals are offered naltrexone or attendance at Narcotics Anonymous (NA) meetings afterwards. O'Connor and Kosten (1998) reviewed studies of this approach and found small sample size, lack of randomised design and lack of control groups. They concluded that more rigorous research methods were needed. This, taken together with concerns about safety, ethics and applicability, means that this approach cannot be supported in terms of both risk and benefit.

Maintenance prescribing

The length of time spent in methadone maintenance treatment is positively linked to the outcome, measured in terms of reduction of illicit use and improved psychological functioning. Adequate dose levels are important and retention in treatment is a goal in itself, with precipitous termination of treatment associated with a return to illicit use (Ball 1991). Nevertheless, Seivewright (2000) states that '[c]ommunity treatment of drug misuse [means] more than methadone', indicating a widespread concern that maintenance may be perceived as a panacea rather than an essential part of the armamentarium of treatment approaches. The comprehensiveness of the original maintenance programmes (including high-dose oral methadone, daily contact, counselling, employment and educational placements), as advocated by Dole and Nyswander (1965) has been diluted, resulting in some programmes consisting of little more than prescribing and token contact (Rosenbaum 1995).

Pharmacological adjuncts to relapse prevention

Naltrexone is a long-acting competitive opioid antagonist with a proven adjunctive role in relapse prevention (Shufman *et al.* 1994). It works by blocking the relevant receptors in the brain, such that any opioid drug taken has negligible effect. It interrupts the behavioural reinforcement of drug-taking and reduces the chance of the reinstatement of dependence.

Preventing overdose

Of illicit drug users interviewed in a study by Loxley *et al.* (1995), 53 per cent had experienced a non-fatal overdose. In this group, 81 per cent had overdosed on heroin. There is still an upward trend in overdoses. The risk of death for a young person injecting heroin is about fourteen times greater than for someone smoking it (Advisory Council of the Misuse of Drugs 2000).

Routinely, all services should give comprehensive advice to drug misusers on the hazards of opioids, including methadone, particularly at the commencement of prescribing and after a period of abstinence, when loss of tolerance occurs. Reminders should be provided at review. This could include teaching of basic first aid to patients, friends and family.

Mortality in specified clinical populations is an important inverse index of treatment effectiveness (Ghodse *et al.* 1998). There is increased risk of fatal overdose when two or more drugs are combined. Oyefeso *et al.* (2000)

found increased mortality among drug misusers who were also taking antidepressants, especially among patients over 45 years of age.

Some drug-dependent individuals suffer from depressive disorders in conjunction with methadone treatment. Antidepressants are very effective in treating the depressive disorder but have no specific effect on the narcotic addiction.

Cocaine misuse

Attempts to find pharmacological treatments for cocaine misuse have been unsuccessful and have included trying to block cocaine-induced euphoria and reversing the neuroadaptation in the brain (Dackis and O'Brien 2002). The National Institute for Drug Abuse Collaborative Cocaine Treatment Study randomly allocated 487 patients to one of four manual-guided treatments:

- group drug counselling (GDC)
- individual drug counselling (IDC) plus GDC
- cognitive therapy plus GDC
- supportive expressive therapy plus GDC.

Contrary to expectations, IDC plus GDC was the most effective using a battery of outcome measures. However, even for this modality 40 per cent continued to use cocaine (Critschristoph *et al.* 1999).

Amphetamine misuse

Amphetamines are used more commonly than opioids and are often injected (see Bruce 2000). The case for substitute prescribing is not proven: there may be a role in harm minimisation for patients who inject. Tolerance occurs but there is no physiological withdrawal syndrome. Craving is a prominent feature. Manualised psychosocial treatments similar to those offered to cocaine misusers have been found to be of some benefit (Huber *et al.* 1997).

Benzodiazepine misuse

Physical dependence on benzodiazepines is, in some ways, more dangerous than opioid dependence. Withdrawal is dangerous if carried out too quickly. People misusing longer-acting benzodiazepines may not show withdrawal signs for several days.

Stabilisation

If there is evidence of withdrawal symptoms, a long-acting benzodiazepine such as diazepam should be given. Longer-acting medication yields more stable blood levels. The dose should be adjusted according to the dependent person's history and observed condition. Occasionally, epileptiform convulsions may occur, suggesting that the dose is inadequate, and may indicate short-term use of an anticonvulsant such as carbamazepine.

Assisted withdrawal

Rapid withdrawal (over a period of seven to twenty-eight days, depending on the dose) is only appropriate in hospital. Typically, community-based withdrawal lasts from several months to a year. Observation is required for about ten days after the end of a detoxification programme because of late-onset events such as seizures.

Relapse prevention

Supportive counselling, including empowering and problem-solving approaches should be offered. Advice regarding insomnia ('sleep hygiene') and anxiety management training should be included in a range of psychological interventions geared to the individual's needs.

Barbiturate misuse

Dependence, complications and treatment are similar to those for benzodiazepines, but the risks of fatal overdose (deliberate or accidental) are higher. Fortunately, there is cross-tolerance between the two classes of drug, such that benzodiazepines should be used for stabilisation and withdrawal in people with physical dependence on barbiturates.

Cannabis misuse

A cannabis withdrawal syndrome has been demonstrated after long-term misuse (Haney *et al.* 1999). It prolongs misuse of the substance and increases the risks of adverse physical and psychological effects (Copeland *et al.* 2001a). There is mounting demand for treatment, and modest benefits have been reported with cognitive methods (Copeland *et al.* 2001b). There is no evidence of any effective pharmacological treatment of cannabis addiction.

Poly-drug misuse

This is associated with high-risk injecting practices (Frischer *et al.* 1993) and is an indication for inpatient treatment in chaotic individuals who are at significant risk. Alcohol misuse is hazardous for drug misusers because of its multiple system toxicity (e.g. hepatobiliary, cardiac and central nervous systems) that can work synergistically with complications of drug use (e.g. hepatitis B or C infection). Alcohol dependence syndrome is associated with

Level and type of intervention

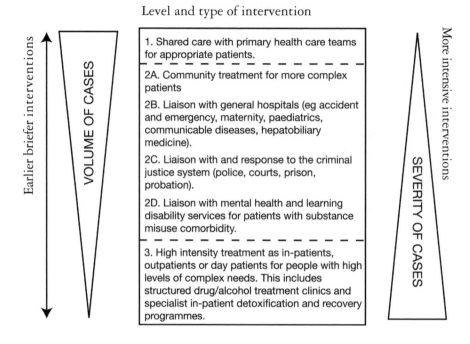

Figure 3.3: Overview of levels of intervention

a potentially fatal withdrawal syndrome that can include epileptiform seizures and is linked with encephalopathy and consequent memory impairment (Wernicke–Korsakov syndrome). Individuals with poly-drug misuse may substitute one substance for another, especially if their drug of choice is not available.

Stratifying the response

Typically, earlier interventions are briefer, whereas later ones are more complex. Treatment matching is not exact, but the formulation matrix and the dimensions of therapeutic mapping indicate the degree of complexity. Three levels, approximating to primary (shared), secondary and tertiary care, are derived, associated with decreasing numbers and increasing severity of patients. (See Figure 3.3.)

Care planning and review

Therapeutic plans should include aims achievable within a reasonable timescale and have contingencies if progress is too slow or absent. Ideally, they should be measurable, yielding identifiable outcomes in the immediate, intermediate and long-term future. This future timeline includes a recursive element, allowing for lapse and relapse.

Outcome variables will include:

- physical health
- psychological health and well-being
- social well-being
- legal status
- substance use
- overall global function.

Qualitative and quantitative measures contribute to the assessment of these variables and allow structured review of care plans, adjustment of the range of interventions and adjustment of the aims.

Collaborative approaches

Drug misusers usually have significant psychosocial needs identified at initial and ongoing assessment. Social stability, including housing, occupation, education and close relationships, is an important factor in minimising the chances of relapse. Some psychological approaches are provided within health systems, while others are given by non-statutory providers or in self-help settings (e.g. NA). Failure to co-ordinate therapeutic input and poor collaboration between agencies can lead to fragmented, ineffective care, with increased relapse rates and higher complication rates.

Increased attention is now being paid to a tiered or stratified response to drug misusers because that specifies the role of different services and interventions and helps identify entry and exit criteria at each level. This assists in delineating the target group and in targeting resources and providing a framework for planning and commissioning comprehensive care systems within any given area. In relation to assessment and care co-ordination, this helps to define appropriate thresholds. In England, the tiers are based on those identified for young people with substance misuse (Health Advisory Service 2001):

1 non-substance misuse (SM) specific services
2 open access substance misuse services
3 structured community-based substance misuse services
4a residential substance misuse specific services
4b highly specialist non-substance misuse specific services.

These tiers complement the levels of intervention in Figure 3.3.

The application of a tiered model recognises that inpatient substance misuse treatment services are a crucial part of the spectrum of care that must be provided. They can be based in dedicated specialist units, in general hospitals (general medical beds) or in psychiatric services. There is good evidence that drug misusers treated in dedicated units achieve better outcomes that others (Department of Health 1996). Some inpatient treatment facilities are provided in the non-statutory sector.

The principle of ICPs is being applied in England to deliver packages of care in a co-ordinated and integrated way through the Models of Care project (Department of Health 2002). For any individual with a plan of treatment, an ICP attempts to describe the nature and projected course. It is based on the notion that drug misusers require inter-agency connections or pathways that usually involve movement between the four treatment tiers over a period of time. To facilitate access to interventions and deliver seamless, co-ordinated treatment, there should be explicit, locally defined and agreed protocols between agencies, clear eligibility criteria and joint working arrangements. Thus, there is a means of agreeing local referral and treatment interfaces to ensure individuals do not slip through the network of diverse complementary services.

Each ICP will have:

- definitions of the care provided
- aims and objectives
- definitions of the service user group served
- eligibility criteria (including priority groups) and exclusions/contraindications
- referral pathway
- screening and assessment processes
- description of the treatment process/phases
- care co-ordination
- departure planning/aftercare and support and onward referral pathways
- services with which the modality interfaces.

(Department of Health 2002)

The Models of Care approach complements other care co-ordination practices (e.g. the Care Programme Approach for patients accepted by specialist mental health services in England and Wales).

Special groups

Female drug misusers

Women are more susceptible to the adverse effects of drug use than men and show relatively poor uptake of drug treatment services. Childcare responsibilities and fears of having children removed form their care act as reasons both for and against women coming for help (Thom and Green 1996). Specific facets of treatment programmes should include: facilities for children; shared care with other services (e.g. obstetrics, paediatrics); access to housing and education services; help for women involved in prostitution; and counselling geared to the needs of women (e.g. female therapists), covering issues such as sexual abuse, domestic violence, depression and deliberate self-harm, and eating disorders (Hodgins *et al.* 1997). Many of these issues are also important for men (e.g. sexual abuse, prostitution, mental health issues).

Ethnic minority populations

The British Crime Survey shows higher levels of drug misuse in Afro-Caribbean people compared to Asians, especially in the 16–29 age range (Ramsey and Spiller 1997). Despite significant disadvantage, Afro-Caribbean people are less likely to receive health and social care than white British people. A number of factors limit the use of drug treatment services by ethnic minorities (Perera *et al.* 1993). These include a focus on opioids rather than other substances such as cocaine and other stimulants; suspicion about lack of confidentiality; a perception that staff understand poorly the needs of ethnic groups; and ignorance of relevant cultural and social factors. It is important that these issues are addressed despite the challenge that in most local authorities in the UK ethnic minorities make up less than 2 per cent of the population.

Drug misuse in the family

Children (individuals under 18 years of age) form a diverse group but there are key differences from adults in relation to legal competence, confidentiality, parental responsibility and protection from harm (the overall welfare of the child being paramount). Drug services for children should address these issues and be child-centred.

The primacy of the child's well-being is a major factor when it is the parents who are misusing drugs. Assessment and support for parenting behaviour should be available as a component of all drug treatment programmes, including inpatient and residential settings.

Predictors of good treatment outcomes

Individuals with greater confidence in and commitment to a treatment programme have been shown to yield better outcomes (Broome *et al.* 1999). Readiness to engage in treatment is a clear indicator of therapeutic involvement, and for people misusing multiple drugs, cocaine misuse reduces retention (Joe *et al.* 1999).

Dual diagnosis

The concept of dual diagnosis or the mentally ill chemical abuser (MICA) is very important (Lehman *et al.* 1989):

- primary mental illness with subsequent (consequent) substance abuse
- primary substance abuse with psychiatric sequelae
- dual primary diagnosis
- common aetiological factor causing mental illness and substance abuse.

There is emerging evidence to support a greater than chance association between schizophrenia and alcohol misuse, with a more definitive community survey in the UK (London) showing that alcohol problems occur at a rate of 36 per cent and drug problems at a rate of 16 per cent in people with severe mental disorders in contact with psychiatric services (Menezes *et al.* 1996). Rates of dual diagnosis are high in the USA and are associated with homelessness, violence and high service costs (Johnson 1997).

Treatment approaches rely on robust assessment, effective collaborative care planning and appropriate crisis management (Checinski 2002).

Conclusion

The nature of the relationship between the types of individual with drug problems and the diverse modalities of treatment available remains a complex one. However, there has been marked progress in understanding and clarifying each of the four dimensions linking treatment and outcome: the significance of individual patient factors; the impact of chronological factors; the efficacy of treatments; and the multi-axial outcome expectations.

Dimension one (patient factors) depends on rigorous biopsychosocial assessment both initially and over a period of time. The level of readiness to change is a major factor determining adherence to treatment and achievement of positive outcomes.

Dimension two (chronological factors) depends on the ability to 'place' the patient along a timeline, being able to assess motivation (readiness to change) at this point and then offering an appropriate treatment plan.

Dimension three (treatment factors) relies on the availability of evidence-based treatments tailored to meet the needs of an individual along a specific timeline Such treatments sit under the broad headings of motivational enhancement, harm minimisation and relapse prevention, and have physical, psychological and social components.

Dimension four (outcome factors) is delineated by the multiple systems identified at assessment and, typically involved in care planning. The nature of such a set of outcomes is that they may be complementary (e.g. the provision of detoxification when abstinence is an agreed goal) or contradictory (e.g. the use of harm minimisation approaches when the agreed ultimate aim is abstinence from drug misuse), but should be seen as milestones along a pathway from disease and dysfunction to relative well-being.

The systematic application of these principles of assessment and treatment will help to reduce risk and generate improved outcomes for drug misusers and society at large.

References

Advisory Council on the Misuse of Drugs (2000) *Reducing Drug Related Deaths*, London: The Stationery Office.

Baker, A., Kochan, N., Dixon, J., Wodack, A. and Heather, N. (1995) 'HIV Risk Taking Behaviour among Injecting Drug Users Currently, Previously and Never Enrolled in Methadone Treatment', *Addiction* 90: 545–54.

Ball, J. C. (1991) 'The Similarity of Crime Rates among Male Heroin Addicts in New York City, Philadelphia and Baltimore', *Journal of Drug Issues* 21: 413–27.

Bearn, J., Gossop, M. and Strang, J. (1996) 'Randomised Double-blind Comparison of Lofexidine and Methadone in the Inpatient Treatment of Opiate Withdrawal', *Drug and Alcohol Dependence* 43: 87–91.

Bien, T., Miller, W. and Tonigan, J. (1993) 'Brief Interventions for Alcohol Problems: A Review', *Addiction* 88: 315–36.

Broome, K. M., Simpson, D. D. and Joe, G. W. (1999) 'Patient and Program Attributes Related to Treatment Process Indicators in DATOS', *Drug and Alcohol Dependence* 57: 127–35.

Bruce, M. (2000) 'Managing Amphetamine Dependence', *Advances in Psychiatric Treatment* 6: 33–40.

Checinski, K. (2002) 'Treatment Strategies and Interventions', in G. H. Rassool (ed.) *Dual Diagnosis. Substance Misuse and Psychiatric Disorders*, Oxford: Blackwell Science.

Copeland, J., Swift, W. and Rees, V. (2001a) 'Clinical Profile of Participants in a Brief Intervention Program for Cannabis Use Disorders', *Journal of Substance Abuse Treatment* 21: 45–52.

Copeland, J., Swift, W. and Rees, V. (2001b) 'A Randomised Controlled Trial of Brief Cognitive-behavioural Interventions for Cannabis Use Disorder', *Journal of Substance Abuse Treatment* 21: 55–64.

Critschristoph, P., Siqueland, L., Blaine, J., Frank, A., Luborsky, L., Onken, L. S., Muenz, L. R., Thase, M. E., Weiss, R. D., Gastfriend, D. R., Woody, G. E., Barber, J. P., Butler, S. F., Daley, D., Salloum, I., Bishop, S., Najavits, L. M., Lis, J., Mercer, D., Griffin, M. L., Moras, K. and Beck, A. T. (1999) 'Psychosocial Treatments for Cocaine Dependence: National Institute for Drug Abuse Collaborative Cocaine Treatment Study', *Archives of General Psychiatry* 56: 493–502.

Dackis, C. A. and O'Brien, C. P. (2002) 'Cocaine Dependence: The Challenge for Pharmacotherapy', *Current Opinion in Psychiatry* 15: 261–7.

De Leon, G. (1995) 'Therapeutic Communities for Addictions: A Theoretical Framework', *International Journal of the Addictions* 30(12): 1,603–45.

Department of Health (1996) *The Task Force to Review Services for Drug Misusers*, London: HMSO.

Department of Health (1999) *Drug Misuse and Dependence – Guidelines on Clinical Management*, London: HMSO.

Department of Health (2002) *Models of Care for Substance Misuse Treatment*, London: HMSO.

Dole, V. P. and Nyswander, M. (1965) 'A Medical Treatment for Diacetylmorphine (Heroin) Addiction', *Journal of the American Medical Association* 193: 80–4.

Donoghoe, M. C., Stimson, G. V. and Dolan, K. A. (1992) *Syringe Exchange in England: An Overview*, London: Tufnell Press.

Drummond, D. C. and Glautier, S. (1994) 'A Controlled Trial of Cue Exposure Treatment in Alcohol Dependence', *Journal of Consulting and Clinical Psychology* 62: 802–17.

Drummond, D. C., Thom, B., Brown, C., Edwards, G. and Mullan, M. J. (1990) 'Specialist versus General Practitioner Treatment of Problem Drinkers', *Lancet* 336: 915–18.

Frischer, M., Haw, S. and Bloor, M. (1993) 'Modelling the Behaviour and Attitudes of Injecting Drug Users: A New Approach to Identifying HIV Risk Practices', *International Journal of the Addictions* 28: 129–52.

Ghodse, A. H. (2002) 'Assessment', in *Drugs and Addictive Behaviour: A Guide to Treatment*, 3rd edition, Cambridge: Cambridge University Press.

Ghodse, A. H., Priestley, J. and Saunders, V. (1997) *Addiction Prevention in Primary Care*, London: St George's Hospital Medical School.

Ghodse, A. H., Oyefeso, A. and Kilpatrick, B. (1998) 'Mortality of Drug Addicts in the United Kingdom 1967–1993', *International Journal of Epidemiology* 27: 473–8.

Gossop, M. and Strang, J. (2000) 'Price, Value and Costs of Opiate Detoxification Treatments', *British Journal of Psychiatry* 177: 262–6.

Haney, M., Ward, M. S., Comer, S. D., Foltin, R. W. and Fischman, M. W. (1999) 'Abstinence Symptoms following Smoked Marijuana in Humans', *Psychopharmacology* 141: 395–404.

Health Advisory Service (2001) *The Substance of Young Needs*, London: Health Advisory Service.

Hodgins, D., El-Guebaly, N. and Addington, J. (1997) 'Treatment of Substance Abusers: Single or Mixed Gender Programmes', *Addiction* 92: 805–12.

Huber, A., Ling, W., Shoptaw, S., Gulati, V., Brethen, P. and Rawson, R. (1997) 'Integrating Treatments for Methamphetamine Abuse: A Psychosocial Perspective', *Journal of Addictive Disorders* 16: 41–50.

Joe, G. W., Simpson, D. D. and Broome, K. M. (1999) 'Retention and Patient Engagement Models for Different Treatment Modalities in DATOS', *Drug and Alcohol Dependence* 57: 113–25.

Johnson, R. E., Chutuape, M. A., Strain, E. C., Walsh, S. L., Stitzer, M. L. and Bigelow, G. E. (2000) 'A Comparison of Levomethadyl Acetate, Buprenorphine and Methadone Opiate Dependence', *New England Journal of Medicine* 343: 1,290–7.

Johnson, S. (1997) 'Dual Diagnosis of Severe Mental Illness and Substance Misuse: A Case for Specialist Services', *British Journal of Psychiatry* 171: 205–8.

Lehman, A. F., Myers, C. P. and Corty, E. C. (1989) 'Assessment and Classification of Patients with Psychiatric and Substance Abuse Syndromes', *Hospital and Community Psychiatry* 40: 1,019–30.

Ling, W., Charuvastra, C., Collins, J. F., Batki, S., Brown, L., Kintausi, P., Wesson, D., McNicholas, L., Tusel, D., Malkkerneker, U., Renner, J., Santos, E., Casadonte, P., Fye, C., Stine, S., Wang, R. and Segal, D. (1998) 'Buprenorphine Maintenance Treatment of Opiate Dependence: A Multicentre, Randomised Clinical Trial', *Addiction* 93: 119–28.

Loxley, W., Carruthers, S. and Bevan, J. (1995) *In the Same Vein: First Report of the Australian Study of HIV and Injecting Drug Use (ASHIDU) (Perth, National Centre for Research into the Prevention of Drug Abuse)*, Perth: Curtin University of Technology.

Marlatt, G. A. and Gordon, J. R. (1985) *Relapse Prevention*, New York: Guilford Press.

Marsden, J., Strang, J. with Lavoie, D., Abdulrahim, D., Hickman, M. and Scott, S. (2000) 'Epidemiologically-based Needs Assessment: Drug Misuse', in A. Stevens and J. Raftery (eds) *Health Care Needs Assessment*, Oxford: Radcliffe.

Menezes, P. R., Johnson, S., Thornicroft, G., Marshall, J., Prosser, D., Bebbington, P. and Kuipers, E. (1996) 'Drug and Alcohol Problems among Individuals with Severe Mental Illness in South London', *British Journal of Psychiatry* 168: 612–19.

Miller, W. R. (1983) 'Motivational Interviewing with Problem Drinkers', *Behavioural Psychotherapy* 11: 147–72.

Miller, W. R. and Tonigan, J. S. (1996) 'Assessing Drinkers' Motivations for Change: The Stages of Change Readiness and Treatment Eagerness Scale (SOCRATES)', *Psychology of Addictive Behaviors* 10(2): 81–9.

O'Connor, T. G. and Kosten, T. R. (1998) 'Rapid and Ultrarapid Opioid Detoxification Techniques', *Journal of the American Medical Association* 279: 229–34.

Oyefeso, A., Valmana, A., Clancy, C., Ghodse, A. H. and Williams, H. (2000) 'Fatal Antidepressant Overdose among Drug Abusers and Non-drug Abusers', *Acta Psychiatriatrica Scandinavica* 102: 295–9.

Perera, J., Power, R. and Gibson, N. (1993) *Assessing the Needs of Black Drug Users in North Westminster*. London: Hungerford Drugs Project and Centre for Research on Drugs and Health Behaviour.

Prochaska, J. O. and DiClemente, C. C. (1986) 'Towards a Comprehensive Model of Change', in W. R. Miller and N. Heather (eds) *Treating Addictive Behaviours: Processes of Change*, New York: Plenum Press.

Project MATCH Research Group (1998) 'Matching Alcoholism Treatments to Client Heterogeneity: Treatment Main Effects and Matching Effects on Drinking during Treatment', *Journal of Studies on Alcohol* 59: 631–9.

Ramsey, M. and Spiller, J. (1997) *Drug Misuse Declared in 1996: Latest Results from the British Crime Survey*, Research Study 172, London: Home Office.

Rosenbaum, M. (1995) 'The Demedicalisation of Methadone Maintenance', *Journal of Psychoactive Drugs* 27: 145–9.

Seivewright, N. (2000) *Community Treatment of Drug Misuse: More than Methadone*, Cambridge: Cambridge University Press.

Shufman, E. N., Porat, S., Witztum, E., Gandacu, D., Bar Hamburger, R. and Ginath, Y. (1994) 'The Efficacy of Naltrexone in Preventing Re-abuse of Heroin after Detoxification', *Society of Biological Psychiatry* 35: 935–45.

Strang, J. and Gossop, M. (eds) (1994) *Heroin Addiction and Drug Policy: The British System*, Oxford: Oxford University Press.

Thom, B. and Green, A. (1996) 'Services for Women: The Way Forward', in L. Harrison (ed.) *Alcohol Problems in the Community*, London: Routledge.

Welch, S. and Strang, J. (1999) 'Pharmacotherapy in the Treatment of Drug Dependence: Options to Strengthen Effectiveness', *Advances in Psychiatric Treatment* 5: 427–34.

4 Developments in the treatment of drug problems

Michael Gossop

The identification of HIV infection among injecting drug users during the 1980s forced a radical rethinking of the nature of the problems and of the appropriateness and effectiveness of existing services. At about the same time, other changes were occurring. These included the appearance of heroin smoking ('chasing the dragon') and the smoking of crack cocaine, and increased numbers of users. In general, the period since the rapid changes of the 1980s has been characterised by gradual developments and the consolidation of treatment responses.

The treatment of drug problems in the UK is provided by many services and agencies, and may include medical, psychiatric, psychological and social interventions. Treatments may vary according to setting, intensity, and duration; and they may be delivered by specialist and non-specialist personnel with different backgrounds and training. Treatments may be directed towards different client needs, and may include (either separately or in combination) forms of detoxification, residential rehabilitation, aftercare, cognitive behavioural therapies, various sorts of drug prescribing, brief counselling, longer-term counselling and support, and psychiatric and medical treatments.

Descriptions of the drug users who seek treatment and of the developments and status of the British treatment system have been provided elsewhere (Strang and Gossop 1994; Gossop *et al.* 1998a; Seivewright 2000; Stewart *et al.* 2000b). The present chapter focuses upon current clinical practice within UK treatment services, and examines areas in which there have been changes in the identification of clinical problems and in the delivery of treatment in recent years.

The problems

Substance use and multiple substance use: consumption behaviours, problems and dependence

Heroin is the most frequently reported main problem drug among drug users in UK treatment services, though cocaine, amphetamines and benzodiazepines are also widely used (Strang and Gossop 1994; Gossop *et al.* 1998b). The use of crack cocaine and associated problems are increasingly found in drug treatment populations (Gossop *et al.* 2002b). However, although drug users in treatment usually present with patterns of multiple drug use, this issue remains relatively neglected and poorly understood (Gossop 2001). Polydrug use may include problematic patterns of drinking. Among drug users in the National Treatment Outcome Research Study (NTORS), more than one-third of those drinking at intake to treatment reported problematic drinking (Gossop *et al.* 2000b). In the US, between 20 and 50 per cent of drug users in treatment are problematic drinkers (Belenko 1979; Hunt *et al.* 1986; Joseph and Appel 1985; Hubbard *et al.* 1989; Lehman and Simpson 1990).

Drug users with multiple drug use problems may require special treatment planning (Strain *et al.* 1991). Heavy drinking may aggravate other drug problems and adversely affect treatment outcomes. Chronic alcohol abuse has been identified as an important cause of medical complications during methadone treatment and is frequently linked to the premature discharge of patients from methadone programmes (Kreek 1981; McLellan 1983; Joe *et al.* 1991). Cocaine misusers with drinking problems have been found to be more likely to relapse to cocaine use after treatment, and drinking is often closely linked to relapse (McKay *et al.* 1999).

The assessment of substance use problems requires investigation along three dimensions (Gossop 2001). These are: consumption behaviour, substance-related problems and severity of dependence. Frequency and quantity of drug use have obvious importance as aspects of consumption behaviour. Route of administration is also important. This is a risk factor for overdose (Gossop *et al.* 1996) and for the transmission of blood-borne infections (Ball and Ross 1991; Gossop *et al.* 1994b; Baker *et al.* 1995; Gibson *et al.* 1999; Alter *et al.* 1999; Best *et al.* 1999b). Injecting and the sharing of injecting equipment are highly problematic behaviours, and the reduction of public health threats associated with injecting is an appropriate treatment goal (McLellan *et al.* 1997). Since the early 1990s most heroin users in the London area have tended to start using heroin by chasing the dragon (Strang *et al.* 1992). Routes of drug administration are not fixed, and many chasers make a subsequent transition to injecting (Griffiths *et al.* 1994).

Research into the addictions has drawn an increasingly clear distinction between substance-related problems and dependence (Edwards and Gross 1976; Edwards *et al.* 1981). Two essential elements of dependence are a strong desire or feeling of compulsion to engage in the particular behaviour and impaired capacity to control the behaviour (Gossop 1989). Severity of dependence is related to route of administration of heroin, cocaine and amphetamines (Gossop *et al.* 1992, 1994a). Severity of heroin dependence is also related both to injecting and sexual HIV risk behaviours (Gossop *et al.* 1993a, 1993b).

Multiple substance use complicates both the assessment and understanding of dependence (Gossop 2001). Few studies have investigated multiple substance use specifically in relation to severity of dependence upon more than one substance. Rawson *et al.* (1981) suggested that dually (drug and alcohol) dependent clients may have worse treatment outcomes than those who are not heavy drinkers, and codependence upon alcohol among opiate users in methadone treatment programmes has been found to affect treatment response and treatment outcome (Chatham *et al.* 1997). Some drug users who have been treated may substitute alcohol as their drug use decreases (Simpson and Lloyd 1977; Hunt *et al.* 1986; DeLeon 1987).

Psychiatric comorbidity

Drug problems often occur in conjunction with psychological and psychiatric disorders. However, the mental health needs of drug users are often not properly met by specialist addiction treatment services (Hall and Farrell 1997), though where drug users present with both psychiatric and substance use problems the failure to address mental health problems leads to poorer outcomes (McLellan *et al.* 1993). The presence of both substance use and psychiatric problems within the same individuals is increasingly recognised as among the more difficult issues to be tackled by psychiatry (Schuckit and Hesselbrock 1994).

Anxiety and depressed mood, in particular, are more prevalent among drug users in treatment than in the general population (Kessler *et al.* 1994; Farrell *et al.* 1998). High symptom levels have been found at intake to treatment among drug misusers admitted to treatment programmes across England, with about one in five having previously received treatment for a psychiatric health problem other than substance use (Marsden *et al.* 2000). Improvement in psychological health and functioning is an important treatment goal for drug users. The prevalence of psychiatric symptoms among drug users seeking treatment indicates the importance of conducting as thorough a psychiatric assessment as is practicable in the context of routine clinical practice. Staff in both psychiatry and addiction treatment settings may require training to detect, assess and respond to comorbid disorders (Scott *et al.* 1998).

Blood-borne infections

There is now an increased awareness of hepatitis B (HBV) and hepatitis C (HCV) as well as HIV infection. HCV is extremely prevalent amongst injecting drug users. Among opiate addicts in London, Best *et al.* (1999b) found 86 per cent were HCV seropositive and 55 per cent were HBV seropositive. In a study of opiate addicts attending a treatment service in London, Noble *et al.* (2000) found prevalence rates for markers of prior infection with HCV of 80 per cent, and 50 per cent for HBV. HCV-positive patients were older, had been injecting for a longer period, and had been attending treatment for longer. There was a strong association between years of injecting drug use and hepatitis infection rates. Drug users were generally aware of the risks of HCV and HBV, but their beliefs about their own viral status were frequently inaccurate. Many addicts mistakenly believed they were HBV or HCV negative. This may have serious public health consequences. Clinicians should encourage hepatitis screening among drug injectors and use this as a catalyst for interventions.

In addition to the direct sharing of needles and syringes, injectors are at risk through indirect forms of sharing, such as 'backloading' as well as exposure to contaminated cookers, filters and rinse water (Gossop *et al.* 1993a, 1994b). Shared use of all injecting equipment can lead to transmission of HIV and other blood-borne infections.

Heavy drinking among HCV-infected drug users is a risk factor for mortality because of its adverse effects upon the physical health of the user. For individuals chronically infected with HCV, even low levels of alcohol consumption are associated with increased risk of viraemia and hepatic fibrosis (Pessione *et al.* 1998).

The risk behaviour of drug users has been the focus for various preventive activities. Dissemination of information about the transmission of blood-borne infections is one of the least controversial prevention responses. This has been widely used, and in some circumstances such measures can be effective (Selwyn 1987). Needle and syringe exchange schemes have also been established in many countries. It has been suggested that these have been effective in the UK in helping to keep HIV seroprevalence at a relatively low level (Stimson 1995).

Treatment services play an important role in tackling blood-borne infections and most drug treatment programmes have incorporated interventions targeted at injecting risk and sex risk behaviours. Methadone maintenance can reduce HIV risk behaviours and HIV seroconversion (Gibson *et al.* 1999; Marsch 1998; Ward *et al.* 1998; Sorensen and Copeland 2000). Needle sharing has been found to be lower among patients in methadone maintenance programmes than among those not in treatment (Longshore *et al.* 1993), and treatment involvement has been found to be predictive of reduced HIV seroconversion rates (Friedman *et al.* 1995; Williams *et al.* 1992; Metzger *et al.* 1993). Higher methadone doses and longer duration of treatment are related to lower rates of HIV infection (Hartel and Schoenbaum 1998). Among NTORS clients, injecting and sharing injecting equipment (and having unprotected sex) were substantially reduced one year after treatment entry (Gossop *et al.* 2002c). Improvements were found both among drug users admitted to methadone treatment and among those admitted to residential treatment programmes.

Overdose

In a study of over 400 heroin users in London, almost one-quarter reported having taken at least one overdose (on a mean of 3.6 occasions) (Gossop *et al.* 1996). A more recent study of opiate addicts in methadone maintenance treatment found that 97 per cent of the sample had witnessed at least one overdose, with 112 people witnessing a total of more than 700 overdoses (Strang *et al.* 2000a). Increases in overdose deaths have been reported among drug users in several countries in recent years. Neeleman and Farrell (1997) noted a ninefold increase in opiate-related deaths in England and Wales between 1974 and 1992, and in Australia Hall (1999) described a 55-fold increase in drug overdose deaths between 1964 and 1997. Simpson and Sells (1982) found the death rate of US drug users to be 3–14 times higher than that of their peers.

Deaths among drug users have many causes, including accidents, suicide, violence, AIDS, and various drug-related and other illnesses (Rivara *et al.* 1997; Rossow and Lauritzen 1999; Hulse *et al.* 1999). Despite the greater awareness of HIV and AIDS as potential causes of death among drug users, drug overdose continues to be one of the most frequent causes of death in this group (Ghodse *et al.* 1978; Powis *et al.* 1999; Strang *et al.* 1999b). In Scotland, Frischer *et al.* (1993) found that more than 90 per cent of drug user deaths were due to overdose or suicide, and only 2 per cent to HIV/AIDS.

Heroin is frequently linked to fatal overdoses, though other drugs, and particularly benzodiazepines, are also often associated with overdose deaths (Strang *et al.* 1999b; Darke and Ross 1999; Risser *et al.* 2000). The mechanism by which opiate overdose leads to death is generally attributed to respiratory depression mediated by inhibition of medullary centres (White and Irvine 1999). However, overdoses which are commonly attributed to the use of opiates are generally more likely to involve the combined use of opiates and alcohol or other sedatives (Darke and Zador 1996; Best *et al.* 1999a).

The mortality rate among drug misusers in the NTORS cohort was 1.2 per cent (Gossop *et al.* 2001b). The majority of deaths (68 per cent) were associated with overdoses. Opiates were most commonly detected during post mortem examinations. In the majority of cases more than one drug was detected. In more than half of the overdose deaths three or more drugs were detected. The most common combinations involved opiates and alcohol, or opiates and benzodiazepines.

Drug overdoses may be taken with suicidal intent, and in this respect overdoses may be related to psychiatric problems, and especially to depressive disorders. About one-third of the NTORS clients had thoughts of killing themselves at admission to treatment (Gossop *et al.* 1998a). In a previous study of non-fatal overdoses, 10 per cent reported taking a deliberate overdose (Gossop *et al.* 1996). The distinction between accidental and intentional overdose is a precarious one (Farrell *et al.* 1996), and official data systems may underestimate suicide among addicts since evidence of intent is required before overdose deaths can be recorded as suicide. It may be useful to think in terms of a continuum between non-fatal, fatal accidental and fatal deliberate overdoses.

Treatment responses

Withdrawal and detoxification

A preliminary phase of treatments aimed at abstinence may involve withdrawal from drugs or 'detoxification'. Although many drugs of abuse have a clearly defined withdrawal syndrome (such as opiates, benzodiazepines and alcohol), some do not. For the stimulant drugs such as cocaine and amphetamines there is some uncertainty about whether a true withdrawal syndrome can be identified. Unquestionably, users can develop a strong dependence upon stimulants. This may be manifested in feelings of strong, and sometimes subjectively overpowering, psychological feelings of need to use the drugs and in impaired behavioural control over their use. A number of physiological disturbances and symptoms occur after the abrupt discontinuation of stimulants. Gossop, Bradley and Brewis (1982) found that abstinence after regular use of amphetamines led to a period of prolonged disturbances in sleep patterns, with daytime drowsiness and night-time wakefulness. Some clinicians regard the withdrawal responses after stopping stimulant use as a withdrawal syndrome requiring treatment. For example, in a double-blind placebo-controlled trial, Kampman *et al.* (2000) found amantidine to be an effective treatment for cocaine withdrawal symptoms.

The importance of detoxification is often overestimated and there have been inappropriate expectations that detoxification procedures alone could be expected to produce long-term abstinence. Detoxification alone is not effective in this respect (Lipton and Maranda 1983). Nonetheless, this should not lead to an underestimation of the importance of the treatment and management of withdrawal. Fear of withdrawal may act as a barrier to treatment entry, and withdrawal discomfort may lead to treatment dropout.

For many years, the most widely used opiate detoxification procedure involved giving reducing doses of methadone. Typically, reducing doses were given over several weeks (Gossop *et al.* 1987). As well as being a lengthy process, this type of detoxification was associated with prolonged, residual, post-detoxification withdrawal symptoms (Gossop *et al.* 1989b). Recent research has sought to identify more rapid and more effective procedures.

A more rapid detoxification can be achieved using centrally acting alpha–2 adrenergic agonists which reduce noradrenergic neuronal firing and noradrenaline turnover. Clonidine is one such treatment but its clinical use has also been compromised by side-effects, including postural hypotension (Gossop 1988). Lofexidine has comparable clinical efficacy to clonidine, with a more favourable side-effect profile (Buntwal *et al.* 2000). Detoxification with lofexidine can also be achieved over periods as short as five to seven days (Bearn *et al.* 1996, 1998). Encouraging results regarding the effectiveness of lofexidine have been reported from a number of studies, including double-blind, controlled clinical trials (Strang *et al.* 1999a). Within the past decade lofexidine has been increasingly widely used in UK detoxification programmes. There is also increasing interest in the possible uses and effectiveness of buprenorphine in the management of opiate withdrawal (Gowing *et al.* 2000).

A dramatic rapid detoxification procedure involves the use of opiate antagonists such as naloxone or naltrexone delivered under anaesthesia or deep sedation (Loimer *et al.* 1991). There is inadequate evidence of the effectiveness or safety of such procedures, and at this time it is questionable whether they should be used outside research settings (Gossop and Strang 1997).

Detoxification is not simply a 'physical' treatment. The manner in which addicts respond to drug withdrawal is powerfully influenced by psychological factors. Anxiety increases withdrawal severity, and can be a more powerful influence upon withdrawal symptoms than heroin dose levels (Phillips *et al.* 1986). Psychological procedures which reduce fears and anxieties about withdrawal can reduce withdrawal symptomatology. Green and Gossop (1988) showed that providing addicts with accurate but reassuring information about withdrawal reduced the severity of heroin withdrawal symptoms and helped to improve detoxification completion rates.

Methadone treatments

Methadone treatments are extremely diverse. Apart from the prescription of methadone as a pharmacological agent, they differ in many respects. Studies have found marked variability in the content and structure of methadone programmes (Gossop and Grant 1991; Ball and Ross 1991; Stewart *et al.* 2000b). Programmes differed in entry criteria, dose levels, time limits for prescribing, frequency of attendance, the manner of dispensing (supervised or unsupervised), and drug formulation (syrup, tablets or ampoules). This variation was of direct relevance to the nature and probable effectiveness of the interventions.

The provision of methadone treatments to opiate addicts in the UK has a different history to that in other countries. Unlike the United States, where methadone treatments were introduced with specific protocols and often with stringent controls, in the UK they have been subject to only the most general controls. Increasing concern is being expressed (Department of Health 1999) about the widespread UK practice of issuing prescriptions for methadone to be consumed without supervision. In virtually all other countries maintenance drugs are usually (or always) consumed under direct supervision.

There is an established illicit UK market involving the diversion and sale of methadone. Estimates of the proportion of drug users in treatment who sell prescribed drugs range from 5 to 34 per cent (Fountain *et al.* 2000). Prior to intake, almost half of the drug users approaching the NTORS methadone programmes and about one-third of those approaching the residential programmes reported having used non-prescribed methadone. In the rethinking of British practice, the Department of Health guidelines, whilst allowing for exceptions, state that 'Supervised dispensing is recommended for new prescriptions for a minimum of three months' (1999: 28). A stronger statement from the Advisory Council on the Misuse of Drugs (ACMD) recommended that 'methadone should be taken under daily supervision for at least 6 months and often longer....The bigger the dose of methadone which is being prescribed, the greater will be the need for supervision' (2000: 65).

Gossop, Grant and Wodak noted that

> insufficient attention has been paid to the manner in which the effectiveness of methadone treatment...might be maximised...there remains considerable confusion both about the identification of goals for the treatment and management of opioid dependence and also about how such goals are related to treatment methods.
>
> (Gossop *et al.* 1989a: 35–6)

Both in the UK and in other countries, there is a tension between the use of methadone as a treatment intended to meet a goal of harm reduction and the use of methadone as an intermediate phase of treatment aimed at abstinence.

Methadone reduction treatment (MRT) has been widely used in the UK for many years. Seivewright commented that 'it would be impossible to overstate the importance of this form of methadone prescribing in the UK' (2000). Typically, MRT involves prescribing methadone over relatively long periods, with the expectation that doses will gradually be reduced and that the patient will eventually be withdrawn from the drug and become abstinent from opiates.

Methadone maintenance treatment (MMT) is also widely used and differs from MRT in that it involves the provision of methadone in *stable* doses. MMT is intended to reduce problematic behaviours associated with illicit drug use (but is not, in itself, an abstinence-oriented treatment, and entails continuing use of prescribed methadone).

A problem with MRT is that this form of treatment is frequently not delivered as intended. In NTORS, only about one-third of the patients allocated to MRT actually received reduction (Gossop *et al.* 2001a), with many patients having received some form of maintenance. Where MRT was delivered as intended, it was associated with poorer outcomes. The more reducing doses they received, the worse their outcomes; and the more rapidly the methadone was reduced, the worse their heroin use outcomes. These findings suggest that where MRT patients achieved improved outcomes after treatment this may have occurred *despite* the specific characteristics of their intended treatment programmes (i.e. reducing doses). The outcomes of the reduction patients may be reflective of some generic treatment effect conferred by receiving a medically prescribed supply of methadone.

For the methadone maintenance patients in NTORS the primary treatment goal (reductions in illicit heroin use) was associated with higher methadone doses and retention in treatment. The associations between methadone dosage, treatment retention and treatment outcome are still not fully understood, though studies from different treatment settings and in different countries have shown positive associations between higher doses, increased retention and improved outcomes (Ward *et al.* 1998; Strain *et al.* 1999).

Prescribing heroin and injectable methadone

Heroin prescribing is sometimes regarded as a key feature of the 'British system'. However, except for a short period after the establishment of the clinics in the late 1960s, heroin prescribing has not been widely used in this country. By 1992 less than 1 per cent of British opiate addicts were receiving a prescription for heroin. There have been a few advocates of heroin prescribing in the UK and some local enthusiasm for an expansion of heroin maintenance, but little sign of any change in practice. Current policy reflects little enthusiasm for any expansion of heroin prescribing. Department of Health guidelines devote only a single brief paragraph to this issue, and state that as a treatment for opiate addiction 'there is very little clinical indication for prescribed [heroin]' (1999: 57).

Greater interest in heroin prescribing has been found in Switzerland, the Netherlands and Germany, where clinical trials have been (or are currently being) carried out. The Swiss trial was conducted with drug users with a history of chronic heroin addiction, failed previous treatments, and marked health and social integration problems (Uchtenhagen *et al.* 1999). In a complicated study design, where the results are sometimes difficult to interpret, the authors concluded that supervised heroin dispensing could be safely carried out with the designated target group, that there were good retention rates, and that improvements were found in illicit drug use, in health and in other outcome areas.

The prescribing of injectable methadone to opiate addicts is of greater relevance as a treatment option in the UK (Mitcheson 1994). There are no legal restrictions in the UK to prevent doctors prescribing methadone in either its oral or injectable form, and a 1995 national survey found that 10 per cent of all methadone prescriptions to addicts were for injectable methadone ampoules (Strang and Sheridan 1998). There are regional variations in this form of prescribing. Injectable methadone appears to be rarely, if ever, prescribed in Scotland, Wales or Northern Ireland.

In a randomised clinical trial, Strang *et al.* (2000b) found that the supervised dispensing of injectable methadone was acceptable to patients and most patients were well retained within this form of treatment. Outcomes among the injectable patients were directly comparable, in terms of drug taking and other outcome domains, to those found among patients receiving oral methadone. The main difference between the treatments concerns their cost. The direct operational costs of providing injectable methadone were about five times greater than for oral methadone.

Cognitive behavioural and psychological treatments

A number of promising treatments based upon psychological principles have been developed in recent years. The limitations of space within this chapter do not permit any attempt at a comprehensive review and only a few can be mentioned.

One form of intervention which has been found to be useful is contingency management. Based upon operant conditioning principles, this sees addictive behaviour as being maintained by environmental and other reinforcers, and as being able to be changed by altering its consequences. As described by Stitzer *et al.*, contingency management 'organizes treatment delivery, sets specific objective behavioural goals, and attempts to structure the [drug user's] environment in a manner that is conducive to change' (1989: 1,438). Contingency management provides a system of incentives and disincentives which are designed to make continued drug use less attractive and abstinence more attractive. Contingency management techniques can be effective in reducing continued drug use among methadone patients (Stitzer *et al.* 1989) and has been found to be a useful form of treatment for 'non-responsive' patients who do not get better as a result of their contact with treatment.

Motivational interviewing has been popular and clinically influential in recent years. Miller's original account of motivational interviewing described its application with problem drinkers (Miller 1983). It has been found to be a useful tool in many stages of treatment but particularly for drug users who are still at an early stage of committing themselves to treatment or to changing their behaviour. Motivation is conceptualised as the product of an interpersonal process in which the behaviour of the therapist has considerable influence on the subsequent attributions and behaviour of the client. The aim of therapy is to increase levels of cognitive dissonance until a critical mass of motivation is achieved, at which point the client is willing to consider change alternatives.

One limitation of many treatments in the addictions is that they presume a prior commitment to change on the part of the drug user. This commitment is often somewhat shaky, and in some cases it may be almost entirely hidden. Motivational interviewing explicitly assumes that the drug user is likely to be ambivalent about their drug taking. Motivational interviewing is described as 'an approach designed to help clients build commitment and reach a decision to change' (Miller and Rollnick 1991). In this respect, motivational interviewing differs from some other treatment approaches in that it avoids trying to persuade or convince the client to do something about their drug use, but seeks to supervise a process of decision making in which the client makes the decisions.

Motivation is seen as 'a state of readiness ... to change, which may fluctuate from one time or situation to another. This state is one that can be influenced' (Miller and Rollnick 1991: 14). In this respect, motivational interviewing challenges the idea of 'denial' as a characteristic of people with drug problems, and challenges treatment interventions based upon aggressive confrontation. Denial, for example, is seen not as an attribute of the drug user, but as a product of the way in which the counsellor interacts with the client. In the strongest assertion of this view, Miller and Rollnick state that 'client resistance is a therapist problem' (1991: 100).

Although the therapist initially adopts an empathic 'Rogerian' stance, this process is soon modified to reinforce statements of concern and elicit self-motivational statements. Miller and Rollnick (1991) state that a wholly non-directive Rogerian approach can leave the client confused and directionless. The therapist is not just being reflective but is subtly steering the client towards change.

The role of the therapist is to encourage the active involvement of the client in the identification of the problem and in the analysis of the various available options for continued drug taking or change according to the costs and benefits of different courses of action (Janis and Mann 1977). The approach is intended to enhance the importance of personal responsibility and the internal attribution of choice and control, and the therapist must help the client to avoid treatment 'short-circuits' due to low self-esteem, low self-efficacy and denial.

The notion of 'stages of change' is often linked with motivational interviewing. The stages of change as originally outlined by Prochaska and DiClemente (1982) were described as *precontemplation, contemplation, action* and *maintenance*. Slight variations of these stages have since been described; for example, a further stage of *relapse* was added by Prochaska and DiClemente (1986). This sort of model draws attention to different interventions that may be appropriate to different stages of change. For example, patients in precontemplation should be helped to develop an awareness of their problems rather than being guided directly towards change. Patients in contemplation are most open to consciousness-raising interventions (such as self-monitoring procedures or educational methods) and may be resistant to the interventions of a directive action-oriented therapist. During the action stage patients are likely to require specific practical help with behaviour change procedures and/or skills training.

Even for the heavily dependent drug user it is relatively easy to stop taking drugs. It is more difficult to remain drug free, and the problems associated with avoiding a return to use are at the heart of what we mean by an addiction. The problem of relapse is how to maintain habit change. The treatment and management of relapse is, therefore, central to the treatment of addictive behaviours.

Relapse prevention (RP) treatments (e.g. Marlatt and Gordon 1985) have influenced many treatment approaches. Former views of relapse as merely a poor outcome of treatment have been replaced by a view of relapse as a process which can be understood, anticipated and avoided. RP has provided a model for treatment intervention and given direction and purpose to treatment in the day-to-day clinical setting, especially by showing how assessment should be conducted and targeted at key problem areas.

The key components of RP are identifying high-risk situations for relapse; instruction and rehearsal of coping skills and strategies; self-monitoring and behavioural analysis of substance use; and planning for emergencies and lapses.

High-risk situations may be situations, events, objects, cognitions or mood states which have become associated with drug use and/or relapse. They may include negative mood states, social pressure, social networks, interpersonal conflicts, negative physical states and some positive emotional states (Litman *et al.* 1983; Gossop *et al.* 1990; Unnithan *et al.* 1992). Risk factors often occur together, either in clusters or in sequence (Bradley *et al.* 1989). Clients are taught to recognise the particular factors which increase the risk of their returning to the problematic behaviour, and to avoid or to cope with these factors. To support the maintenance of change, RP requires the development of specific coping strategies to deal with high-risk situations. These may include skills training and the development or strengthening of more global coping strategies that address issues of lifestyle imbalance and antecedents of relapse.

Treatment intensity and duration

Brief interventions have been found to be useful with some problem drinkers (Heather 1995). Similarly, some drug users may not need long-term and/or intensive treatment. Brief interventions may be used in primary care settings and in non-medical settings, and may include self-help manuals. Relatively little is known about the effectiveness of such interventions when applied to problem drug users and particularly when used with severely dependent drug users. However, it is known that many of the people who attend drug treatment services only attend the first session and do not present for any of the further treatment. Current practice may fail to make best use of the first session, which for many patients may also be the only session. Also, opiate addicts attending treatment services often have had many experiences of self-detoxification or other forms of self-treatment (Gossop *et al.* 1991). Brief interventions are an interesting option for supporting and strengthening such attempts.

On the other hand, many people who have long-term dependence upon heroin and/or other drugs experience great difficulty in giving up drugs.

Patients with more severe problems may require more intensive treatment input, and longer periods of time in treatment have also been found to be especially important for drug users with more severe problems (Simpson *et al.* 1999). If treatment is to produce improved outcomes, clients should stay for long enough to be exposed to and to participate in treatment components of sufficient quality and intensity to facilitate change, and length of time in treatment has been found to be one of the most consistent predictors of favourable post-treatment outcomes among drug users (Simpson 1997). Clients from the NTORS residential programmes who remained in treatment for the critical times achieved better one-year outcomes than those who left earlier in terms of abstinence from opiates and stimulants, and in reduction in injecting drug use, and for both drug selling and acquisitive crimes (Gossop *et al.* 1999a). The observation that time in treatment is predictive of outcome is consistent with the findings of other studies, which have shown that treatment duration is associated with improved outcomes when compared both with the clients' own pre-treatment baseline behaviours and with comparison groups (Simpson 1981; Anglin and Hser 1990; DeLeon 1989; Gerstein and Harwood 1990; Hubbard *et al.* 1989; Simpson *et al.* 1995).

Time spent in treatment is not in itself *sufficient* for clinical improvement (Joe and Simpson 1975). Patients who were randomly assigned to longer stays in residential treatment did not have better outcomes than those assigned to shorter stays (Longabaugh *et al.* 1995), and clients who actively participate in programmes and make cognitive and behavioural changes during treatment achieve superior outcomes to others who stay for comparable periods but who do not make such changes (Simpson *et al.* 1995; McLellan *et al.* 1993). Time in treatment is a complex measure and should, in many respects, be regarded as a proxy indicator of other factors. Many factors that predict treatment retention are the same as those that predict improved outcomes (Anglin and Hser 1990).

An unfortunate recent trend is towards a 'ledger clerk culture' in which treatment provision is determined simply by price rather than effectiveness. Decisions about treatment duration are frequently not made on clinical grounds but as cost-cutting measures by outside purchasers of services, who take decisions about what constitutes a basic 'unit' for treatment episodes (Leshner 1997). Residential treatment programmes have been especially vulnerable to the erosion of their services through the withdrawal of financial support. Many programmes have been forced to reduce the duration and the range of available treatment services (Etheridge *et al.* 1997; Horgan 1997). It would be self-defeating if services were to be cut back below effective levels of functioning. In NTORS, the planned duration of several inpatient programmes was shorter than the minimum thresholds for improved outcomes. Treatment durations can be made too short to provide the most effective client outcomes.

The planning and delivery of treatment programmes should be driven by a thorough initial and continuing assessment of the type and severity of client problems, and clients should receive at least the minimum therapeutic dose or exposure to interventions (Simpson 1997). Within the longer-term residential programmes, it seems likely that several months of counselling and treatment are required to optimise therapeutic benefits. Far from seeking to reduce treatment duration, attempts to maximise the cost-effectiveness of services should seek to increase rates of client retention in treatment.

Setting

Drug abuse treatment is provided in medical, psychiatric and in a variety of non-medical settings. It is provided both by specialists and by generalists, and delivered in residential and in community settings. The question of how treatment effectiveness is related to treatment setting is a question that has only recently attracted attention.

Among the studies which have shown setting effects is a study of detoxification completion rates in which heroin-dependent patients were assigned to treatment in either a dedicated inpatient setting or a specialist drug dependence outpatient clinic (Gossop *et al.* 1986). Successful detoxification completion rates of 81 per cent were reported for patients treated in an inpatient unit, and 17 per cent for patients treated in the outpatient clinic. These figures are consistent with the findings from a range of other studies in inpatient and outpatient settings with different groups of patients and using different treatment interventions (Gossop *et al.* 1989b; Strang and Gossop 1990; Dawe *et al.* 1991; Unnithan *et al.* 1992).

Clear setting differences were also reported by Strang *et al.* (1997) in a comparison of outcomes for drug users randomly assigned to treatment either in a specialist inpatient drug dependence unit or on a general psychiatric ward. The successful detoxification completion rates were 45 per cent and 18 per cent of the original randomised cohort for the specialist inpatient unit and the general psychiatric ward, respectively; or, if the analysis is restricted to only those patients who subsequently entered the inpatient wards, 75 per cent and 43 per cent, respectively. Longer-term outcome data at two months and at seven months post-treatment showed abstinence rates at two months of 65 per cent of the specialist treatment sample and 23 per cent of the general psychiatric treatment sample, and at 7 months of 79 per cent and 31 per cent of the samples respectively. With the less stringent outcome criterion of avoidance of daily opiate use, improvement at two months was found for 80 per cent of the specialist treatment sample and 61 per cent of the general psychiatric treatment sample, with comparable figures at seven months being 83 per cent and 46 per cent, respectively. The results of these studies strongly suggest the importance of treatment setting as a determinant of outcome.

In normal clinical practice, it is to be expected that there would be case-mix differences between the characteristics and problems of drug users who seek treatment with and attend different treatment services. Those seeking residential treatment tend to be more seriously problematic than those in community settings. In NTORS these differences were most evident in comparisons of the residential rehabilitation and methadone reduction clients (Gossop *et al.* 1998b). Drug users in methadone reduction programmes tended to be younger; they had used heroin for the shortest time; they were more likely to confine their drug use to heroin and less likely to have broad patterns of polydrug or alcohol use, and less likely to share injecting equipment. Residential clients included the more chronic, long-term users with the longest heroin careers, more regular users of stimulants (especially cocaine) and more heavy drinkers; they were more likely to have shared injecting equipment and were more actively involved in crime.

These differences between drug users in different settings reflect a complex interaction of service referral and self-selection processes. They can be expected to have an important impact upon clinical assessment procedures and upon the delivery of treatment interventions. Treatment outcome itself can be expected to be affected by client characteristics, and specifically by the nature and severity of the client's pre-admission problems.

One issue which has attracted recent attention is the extent to which drug users can benefit from treatments delivered under various forms of coercion. The published literature on this subject is equivocal. In a study of drug users being treated within the criminal justice system, Pitre *et al.* (1998) found that it was possible to engage drug users in coerced treatment, though no outcome data were reported. Hiller *et al.* (2000) found no differences in treatment response to methadone maintenance among drug users who were on probation, on parole or awaiting trial when compared to others with no official legal status, and in a study of a prison-based treatment therapeutic community DeLeon *et al.* (2000) found that motivation for treatment was one of the strongest predictors of retention and outcomes in a prison treatment programme.

With the rapid expansion in the number of heroin users in the UK during the 1980s and subsequently in the numbers of addicts approaching treatment services, there has been an increased willingness to re-engage general practitioners (GPs) in the treatment and management of problem drug users. Current national policy is to encourage and expand the role of GPs in this area. A survey found that British GPs issued more than 40 per cent of methadone prescriptions given to addicts and filled by retail pharmacists (Strang *et al.* 1996).

Some GPs have a substantial involvement with drug users (Glanz and Taylor 1986), and one recommended form of GP involvement is 'shared care', which involves

> the joint participation of specialists and GPs...in the planned delivery of care for patients with a drug use problem, informed by an enhanced

information exchange beyond routine discharge and referral letters....
This may include prescribing substitute drugs under appropriate
circumstances.

(Department of Health 1995: p10)

Clients receiving methadone treatment in clinics or in GP settings have
been found to show similar levels of overall improvements in response to the
provision of methadone treatment, with substantial reductions in their use
of illicit drugs, alcohol, crime, and improvements in mental and physical
health (Gossop *et al.* 1999b). However, one limitation to increased primary
care involvement is the resistance of many GPs to taking a more active role
in the treatment of drug addiction (Bell *et al.* 1990).

Treatment outcomes

The role played by treatment in helping addicts to give up drugs is
complex, and evidence about the impact of treatment is often difficult to
interpret. Large-scale, prospective, multi-site treatment outcome studies
provide important information about treatment effectiveness (Simpson
1997). An important feature of NTORS (as in the Drug Abuse Reporting
Program (DARP), Treatment Outcome Prospective Study (TOPS) and Drug
Abuse Treatment Outcome Study (DATOS)) is that it investigates outcomes
after treatment provided in existing services under day-to-day clinical
circumstances. The investigation of treatment outcome in field settings is
valuable in helping to identify what works in practice, even though the
possibilities for control over treatment assignment and other aspects of evaluation design are more limited than in clinical trials or other experimental
studies (Simpson 1997). The US outcome studies showed that patients
entering the major drug treatment modalities made significant reductions in
their use of heroin, cocaine and other illicit drugs (Simpson and Sells 1982;
Hubbard *et al.* 1989; Anglin *et al.* 1997; Etheridge *et al.* 1997).

Similarly, the NTORS clients presented with a range of serious and
chronic drug use and other problems, and showed substantial and important
reductions in their problem behaviours at follow-up (Gossop *et al.* 1998b).
These were most evident for reductions in use of heroin and other illicit
drugs, reduced injecting and sharing of injecting equipment, improvements
in psychological health and reductions in crime. Frequency of heroin use
after one year, for example, was reduced to about half of the intake levels,
and heroin use remained at this lower level throughout the full follow-up
period. Substantial reductions in frequency of heroin use were found for
clients from both the residential programmes and the methadone
programmes.

The most stringent criterion for treatment outcome is that of abstinence,
and this was an explicit treatment goal of the residential treatment
programmes. In addition to the decreases in frequency of illicit drug use

already reported, significant increases in rates of abstinence from illicit drug use were also found among clients from both the residential and the methadone programmes.

In view of the concern about the treatment of stimulant problems, the NTORS results are interesting. Stimulants, and especially crack cocaine, were widely used by drug users approaching treatment programmes. Among those for whom stimulants were the main problem drug, use of crack cocaine, powder cocaine and amphetamines at one-year follow-up was reduced to approximately one-quarter of the intake levels (Gossop *et al.* 2000a). The five-year results give rise to concern, in that there was a gradual increase in the use of crack cocaine among those who were not using crack at intake (Gossop *et al.* 2002b).

NTORS found substantial reductions in other problem behaviours. Injecting and the sharing of injecting equipment were both reduced, with reductions occurring among the residential and the methadone clients. The overall sharing of injecting equipment, for example, fell to less than 5 per cent, about one-quarter of the level at intake.

The clients in the NTORS programmes reported committing a very large number of acquisitive crimes prior to treatment (Stewart *et al.* 2000a). At follow-up there were substantial reductions both in the numbers of crimes committed and in the percentage of clients engaged in acquisitive crime. Overall, acquisitive crimes were reduced to one-third of intake levels, and the rate of involvement in crime was reduced to about half of intake levels (Gossop *et al.* 2000c). Much of the crime reduction appeared to be linked to reductions that also occurred in the regular, dependent use of drugs, and particularly of heroin. This link between heroin use and crime was especially evident among the most criminally active drug users, where the likelihood of committing an acquisitive crime at follow-up was more than 10 times higher among those who continued to be regular heroin users.

Although the overall clinical outcomes as described in NTORS are encouraging, the outcomes for alcohol consumption were less satisfactory. With the exception of a fluctuation in frequency of drinking (a reduction at one year immediately followed by an increase at two-year follow-up), there was no reduction in drinking among the clients from the residential treatment programmes. Among the methadone clients no change was found at any point during the follow-up period, and for clients from both settings alcohol consumption after five years was no different from intake levels. The poor drinking outcomes represent an area of weakness requiring urgent attention by drug use treatment services, and especially by methadone treatment services.

It was anticipated that there would be differences between the agencies in terms of the characteristics of the clients who went to those programmes, in terms of the treatments provided and possibly also in terms of the outcomes achieved by clients in the different programmes. The results at one year show a huge variation in the behavioural changes of clients from different agencies. Although overall levels of improvement were satisfactory, some agencies, for whatever reason, were not achieving satisfactory client outcomes. Clients from the 'best'-performing agencies showed reductions in heroin use three times greater than those from the 'worst'-performing agencies within the same modality (Gossop *et al.* 1998a). The reasons for this variation between agencies which are apparently offering the same (or very similar) services is not properly understood, though the marked and often unacceptable variation in programme delivery may lead to situations in which key elements of treatment may be neglected or even omitted. Identification of the effective treatment components would provide a strong foundation for improving existing treatment interventions.

So where next? Although there is broad agreement that many treatment factors may be related to outcome, relatively little is known about what these factors are or how they affect outcome. An important question for clinicians and researchers, and one to which we currently have no good answer, is how can we identify and measure the impact of treatment process variables? The answer to this question may improve treatment effectiveness by helping to discriminate between 'active' and 'inert' components of treatment and enabling the elimination of the inert components (McLellan *et al.* 1997). The important developments in addiction treatments during the next decades are likely to occur, not as a result of radical new discoveries, but through the improvement of existing interventions and through improved provision of effective treatments.

References

Advisory Council on the Misuse of Drugs (2000) *Reducing Drug Related Deaths*, London: The Stationery Office.

Alter, M. J., Kruszon-Moran, D., Nainan, O. V., McQuillan, G. M., Gao, F., Moyer, L. A., Kaslow, R. A. and Margolis, H. S. (1999) 'The Prevalence of Hepatitis C Virus Infection in the United States, 1988 through 1994', *New England Journal of Medicine* 341(8): 556–62.

Anglin, M. D. and Hser, Y. I. (1990) 'Treatment of Drug Abuse', in M. Tonry and J. Q. Wilson (eds) *Drugs and Crime*, Chicago: University of Chicago Press.

Anglin, M. D., Hser, Y.-I., Grella, C. E. (1997) 'Drug Addiction and Treatment Careers among Clients in the Drug Abuse Treatment Outcome Study (DATOS)', *Psychology of Addictive Behaviors* 11(4): 308–23.

Baker, A., Kochan, N., Dixon, J. and Wodak, A. (1995) 'HIV Risk Taking Behaviour among Injecting Drug Users Currently, Previously, and Never Enrolled in Methadone Treatment', *Addiction* 90(4): 545–54.

Ball, J. and Ross, A. (1991) *The Effectiveness of Methadone Maintenance Treatment*, New York: Springer.

Bearn, J. A., Gossop, M. and Strang, J. (1996) 'A Randomised Double-blind Comparison of Lofexidine and Methadone in the In-patient Treatment of Opiate Withdrawal', *Drug and Alcohol Dependence* 43: 87–91.

Bearn, J. A., Gossop, M. and Strang, J. (1998) 'Accelerated Lofexidine Treatment Regimen Compared with Conventional Lofexidine and Methadone Treatment for In-patient Opiate Detoxification', *Drug and Alcohol Dependence* 50: 227–32.

Belenko, S. (1979) 'Alcohol Abuse by Heroin Addicts: Review of Research Findings and Issues', *International Journal of the Addictions* 14: 965–75.

Bell, G., Cohen, J. and Cremona, A. (1990) 'How Willing Are General Practitioners to Manage Narcotic Misuse?', *Health Trends* 2: 56–7.

Best, D., Gossop, M., Lehmann, P., Harris, J. and Strang, J. (1999a) 'The Relationship between Overdose and Alcohol Consumption among Methadone Maintenance Patients', *Journal of Substance Use* 4: 41–4.

Best, D., Noble, A., Finch, E., Gossop, M., Sidwell, C. and Strang, J. (1999b) 'Accuracy of Perceptions of Hepatitis B and C Status: Cross Sectional Investigation of Opiate Addicts in Treatment', *British Medical Journal* 319: 290–1.

Bradley, B., Phillips, G., Green, L. and Gossop, M. (1989) 'Circumstances Surrounding the Initial Lapse to Opiate Use following Detoxification', *British Journal of Psychiatry* 154: 354–9.

Buntwal, N., Bearn, J., Gossop, M. and Strang, J. (2000) 'Naltrexone and Lofexidine Combination Treatment Compared with Conventional Lofexidine Treatment for Inpatient Opiate Detoxification', *Drug and Alcohol Dependence* 59: 183–8.

Chatham, L. R., Rowan-Szal, G. A., Joe, G. W. and Simpson, D. D. (1997) 'Heavy Drinking, Alcohol Dependent vs. Nondependent Methadone Maintenance Clients: A Follow-up Study', *Addictive Behaviours* 22(1): 69–80.

Darke, S. and Ross, J. (1999) 'Heroin-related Deaths in South Western Sydney, Australia, 1992–96', *Drug and Alcohol Review* 18(1): 39–45.

Darke, S. and Zador, D. (1996) 'Fatal Heroin "Overdose": A Review', *Addiction* 91: 1,765–72.

Dawe, S., Griffiths, P., Gossop, M. and Strang, J. (1991) 'Should Opiate Addicts Be Involved in Controlling Their Own Detoxification? A Comparison of Fixed versus Negotiable Schedules', *British Journal of Addictions* 86(8): 977–82.

DeLeon, G. (1987) 'Alcohol Use among Drug Abusers: Treatment Outcome in a Therapeutic Community', *Alcoholism* 11: 430–6.

DeLeon, G. (1989) 'Psychopathology and Substance Abuse: What Is Being Learned from Research in Therapeutic Communities', *Journal of Psychoactive Drugs* 21: 177–88.

DeLeon, G., Melnick, G., Thomas, G., Kressel, D. and Wexler, H. (2000) 'Motivation for Treatment in a Prison-based Therapeutic Community', *American Journal of Drug and Alcohol Abuse* 26: 33–46.

Department of Health (1995) *The Task Force to Review Services for Drug Misusers: Report of an Independent Review of Drug Treatment Services in England*, London: Department of Health.

Department of Health (1999) *Drug Misuse and Dependence – Guidelines on Clinical Management*, London: Department of Health.

Edwards, G. and Gross, M. M. (1976) 'Alcohol Dependence: Provisional Description of a Clinical Syndrome', *British Medical Journal* 1: 1,058–61.

Edwards, G., Arif, A. and Hodgson, R. (1981) 'Nomenclature and Classification of Drug- and Alcohol-related Problems: A WHO Memorandum', *Bulletin of the World Health Organization* 59(2): 225–42.

Etheridge, R. M., Hubbard, R. L., Anderson, J., Craddock, S. G. and Flynn, P. M. (1997) 'Treatment Structure and Programme Services in the Drug Abuse Treatment Outcome Study (DATOS)', *Psychology of Addictive Behaviours* 11(4): 224–60.

Farrell, M., Neeleman, J., Griffiths, P. and Strang, J. (1996) 'Suicide and Overdose among Opiate Addicts', *Addiction* 91(3): 321–3.

Farrell, M., Howes, S., Taylor, C., Lewis, G., Jenkins, R., Bebbington, P., Jarvis, M., Brugha, T., Gill, B. and Meltzer, H. (1998) 'Substance Misuse and Psychiatric Comorbidity: An Overview of the OPCS National Psychiatric Morbidity Survey', *Addictive Behaviors* 23: 909–18.

Fountain, J., Strang, J., Gossop, M., Farrell, M. and Griffiths, P. (2000) 'Diversion of Drugs Prescribed to Drug Users in Treatment: Analysis of the UK Market and New Data from London', *Addiction* 95: 393–406.

Friedman, S., Jose, B., DesJarlais, D. and Neaigus, A. (1995) 'Risk Factors for Human Immunodeficiency Virus Seroconversion among Out-of-treatment Drug Injectors in High and Low Seroprevalence Cities. The National AIDS Research Consortium', *American Journal of Epidemiology* 142: 864–74.

Frischer, M., Bloor, M., Goldberg, D., Clark, J., Green, S. and McKeganey, N. (1993) 'Mortality among Injecting Drug Users: A Critical Reappraisal', *Journal of Epidemiology and Community Health* 47: 59–63.

Gerstein, D. R. and Harwood, H. J. (1990) *Treating Drug Problems*, vol. 1: *A Study of Evolution, Effectiveness and Financing of Public and Private Drug Systems*, Washington, DC: National Academy Press.

Ghodse, A. H., Sheehan, M., Stevens, B., Taylor, C. and Edwards, G. (1978) 'Mortality among Drug Addicts in Greater London', *British Medical Journal* 2: 1,742–4.

Gibson, D. R., Flynn, N. M. and McCarthy, J. J. (1999) 'Effectiveness of Methadone Treatment in Reducing HIV Risk Behaviour and HIV Seroconversion among Injecting Drug Users', *AIDS* 13(14): 1,807–18.

Glanz, A. and Taylor, C. (1986) 'Findings of a National Survey of the Role of General Practitioners in the Treatment of Opiate Misuse: Extent of Contact with Opiate Misusers', *British Medical Journal* 293: 427–30.

Gossop, M. (1988) 'Clonidine and the Treatment of the Opiate Withdrawal Syndrome', *Drug and Alcohol Dependence* 21: 253–9.

Gossop, M. (1989) *Relapse and Addictive Behaviour*, Routledge, London.

Gossop. M. (2001) 'A Web of Dependence', *Addiction* 96: 677–8.

Gossop, M. and Grant, M. (1991) 'A Study of the Content and Structure of Heroin Treatment Programmes Using Methadone in Six Countries', *British Journal of Addiction* 86: 1,151–66.

Gossop, M. and Strang, J. (1997) 'Rapid Anaesthetic-antagonist Detoxification of Heroin Addicts. What Origins, Evidence Base and Clinical Justification?' *British Journal of Intensive Care* 7: 66–9.

Gossop, M., Bradley, B. and Brewis, R. (1982) 'Amphetamine Withdrawal and Sleep Disturbance', *Drug and Alcohol Dependence* 10: 177–83.

Gossop, M., Johns, A. and Green, L. (1986) 'Opiate Withdrawal: Inpatient versus Outpatient Programmes and Preferred versus Random Assignation to Treatment', *British Medical Journal* 293: 103–4.

Gossop, M., Bradley, B. and Phillips, G. (1987) 'An Investigation of Withdrawal Symptoms Shown by Opiate Addicts during and Subsequent to a 21-day Inpatient Methadone Detoxification Procedure,' *Addictive Behaviors* 12: 1–6.

Gossop, M., Grant, M. and Wodak, A. (1989a) *The Uses of Methadone in the Treatment and Management of Opioid Dependence*, Geneva: World Health Organisation.

Gossop, M., Griffiths, P., Bradley, B. and Strang, J. (1989b) 'Opiate Withdrawal Symptoms in Response to 10-day and 21-day Methadone Withdrawal Programmes', *British Journal of Psychiatry* 154: 360–3.

Gossop, M., Green, L., Philips, G. and Bradley, B. P. (1990) 'Factors Predicting Outcome among Opiate Addicts after Treatment', *British Journal of Clinical Psychology* 29(2): 209–16.

Gossop, M., Battersby, M. and Strang, J. (1991) 'Self-detoxification by Opiate Addicts: A Preliminary Investigation', *British Journal of Psychiatry* 159: 208–12.

Gossop, M., Griffiths, P., Powis, B. and Strang, J. (1992) 'Severity of Dependence and Route of Administration of Heroin, Cocaine and Amphetamines', *British Journal of Addiction* 87: 1,527–36.

Gossop, M., Griffiths, P., Powis, B. and Strang, J. (1993a) 'Severity of Heroin Dependence and HIV Risk. I. Sexual Behaviour. *AIDS Care* 5: 149–57.

Gossop, M., Griffiths, P., Powis, B. and Strang, J. (1993b) 'Severity of Heroin Dependence and HIV Risk. II. Sharing Injecting Equipment', *AIDS Care* 5: 159–68.

Gossop, M., Griffiths, P., Powis, B. and Strang, J. (1994a) 'Cocaine: Patterns of Use, Route of Administration, and Severity of Dependence', *British Journal of Psychiatry* 164: 101–4.

Gossop, M., Powis, B., Griffiths, P. and Strang, J. (1994b) 'Multiple Risks for HIV and Hepatitis B Infection among Heroin Users', *Drug and Alcohol Review* 13(3): 293–300.

Gossop, M., Griffiths, P., Powis, B., Williamson, S. and Strang, J. (1996) 'Frequency of Non-fatal Heroin Overdoses', *British Medical Journal* 313: 402.

Gossop, M., Marsden, J. and Stewart, D. (1998a) *NTORS at One Year. The National Treatment Outcome Research Study: Changes in Substance Use, Health and Criminal Behaviours at One Year after Intake.* London: Department of Health.

Gossop, M., Marsden, J., Stewart, D., Lehmann, P, Edwards, C., Wilson, A. and Segar, G. (1998b) 'Substance Use, Health and Social Problems of Clients at 54 Drug Treatment Agencies: Intake Data from the National Treatment Outcome Research Study (NTORS)', *British Journal of Psychiatry* 173: 166–71.

Gossop, M., Marsden, J., Stewart, D. and Rolfe, A. (1999a) 'Treatment Retention and 1 Year Outcomes for Residential Programmes in England', *Drug and Alcohol Dependence* 57: 89–98.

Gossop, M., Marsden, J., Stewart, D., Lehmann, P. and Strang, J. (1999b) 'Methadone Treatment Practices and Outcome for Opiate Addicts Treated in Drug Clinics and in General Practice: Results from the National Treatment Outcome Research Study', *British Journal of General Practice* 49: 31–4.

Gossop, M., Marsden, J. and Stewart, D. (2000a) 'Treatment Outcomes of Stimulant Misusers: One Year Follow-up Results from the National Treatment Outcome Research Study (NTORS), *Addictive Behaviors* 25: 509–22.

Gossop, M., Marsden, J., Stewart, D. and Rolfe, A. (2000b) 'Patterns of Drinking and Drinking Outcomes among Drug Misusers: 1-year Follow-up Results', *Journal of Substance Abuse Treatment* 19: 45–50.

Gossop, M., Marsden, J., Stewart, D. and Rolfe, A. (2000c) 'Reductions in Acquisitive Crime and Drug Use after Treatment of Addiction Problems: One Year Follow-up Outcomes', *Drug and Alcohol Dependence* 58: 165–72.

Gossop, M., Marsden, J., Stewart, D. and Treacy, S. (2001a) 'Outcomes after Methadone Maintenance and Methadone Reduction Treatments: Two-year Follow-up Results from the National Treatment Outcome Research Study', *Drug and Alcohol Dependence* 62: 255–64.

Gossop, M., Marsden, J., Stewart, D. and Treacy, S. (2001b) 'A Prospective Study of Mortality among Drug Misusers during a Four Year Period after Seeking Treatment', *Addiction* 97: 39–47.

Gossop, M., Marsden, J. and Stewart, D. (2002a) 'Dual Dependence: Assessment of Dependence upon Alcohol and Illicit Drugs, and the Relationship of Alcohol Dependence among Drug Misusers to Patterns of Drinking, Illicit Drug Use, and Health Problems', *Addiction* 97: 169–78.

Gossop, M., Marsden, J., Stewart, D. and Kidd, T. (2002b) 'Changes in Use of Crack Cocaine after Drug Misuse Treatment: 4–5 Year Follow-up Results from the National Treatment Outcome Research Study (NTORS)', *Drug and Alcohol Dependence* 66: 21–8.

Gossop, M., Marsden, J., Stewart, D. and Treacy, S. (2002c) 'Reduced Injection Risk and Sexual Risk Behaviour after Drug Misuse Treatment: Results from the National Treatment Outcome Research Study (NTORS)', *AIDS Care* 14: 77–93.

Gowing, L., Ali, R. and White, J. (2000) 'The Management of Opiate Withdrawal', *Drug and Alcohol Review* 19: 309–18.

Green, L. and Gossop, M. (1988) 'The Effects of Information on the Opiate Withdrawal Syndrome', *British Journal of Addiction* 83: 305–9.

Griffiths, P., Gossop, M., Powis, B. and Strang, J. (1994) 'Transitions in Pattern of Heroin Administration: A Study of Heroin Chasers and Heroin Injectors', *Addiction* 89: 321–9.

Hall, W. (1999) 'Reducing the Toll: Opioid Overdose Deaths in Australia', *Drug and Alcohol Review* 18(2): 213–20.

Hall, W. and Farrell, M. (1997) 'Comorbidity of Mental Disorders with Substance Misuse', *British Journal of Psychiary* 171: 4–5.

Hartel, D. M. and Schoenbaum, E. E. (1998) 'Methadone Treatment Protects against HIV Infection: Two Decades of Experience in the Bronx, New York City', *Public Health Reports* 113 (Suppl. 1): 107–15.

Heather, N. (1995) 'Brief Intervention Strategies', in R. Hester and W. Miller (eds) *Handbook of Alcoholism Treatment Approaches*, London: Allyn and Bacon.

Hiller, M., Simpson, D., Broome, K. and Joe, G. (2000) 'Legal Status at Intake and Posttreatment Incarceration: 12 Month Follow-up of Methadone Maintenance Treatment', *Journal of Maintenance in the Addictions* 1: 27–43.

Horgan, C. M. (1997) 'Need and Access to Drug Abuse Treatment', in J. Egertson, D. Fox and A. Leshner (eds) *Treating Drug Abusers Effectively*, Oxford: Blackwell.

Hubbard, R. L., Marsden, M. E., Rachal, J. V., Harwood, H. J., Cavanaugh, E. R. and Ginzburg, H. M. (1989) *Drug Abuse Treatment: A National Study of Effectiveness*, London: Chapel Hill.

Hulse, G. K., English, D. R., Milne, E. and Holman, C. D. J. (1999) 'The Quantification of Mortality Resulting from the Regular Use of Illicit Opiates', *Addiction* 94(2): 221–9.

Hunt, D. E., Strug, D. L., Goldsmith, D. S., Lipton, D. S., Spunt, B., Robertson, K. and Truitt, L. (1986) 'Alcohol Use and Abuse: Heavy Drinking among Methadone Clients,' *American Journal of Drug and Alcohol Abuse* 12: 147–64.

Janis, I. and Mann, L. (1977) *Decision Making A Psychological Analysis of Conflict, Choice and Commitment*, London: Collier Macmillan.

Joe, G. W. and Simpson, D. D. (1975) 'Retention in Treatment of Drug Users: 1971–1972 DARP Admissions', *American Journal of Drug and Alcohol Abuse* 2(1): 63–71.

Joe, G. W., Simpson, D. D., Hubbard, R. L. (1991) 'Treatment Predictors of Tenure in Methadone Maintenance', *Journal of Substance Abuse* 3: 73–84.

Joseph, H. and Appel, P. (1985) 'Alcoholism and Methadone Treatment: Consequences for the Patient and Programme', *American Journal of Drug and Alcohol Abuse* 11: 37–53.

Kampman, K., Volpicelli, J., Alterman, A., Cornish, J. and O'Brien, C. (2000) 'Amantidine in the Treatment of Cocaine-dependent Patients with Severe Withdrawal Symptoms', *American Journal of Psychiatry* 157: 2,052–4.

Kessler, R. C., McGonagle, K. A., Zhao, S., Nelson, C. B., Hughes, M., Eshleman, S., Wittchen, H. U. and Kendler, K. S. (1994) 'Lifetime and 12 Month Prevalence of DSM-III-R Psychiatric Disorders in the United States: Results from the National Comorbidity Survey', *Archives of General Psychiatry* 51: 8–19.

Kreek, M. J. (1981) 'Medical Management of Methadone-maintained Patients', in J. Lowinson and P. Ruiz (eds) *Substance Abuse: Clinical Problems and Perspectives*, Baltimore, MD: Williams and Wilkins.

Lehman, W. E. R. and Simpson, D. D. (1990) 'Alcohol Use', in D. D. Simpson and S. B. Sells (eds) *Opioid Addiction and Treatment: A 12 Year Follow-Up*, Melbourne, FL: Kreiger.

Leshner, A., (1997) 'Introduction to the Special Issue: The National Institute on Drug Abuse's (NIDA's) Drug Abuse Treatment Outcome Study (DATOS)', *Psychology of Addictive Behaviors* 11(4): 211–15.

Lipton, D. and Maranda, M. (1983) 'Detoxification from Heroin Dependency: An Overview of Method and Effectiveness', in B. Stimmel (ed.) *Evaluation of Drug Treatment Programmes*, New York: Hawarth.

Litman, G. K., Stapleton, J., Oppenheim, A. N., Peleg, M. and Jackson, P. (1983) 'Situations Related to Alcoholism Relapse', *British Journal of Addiction* 78: 381–9.

Loimer, N., Lenz, K., Schmid, R. and Presslich, O. (1991) 'Technique for Greatly Shortening the Transition from Methadone to Naltrexone Maintenance of Patients Addicted to Opiates', *American Journal of Psychiatry* 148: 933–5.

Longabaugh, R., Beattie, M., Noel, N., Stout, R. and Malloy, P. (1995) 'The Effect of Social Investment on Treatment Outcome', *Journal of Studies on Alcohol* 54: 465–78.

Longshore, D., Hsieh, S. C., Danila, B. and Anglin, M. D. (1993) 'Methadone Maintenance and Needle/Syringe Sharing', *International Journal of the Addictions* 28(10): 983–96.

McKay, J. R., Alterman, A. I., Rutherford, M. J., Cacciola, J. S. and McLellan, A. T. (1999) 'The Relationship of Alcohol Use to Cocaine Relapse in Cocaine Dependent Patients in an Aftercare Study', *Journal of Studies on Alcohol* 60(2): 176–80.

McLellan, A. T. (1983) 'Patient Characteristics Associated with Outcome', in J. R. Cooper, F. Altman, B. S. Brown and D. Czechowicz (eds) *Research on the Treatment of Narcotic Addiction: State of the Art* (DHHS Publication No. ADM 83–1281), Washington, DC: US Government Printing Office.

McLellan, A. T., Arndt, I. O., Metzger, D. S., Wood, G. E. and O'Brien, C. P. (1993) 'The Effects of Psychological Services in Substance Abuse Treatment', *Journal of the American Medical Association* 269(15): 1,953–61.

McLellan, A. T., Woody, G. E., Metzger, D., McKay, J., Durell, J., Alterman, A. I. and O'Brien, C. P. (1997) 'Evaluating the Effectiveness of Addiction Treatments: Reasonable Expectations, Appropriate Comparisons', in J. Egertson, D. Fox and A. Leshner (eds) *Treating Drug Abusers Effectively*, Oxford: Blackwell.

Marlatt, G. A. and Gordon, J. R. (1985) *Relapse Prevention: Maintenance Strategies in the Treatment of Addictive Behaviors*, New York: Guilford Press.

Marsch, L. A. (1998) 'The Efficacy of Methadone Maintenance Interventions in Reducing Illicit Opiate Use, HIV Risk Behaviour and Criminality: A Meta-analysis', *Addiction* 93(4): 515–32.

Marsden, J., Gossop, M., Stewart, D., Rolfe, A. and Farrell, M. (2000) 'Psychiatric Symptoms among Clients Seeking Treatment for Drug Dependence: Intake Data from the National Treatment Outcome Research Study', *British Journal of Psychiatry* 176: 285–9.

Metzger, D. S., Woody, G. E., McLellan A. T., O'Brien, C. P., Druley, P., Navaline, H., DePhilippis, D., Stolley, P. and Abrutyn, E. (1993) 'Human Immunodeficiency Virus

Seroconversion among Intravenous Drug Users In and Out of Treatment: An 18 Month Prospective Follow Up', *Journal of Acquired Immune Deficiency Syndromes* 6(9): 1,049–56.

Miller, W. (1983) 'Motivational Interviewing with Problem Drinkers', *Behavioural Psychotherapy* 11: 147–72.

Miller, W. R. and Rollnick, S. (1991) *Motivational Interviewing*, New York: Guilford.

Mitcheson, M. (1994) 'Drug Clinics in the 1970s', in J. Strang and M. Gossop (eds) *Heroin Addiction and Drug Policy: The British System*, Oxford: Oxford University Press.

Neeleman, J. and Farrell, M. (1997) 'Fatal Methadone and Heroin Overdoses: Time Trends in England and Wales', *Journal of Epidemiology and Community Health* 51: 435–7.

Noble, A., Best, D., Finch, E., Gossop, M., Sidwell, C. and Strang, J. (2000) 'Injecting Risk Behaviour and Year of First Injection as Predictors of Hepatitis B and C Status among Methadone Maintenance Patients in South London', *Journal of Substance Use* 5: 131–5.

Pessione, F., Degos, F., Marcellin, P., Duchatelle, V., Njapoum, C., Martinot-Peignoux, M., Degott, C., Valla, D., Erlinger, S. and Rueff, B. (1998) 'Effect of Alcohol Consumption on Serum Hepatitis C Virus RNA and Histological Lesions in Chronic Hepatitis C', *Hepatology* 27(6): 1,717–22.

Phillips, G., Gossop, M. and Bradley, B. (1986) 'The Influence of Psychological Factors on the Opiate Withdrawal Syndrome', *British Journal of Psychiatry* 149: 235–8.

Pitre, U., Dansereau, D., Newbern, D. and Simpson, D. (1998) 'Residential Drug Abuse Treatment for Probationers: Use of Node-link Mapping to Enhance Participation and Progress', *Journal of Substance Abuse Treatment* 15: 535–43.

Powis, B., Strang, J., Griffiths, P., Taylor, C., Williamson, S., Fountain, J. and Gossop, M. (1999) 'Self Reported Overdose among Injecting Drug Users in London: Extent and Nature of the Problem', *Addiction* 94(4): 471–8.

Prochaska, J. and DiClemente, C. (1982) 'Transtheoretical Therapy: Toward a More Integrative Model of Change', *Psychotherapy, Theory, Research and Practice* 19: 276–8.

Prochaska, J. and DiClemente, C. (1986) 'Toward a Comprehensive Model of Change', in W. Miller and N. Heather (eds) *Treating Addictive Behaviours*, New York: Plenum.

Rawson, R., Washton, A., Resnick, R., Tennant, F. (1981) 'Clonidine Hydrochloride Detoxification from Methadone Treatment: The Value of Naltrexone Aftercare', in L. Harris (ed.) *Problem of Drug Dependence 1980*, Research Monograph 34, Rockville, MD: National Institute on Drug Abuse.

Risser, D., Uhl, A., Stichenwirth, M., Honigschabl, S., Hirz, W., Schneider, B., Stellag-Carion, C., Klupp, N., Vycudilik, W. and Bauer, G. (2000) 'Quality of Heroin and Heroin-related Deaths from 1987–1995 in Vienna, Austria', *Addiction* 95: 375–82.

Rivara, F. P., Mueller, B. A., Somes, G., Mendoza, C. T., Rushforth, N. B. and Kellerman, A. L. (1997) 'Alcohol and Illicit Drug Abuse and the Risk of Violent Death in the Home', *Journal of the American Medical Association* 278(7): 569–75.

Rossow, I. and Lauritzen, G. (1999) 'Balancing on the Edge of Death: Suicide Attempts and Life-threatening Overdoses among Drug Addicts', *Addiction* 94(2): 209–19.

Schuckit, M. and Hesselbrock, V. (1994) 'Alcohol Dependence and Anxiety Disorders: What is the Relationship?', *American Journal of Psychiatry* 151: 1,723–34.

Scott, J., Gilvarry, E. and Farrell, M. (1998) 'Managing Anxiety and Depression in Alcohol and Drug Dependence', *Addictive Behaviours* 23: 919–31.

Seivewright, N. (2000) *Community Treatment of Drug Misuse: More than Methadone*. Cambridge: Cambridge University Press.

Selwyn, P. A. (1987) 'Sterile Needles and the Epidemic of Acquired Immunodeficiency Syndrome: Issues for Drug Abuse Treatment and Public Health', *Advances in Alcohol & Substance Abuse* 7(2): 99–105.

Simpson, D. D. (1981) 'Treatment for Drug Abuse: Follow-up Outcomes and Length of Time Spent', *Archives of General Psychiatry* 38: 875–80.

Simpson, D. D. (1997) 'Effectiveness of Drug-abuse Treatment: A Review of Research from Field Settings', in J. Egertson, D. Fox and A. Leshner (eds) *Treating Drug Abusers Effectively*, Oxford: Blackwell.

Simpson, D. D. and Lloyd, M. R. (1977) *Alcohol and Illicit Drug Use: National Follow-up Study of Admissions to Drug Abuse Treatments in the DARP during 1969–1971. Services Research Report*, DHEW Publication No. ADM 77–496, Rockville, MD: National Institute on Drug Abuse.

Simpson, D. D. and Sells, S. B. (1982) 'Effectiveness of Treatment for Drug Abuse: An Overview of the DARP Research Program', *Advances in Alcohol and Substance Abuse* 2: 7–29.

Simpson, D. D., Joe, G. W., Rowan-Szal, G. and Greener, J. (1995) 'Client Engagement and Client Change during Drug Abuse Treatment', *Journal of Substance Abuse* 7(1): 117–34.

Simpson, D. D., Joe, G. W., Fletcher, B. W., Hubbard, R. L., Anglin, M. D. (1999) 'A National Evaluation of Treatment Outcomes for Cocaine Dependence', *Archives of General Psychiatry* 56: 507–14.

Sorensen, J. L. and Copeland, A. L. (2000) 'Drug Abuse Treatment as an HIV Preventative Strategy: A Review', *Drug and Alcohol Dependence* 59(1): 17–31.

Stewart, D., Gossop, M., Marsden, J. and Rolfe, A. (2000a) 'Drug Misuse and Acquisitive Crime among Clients Recruited to the National Treatment Outcome Research Study (NTORS)', *Criminal Behaviour and Mental Health* 10: 10–20.

Stewart, D., Gossop, M., Marsden, J. and Strang, J. (2000b) 'Variation between and within Drug Treatment Modalities: Data from the National Treatment Outcome Research Study (UK)', *European Addiction Research* 6: 106–14.

Stimson, G. V. (1995) 'Aids and Injecting Drug Use in the United Kingdom, 1987–1993: The Policy Response and the Prevention of the Epidemic', *Social Science and Medicine* 41 (5): 699–716.

Stitzer, M., Bigelow, G. and Gross, J. (1989) 'Behavioral Treatment of Drug Abuse', in T. Karasu (ed.) *Treatments of Psychiatric Disorders*, vol. 2. Washington, DC: American Psychiatric Association.

Strain, E. C., Brooner, R. K. and Bigelow, G. E. (1991) 'Clustering of Multiple Substance Use and Psychiatric Diagnoses in Opiate Addicts', *Drug & Alcohol Dependence* 27(2): 127–34.

Strain, E. C., Bigelow, G. E., Liebson, I. A. and Stitzer, M. L. (1999) 'Moderate- vs High-dose Methadone in the Treatment of Opioid Dependence', *Journal of the American Medical Association* 281(11): 1,000–5.

Strang, J. and Gossop, M. (1990) 'Comparison of Linear Versus Inverse Exponential Methadone Reduction Curves in the Detoxification of Opiate Addicts', *Addictive Behaviors* 15: 541–7.

Strang, J. and Gossop, M. (1994) *Heroin Addiction and Drug Policy: The British System*, Oxford: Oxford University Press.

Strang, J. and Sheridan, J. (1998) 'National and Regional Characteristics of Methadone Prescribing in England and Wales: Local Analyses of Data from the 1995 National Survey of Community Pharmacies', *Journal of Substance Misuse* 3: 240–6.

Strang, J., Griffiths, P., Powis, B. and Gossop, M. (1992) 'First Use of Heroin: Changes in Route of Administration Over Time', *British Medical Journal* 304: 1,222–3.

Strang, J., Sheridan, J. and Barber, N. (1996) 'Prescribing Injectable and Oral Methadone to Opiate Addicts: Results from the 1995 National Postal Survey of Community Pharmacists in England and Wales', *British Medical Journal* 313: 270–4.

Strang, J., Marks, I., Dawe, S., Powell, J., Richards, D. and Grey, J. (1997) 'Type of Hospital Setting and Treatment Outcome with Heroin Addicts. Results from a Randomised Trial', *British Journal of Psychiatry* 171: 335–9.

Strang, J., Bearn, J. and Gossop, M. (1999a) 'Lofexidine for Opiate Detoxification: Review of Recent Randomised and Open Controlled Trials', *American Journal on Addictions* 8: 337–48.

Strang, J., Griffiths, P., Powis, B., Fountain, J., Williamson, S. and Gossop, M. (1999b) 'Which Drugs Cause Overdose among Opiate Misusers? Study of Personal and Witnessed Overdoses', *Drug and Alcohol Review,* 18: 253–61.

Strang, J., Best, D., Man, L.-H., Noble, A. and Gossop, M. (2000a) 'Peer-initiated Overdose Resuscitation: Fellow Drug Users Could Be Mobilised to Implement Resuscitation', *International Journal of Drug Policy* 11: 437–45.

Strang, J., Marsden, J., Cummins, M., Farrell, M., Finch, E., Gossop, M., Stewart, D. and Welch, S. (2000b) 'Randomised Trial of Supervised Injectable versus Oral Methadone Maintenance: Report of Feasibility and 6-month Outcomes', *Addiction* 95: 1631–45.

Uchtenhagen, A., Guzwiller, F., Dobler-Mikola, A., Steffen, T. and Rihs-Middel, M. (1999) *Prescription of Narcotics for Heroin Addicts: Main Results of the Swiss Cohort Study,* Basle: Karger.

Unnithan, S., Gossop, M., Strang, J. (1992) 'Factors Associated with Relapse among Opiate Addicts in an Out-patient Detoxification Programme', *British Journal of Psychiatry* 309: 103–4.

Ward, J., Mattick, R. P. and Hall, W. (eds) (1998) *Methadone Maintenance Treatment and Other Opiate Replacement Therapies,* Amsterdam: Harwood Academic Publishers.

White, J. M. and Irvine, R. J. (1999) 'Mechanisms of Fatal Opioid Overdose', *Addiction* 94: 961–72.

Williams, A. B., McNelly, E. A., Willaims, A. E. and D'Aquila, R. T. (1992) 'Methadone Maintenance Treatment and HIV Type 1 Seroconversion among Injecting Drug Users', *AIDS Care* 4(1): 35–41.

5 Psychological and pharmacological components of treatment

Conflict or cooperation?

Colin Brewer

Introduction

Let us start by looking at a type of 'harm reduction' which has very little to do with addiction treatment but which provides some interesting and useful analogies: birth control. Women (and men) seek advice on family planning because they wish to avoid a specific type of harm, namely unwelcome pregnancy. Although the whole area is a moral minefield and was at one time subject to ferocious legal penalties, there has been, for many years, a remarkable degree of consensus on the range of services offered and how the services should be run.

Pregnancy, even unwelcome pregnancy, is not a 'disease', but it so happens that many of the most effective techniques for preventing or managing unwanted pregnancy were developed by doctors. Most people of child-bearing (or child-begetting) age are at least aware of oral contraceptives, intrauterine contraceptive devices, intramuscular depot contraceptives and medical or surgical termination of pregnancy, as well as the various barrier methods which have been around in one form or other for several hundred years.

Not everyone wants to use these medical methods. Apart from a relatively small number of people with strong religious feelings against any sort of fertility control (some of whom demonstrate their respect for sentient human life by bombing clinics or shooting gynaecologists) there are many non-religious people who do not like the idea of doctors interfering with their hormones or putting bits of copper or plastic into their uterus. Others do not like having their Fallopian tubes or their spermatic ducts ligated. For these people, methods of contraception based on a better understanding of the fertile and infertile parts of the menstrual cycle are available. My point is that in a typical family planning clinic all these methods coexist fairly peacefully. The job of the staff is to show and if necessary explain the therapeutic menu and help patients to make an informed choice. Patients often have a good idea of the harm reduction method that they want to use and do not necessarily need much help in their selection. Even if the clinic staff think that a patient's preference is not ideal, they will not usually put too many obstacles in the way of the patient's choice unless there are very clear medical contraindications. If such contraindications exist, most patients are sensible enough to recognise them. Furthermore, if one method proves ineffective, or is effective but causes unacceptable side-effects, the clinic staff will be happy to discuss alternatives.

Finally, although family planning involves moral as well as medical issues, discussions are usually carried on in a fairly value-free atmosphere. The roles of doctors, nurses and counsellors are often interchangeable, but what characterises all of them is that they are well informed about the various treatments that they can provide. Non-medical staff may sometimes need to defer to medical expertise but the training of family planning staff normally ensures that they share and use a large body of medical and technical information.

How different – how very different! – are the typical relationships between medical and non-medical staff in the world of harm reduction as it applies to legal and illegal drugs. Indeed, this part of the chapter could almost be subtitled 'Why drug counsellors hate doctors'. For one of the perennial arguments among those who treat substance abusers is between those who think there is a place for pharmacological treatments in their management and those who think there is no place for them at all. The argument is almost entirely one-sided because not even the most enthusiastic supporters of pharmacological treatment would maintain that there is no place for social, psychological or even spiritual components of treatments as well. In contrast, large areas of the addiction treatment world – especially, but not exclusively, in the residential sector – are so opposed to pharmacological treatment that they will not accept patients for treatment if they are taking any medication at all. If such establishments have any contact with doctors, other than for the treatment of concurrent medical or surgical conditions, it is to assist patients to withdraw completely from psychotropic or maintenance medication so that the 'real' work of spiritual, psychological and/or social renaissance may begin.

Even in non-residential outpatient treatment programmes, there is often a sharp distinction between counselling and methadone, though methadone (or, in some daringly modern centres, buprenorphine) is almost the only long-term pharmacological treatment offered to heroin addicts. And, when it is offered, both counsellors and nurses often pressurise patients to reduce their dose of maintenance medication, even if they don't feel ready to do so.

Methadone and buprenorphine are probably the best-known pharmacological treatments in opiate dependence, but the following drugs have also been shown in controlled studies to have specific effects which reduce symptoms or improve outcome, sometimes considerably: naltrexone for relapse prevention in opiate dependence; clonidine and lofexidine in opiate withdrawal; disulfiram and acamprosate in alcohol abuse; disulfiram in cocaine abuse; octreotide for preventing diarrhoea in opiate withdrawal. This list is not exhaustive and I will not discuss every drug in detail. Incidentally, I insist that interventions for alcohol abuse be not merely mentioned but mentioned prominently in this chapter. Alcohol is, after all, our favourite drug and alcohol abuse is certainly, besides nicotine, our biggest drug problem. Furthermore, it often complicates other types of drug abuse.

The opiate antagonist naltrexone, discussed in more detail below (pp. 102–3, was originally developed to block the effects of heroin and thus reduce relapse rates. However, it has also been shown in the past decade to be quite helpful in reducing relapses in alcoholic patients, though by a rather different mechanism. Yet, though there were good animal studies suggesting that it reduced alcohol consumption, the mainly 12-Step counsellors at some of the prestigious US centres where the first research was done were strongly opposed to studies aimed at finding out whether this effect also applied to human beings. Their opposition was not based on any evaluation of the animal evidence but simply on a visceral hostility to the use of pharmacological treatment (H. Kleber, personal communication).

Before providing detailed evidence for the effectiveness of these pharmacological interventions, it may be helpful to look at the possible reasons for the opposition of counsellors (and to a lesser extent psychologists) to using them in addiction treatment. I suggest the following broad headings.

The influence of '12-Step' treatment programmes

Twelve-Step programmes, based on the principles of Alcoholics Anonymous (AA) and sometimes also described as the 'Minnesota model' of treatment, are still the main treatment ideology in the United States. It has been argued that the 12-Step movement is a religious rather than a scientifically based treatment programme and several recent judgments of US courts have forbidden state-funded treatment programmes – and especially probation-linked treatment programmes – to require patients to take part in 12-Step meetings on the grounds that this violates the constitutional separation of church and state. One of the co-founders of AA, the famous 'Dr Bob', was quite tolerant of non-AA approaches and was not at all ill disposed towards his fellow physicians. (This may in part have been because, although foreswearing alcohol, he was apparently heavily dependent on barbiturates for sleep throughout his life and he also needed medical attention for the emphysema, caused by his addiction to tobacco, which eventually killed him.) Although one important AA publication (Alcoholics Anonymous 1975) states that 'to take or not to take disulfiram [Antabuse], to go into psychotherapy...these are all your own decisions. We respect your right to make them', the attitude of many AA and Narcotics Anonymous (NA) groups[1] is profoundly hostile to disulfiram and naltrexone, not to mention methadone. Such aids to abstinence or control are often derided as 'just a crutch', though many people will wonder what is wrong with a temporary crutch which enables people to get on with their lives while they receive psychological treatment aimed at enabling them to manage without crutches, eventually.

The psychoanalytic tradition and the search for 'underlying problems'

Still heavily influenced by psychodynamic concepts, many counsellors, social workers and psychotherapists seem to think that addiction is usually (or even always) a manifestation of underlying problems or neurotic conflicts. A rare exception in this debate is Brickman (1988). Although it is often implied that it is more important to resolve the alleged underlying problems than to attack the alcohol or heroin use directly, it is clear that most of the 'depression' associated with alcohol abuse is a *consequence* rather than a cause of the drinking, and the same almost certainly applies to heroin abuse (Shuckit 1994; Davidson 1993; McIntosh and Ritson 2001). Nevertheless, it is often asserted by psychoanalysts that simply and crudely attacking such obvious 'symptoms' as heavy drinking will lead to 'symptom substitution'. In reality, controlled studies of cognitive behavioural psychotherapy in other contexts indicate that such fears are generally groundless (Gelder *et al.* 1967).

Misconceptions about the 'medical model'

Many counsellors and psychologists appear to believe that those who think there is a place for pharmacological treatments must therefore espouse a crudely mechanistic and simplistic 'medical model' of addiction and its treatment, and must think treatment is just a matter of adjusting a few receptors here and there and increasing or decreasing a few neurotransmitters. This does not follow. As I mentioned earlier, to prescribe oral contraceptives does not indicate a belief that unwanted pregnancy is a disease. It merely recognises that medical interventions can be highly effective.

There are some echoes here of the now largely defunct anti-psychiatry movement which was so opposed to the use of pharmacological treatments in psychiatry in the 1960s and 1970s. Their motto was 'do not adjust your brain, there is a fault in reality', and in their opposition to pharmacological treatment they were in effect arguing that the brain is the only organ in the body that never malfunctions. Since the brain is by far the most complex organ, the wonder is that it doesn't malfunction more often.

The much greater profitability of inpatient treatment programmes

All the pharmacological treatments discussed shortly are in principle best suited to outpatient programmes. Several authors have noted that organisations that profit from prolonged inpatient programmes are unlikely to welcome treatments that make inpatient care largely unnecessary (Babow 1975; Miller and Hester 1986). Despite their obvious sympathy for the 12-Step ideology, Mathew *et al.* note that while

AA required recovering alcoholics to assist drinking alcoholics, free of charge…the Minnesota model was financially attractive to investors since it used recovering alcoholics and addicts, with minimal, if any, professional training. Helping other substance abusers was part of their own recovery and they were willing to work for low wages. Most rehabilitation centres employed minimal staffs of nurses, social workers and physicians.

(Mathew *et al.* 1994)

While financial factors are especially relevant to private inpatient clinics, the 'edifice complex' is not unknown in state or non-profit organisations.

Ignorance of the literature

It follows from the observations of Mathew *et al.* that many treatment programmes preferentially employ as counsellors people who have been exposed to only one particular model of treatment and who have often been told that no other approach is acceptable. It is therefore not surprising if such counsellors are ignorant of other models. Since many of them have no scientific background, they are also unable to evaluate the very large body of research into treatment effectiveness. However, ignorance is not restricted to non-medical treatment staff. In 1993 I noted that out of 16 current medical alcoholism textbooks five ignored disulfiram altogether or mentioned it only very briefly and three failed to mention the importance of supervised administration (Brewer 1993).

Gunne gives an amusing description of how an overtly anti-physician ideology developed in the Swedish addiction treatment system:

The staff of…treatment homes sometimes had a background of studies in psychology or social sciences, some were ex-addicts, but to a large extent they were merely enthusiastic amateurs. Common to these therapists was in most places a hostile attitude to the medical profession and after a while also to evaluation research based on hard – and sometimes unpleasant-facts.

(Gunne 1990)

This anti-physician (and anti-science) attitude exists in Britain and the US as well as in Sweden. McDonald *et al.*, who teach social work in Britain, noted that 'social workers are usually trained to believe that like religious…affiliation, choice of approach is largely a personal matter. This comfortable view…that all theories are created equal…ignores trends favouring certain methods above others' (1992). However, perhaps the main problem is ignorance rather than antagonism. Harrison (1992) reported that most British social work courses devoted very little time to drug and alcohol abuse and even less to the practical business of management.

Professional rivalries and attitudes

We need not invoke unconscious mechanisms to explain why counsellors and psychologists might be reluctant to endorse treatments which are more effective than those which their training qualifies them to administer if that endorsement means they have to hand over responsibility for the patient to physicians. Many psychiatrists working in addiction undertake or recommend psychological treatments in individual cases, as well as prescribing drugs, but non-medical therapists inevitably offer only a very limited range of treatments. In general, psychotherapists only do psychotherapy and acupuncturists only do acupuncture. As Mark Twain famously observed, 'If your only tool is a hammer, all your problems start to look like nails'.

Doctors are human, and that means that they share many ordinary public attitudes to alcoholics and other substance abusers. Surveys repeatedly show that general practitioners (GPs), who handle well over 90 per cent of all illness episodes, are often hostile to drug abusers and rarely more than moderately supportive. For several decades, many doctors seem to have been happy to abandon the field of addiction treatment to non-physicians, who were naturally delighted to get a toehold in the deeply satisfying world of helping one's fellow human beings in a professional capacity. Demonstrably effective medical treatments can be bad news for the unmedical.

Specific and non-specific effects of treatment

One area where ignorance reigns almost supreme among non-medical treatment staff is the placebo effect, by which I mean the non-specific effects of treatment. It is not just prescribed medicines that can have a placebo effect. All medical students are taught about the placebo effects of medical treatments, but few trainee counsellors seem to be taught about the placebo effects of counselling. Numerous studies show very clearly that counselling and psychotherapy can also have an enormous placebo effect (Prioleau *et al*. 1983). Indeed, in many studies it is difficult to discern any really significant advantage of seemingly intensive and well-intentioned counselling compared with a placebo procedure which consists of little more than making encouraging noises.

In assessing the effectiveness of any intervention – psychological or pharmacological – there are several factors which can make life very difficult for the investigator, chief among which is what one might call 'the fundamental therapeutic delusion'. This is the natural tendency for those involved in therapeutic activity to believe that what they do is useful. People simply don't like to admit to themselves or their patients that what they do may have no specific value or may be actually harmful. This means that enthusiasts often perceive benefit where none really exists and turn an individual or collective blind eye to adverse effects. (As one of our more perceptive prime ministers remarked, 'Considering that enthusiasm moves the world, it is a pity that so few enthusiasts can be trusted to tell the truth'.) Unfortunately, these pitfalls entrap patients as well as those trying to help them. Hence the observation of an eminent Victorian physician that the desire to take medicine is what chiefly distinguishes man from the lower animals. Therapists and investigators can easily confuse the natural history of a particular condition, which is to say the spontaneous improvements and deteriorations that often occur in the absence of treatment, with the consequences of intervention.

The placebo effect conflates these two factors and can be surprisingly powerful. Modern doctors, aware of the placebo effect but forgetting that their forebears rarely prescribed anything that was specifically effective, sometimes find it difficult to understand just how powerful the placebo effect can be. Yet it is constantly being rediscovered. A recent editorial (Andrews 2001) noted almost with surprise that the specific effects of antidepressant drugs were responsible for considerably less overall improvement than the non-specific effects. Acupuncture is popular with both patients and acupuncturists (especially private ones), yet many controlled studies indicate that it doesn't usually matter very much whether or not the needles are placed in what are theoretically the right spots (Ernst and White 1999). All these factors make objective assessment so difficult that adequately controlled studies often require a great deal of time and money, and the quantity of studies is no substitute for their quality.

Good controlled studies show that what is true for antidepressants is even truer for counselling. While a problem shared with a therapist is often a problem halved, or at any rate reduced, the nature of the therapy is usually much less important than the fact that the patient has entered a professional relationship. In one of the most thorough studies, Sloane *et al.* (1975) found that behavioural psychotherapy was more effective than the psychodynamic variety in psychiatric outpatients but most of the subsequent improvement followed the assessment interview rather than the actual therapy. In the Vanderbilt study (Strupp and Hadley 1979) anxious students responded equally well overall, whether they were counselled by interested but untrained faculty members or by trained therapists. This result is consistently found in comparative psychotherapy studies (Durlak 1979). Harris, a non-physician working in a drugs project, is unusual in emphasising this sobering finding. He adds that most counsellor training courses operate 'without recourse to outcomes or research findings....It is ironic that the counselling profession...seems to be inflexible and not able to change' (Harris 2001).

Furthermore, because therapists are human they are very variable. Najavitz and Weiss (1994) found that fourfold differences in outcome and dropout rates between the most effective and the least effective addiction therapists and counsellors were common. In contrast, the therapeutic effects of an adequate dose of methadone or naltrexone rest very largely on their inherent and unvarying pharmacological characteristics. Let us now examine more closely some of these pharmacological treatments.

Disulfiram (Antabuse)

Most alcoholic patients who take disulfiram in adequate dosage would get an unpleasant reaction within a few minutes if they continued drinking alcohol. Much of the alcohol which is absorbed into the blood is broken down by enzymes, first to acetaldehyde, then to acetic acid (vinegar) and then to water and carbon dioxide. Acetaldehyde – closely related to formaldehyde – is rather toxic stuff but is normally broken down so quickly that blood levels remain too low to cause toxic effects. Disulfiram inhibits the enzyme acetaldehyde dehydrogenase (ALDH), which converts acetalde-hyde to acetic acid. Drinking alcohol while taking disulfiram therefore produces high acetaldehyde levels, which can cause a variety of unpleasant but relatively transient effects. As little as half a unit of alcohol (approxi-mately 5g) may be sufficient to cause the disulfiram–alcohol reaction (DAR) (Brewer 1984). It therefore deters patients from drinking, or from repeating the experience if they have already had an unpleasant DAR. Naturally, disul-firam has no effect on drinking behaviour if patients for whom it is prescribed either discontinue it or never take it in the first place.

Interestingly, many Japanese have a genetically determined ALDH defi-ciency and therefore also experience raised acetaldehyde levels after drinking. The increase is not usually as marked as with disulfiram but, as the distin-guished addiction researcher Griffith Edwards notes, this normally inconsequential enzyme variant 'produces an unpleasant reaction to alcohol which can give a degree of protection against the development of alcohol dependence' (2000: 70). In reality such people produce, in effect, a mild built-in disulfiram reaction to alcohol. However, in those who inherit this disposition from both parents, the reaction with alcohol is so strong that alcohol abuse in this sub-group is virtually unknown (Tu *et al.* 1995). In other words, prescribing disulfiram merely offers patients the same degree of deterrence from, and protection against, drinking that is naturally present in some Orientals, and by almost exactly the same mechanism (Sun *et al.* 2002).

Disulfiram was first used in alcoholism treatment in 1948 and is therefore regarded by some treatment professionals as hopelessly old-fashioned, though insulin and penicillin are even older and still give good service. In reality, the effectiveness of disulfiram *when supervised by a third party such as family members or health professionals* is almost unanimously supported by controlled and uncon-trolled studies. This crucially important distinction between studies in which disulfiram administration was supervised and those in which it was not has been ignored by many reviewers. Table 5.1 gives an up-to-date list of these studies, from which I will select a few highlights.

Bourne *et al.* (1966) published the first study in which disulfiram was routinely supervised, generally as one component of a probation order. Although the study was uncontrolled, the results were very encouraging given that virtually all these patients were recurrent 'skid-row' alcoholic offenders

Table 5.1: Clinical trials of supervised disulfiram

Authors	Design	No. of subjects	Frequency of disulfiram supervision	Control Group*	Daily Dose (mg)	Patients	P=†	Comment
Bourne et al. 1966	U	196	Daily	NA	500	Skid-row alcoholics	NA	Compliance approx 60%
Gallant et al. 1968	RCT	84	Thrice weekly	No disulfiram group therapy	500	Recurrent skid-row alcoholic offenders	NA	Few patients in any group attended
Liebson et al. 1971	U	10	?Weekly	NA	250	Skid-row alcoholics	NA	Disulfiram combined in capsule with chlordiazepoxide
Haynes 1973	U	138	Twice weekly	NA	Not stated	Recurrent alcoholic offenders	NA	13-fold reduction in arrests
Gerrein et al. 1973	RCT	49	Twice weekly	Unsupervised	250	Ordinary outpatients	<0.05	Improved longer term retention
Azrin 1976	RCT	20	Daily	Unsupervised	?250	Ordinary outpatients	<0.005	Better results with less counselling. Two-year follow-up
Liebson et al. 1973	RCT	6	Daily	Unsupervised	500–250	Alcoholic methadone maintenance	<0.001	1% v. 17% drinking days
Robichaud et al. 1979	RCT	21	Daily/alternate days	A–B–A				

Table 5.1: Clinical trials of supervised disulfiram continued

Study				Design	500–250	Alcoholic employees	<0.01	Fivefold reduction in absenteeism
Azrin et al. 1982	RCT	43	Daily supervisor with special training	Unsupervised	250	Ordinary rural outpatients	<0.01	Nearly 100% abstinence at six months in treatment group
Brewer and Smith 1983	U	16	Twice weekly	NA	200–800	Recurrent alcoholic offenders	NA	Average abstinence 30 weeks, v. six weeks in previous two years. Nine out of 16 totally successful.
Keane et al. 1984	RCT	25	Daily	Spouse contracting	Not stated ?250	Outpatients	NA	Contracting improved compliance and outcome
Sereny et al. 1986	Before and after	68	Thrice weekly	Patients acted as own controls	250–500	Outpatients, three times previous treatment failures	NA	40% total/18% partial success
Chick et al. 1992	RCT	126	Daily	Supervised vitamin C	200	Ordinary outpatients	<0.05	P<0.01 on some measures

Gerber et al. 1994	Non-randomised	20	Daily	Healthy volunteers	Not stated	Outpatients with liver disease	NA	Quality of life and liver functions normalised at six months
Besson et al. 1998	U†	46	Daily	Acamprosate or placebo	Not stated	Ordinary outpatients	NA	Disulfiram improved acamprosate effects
Carroll et al. 1993	RCT	18	Weekly	Naltrexone 50 mg	250	Alcohol and cocaine abusers	<0.01	Reduced drinking associated with reduced cocaine
Carroll et al. 1998	RCT	122	Twice weekly to weekly	No disulfiram	250–500	Alcohol and cocaine abusers	<0.01	Longer retention in treatment (p<0.05)
Tønnesen et al. 1999	RCT	42	Twice weekly	No treatment	800 twice weekly	Alcoholic outpatients awaiting surgery	<0.02	Complete pre-operative abstinence in treatment group

Note:
RCT randomised controlled trial
U uncontrolled
* in most cases, the control group received at least standard levels of psychosocial treatment
** main outcome measure
† disulfiram patients unrandomised in RCT of acamprosate

Source: Brewer et al. (2000).

with long histories of severe alcohol abuse resistant to other methods. About 60 per cent took disulfiram, supervised by probation officers, during the 30–60 days of their suspended sentence. Most took it for longer than was legally required. The authors concluded modestly that probation-linked supervised disulfiram seemed to be a useful idea and worth developing.

In a retrospective study in Colorado Springs, Haynes (1973) investigated the effectiveness of supervised disulfiram for 12 months as one condition of a probation order in recurrent alcoholic offenders. Some patients left town, often for legitimate reasons, and 12 per cent were jailed for non-compliance. In the remainder, acting as their own controls, he found an almost 13-fold reduction in alcohol-related offences compared with their previous record.

Azrin (1976) published the first of two randomised controlled studies (RCTs) in which he investigated the effects of both supervised and unsupervised disulfiram combined with a package of essentially cognitive behavioural (as opposed to psychodynamic) outpatient interventions which he called community reinforcement therapy (CRT). CRT had already been shown by Hunt and Azrin (1973) to be significantly more effective than conventional outpatient treatment. Disulfiram was supervised both by family members and by counsellors at each counselling session. Apart from the highly significant differences in favour of disulfiram, this study is noteworthy for the unusually long follow-up period (two years) during which the improvements were maintained. Furthermore, these improved results were achieved with 40 per cent less counselling time than was needed by patients in the control group.

Liebson *et al.* (1973) studied supervised disulfiram in a small group of methadone maintenance patients who also abused alcohol – a common and often challenging clinical problem. In the experimental group, dispensing of the daily methadone dose was made contingent on taking disulfiram under professional supervision. Their alcohol consumption was considerably and significantly lower than in the unsupervised control group.

Azrin followed up his earlier studies with another (Azrin *et al.* 1982) which confirmed the effectiveness of properly supervised disulfiram. However, he and his co-authors also made the very important (and unexpected) discovery that for patients with reasonably intact relationships, who constitute, in many studies, a majority or at least a large minority of subjects, involving the non-alcoholic partners and giving them simple training to improve the quality of disulfiram supervision was the most important component of treatment. In such cases, adding more intensive counselling conferred no additional benefit. Disulfiram effects were maintained throughout the six-month study period.

A multi-centre six-month British study by Chick *et al.* (1992) confirmed the effectiveness of supervised disulfiram but was also designed to discover whether the effectiveness was due to the psychological and symbolic impact of supervision or to the deterrent and pharmacological effects of disulfiram. The subjects were patients receiving standard outpatient alcoholism treatment who were randomly assigned to supervised disulfiram or supervised vitamin C. Where possible, supervision was delegated to family members, who were given appropriate instruction, but in other cases medication was supervised by clinic staff or community nurses. The results, which included a significant reduction in the liver enzyme gamma glutamyl transpeptidase (a marker for alcoholic liver damage) very clearly favoured the disulfiram group.

Disulfiram for cocaine abuse

On empirical grounds, disulfiram is sometimes prescribed for patients whose cocaine abuse is associated with excessive drinking. The rationale is that if cocaine use usually follows heavy drinking (a not uncommon sequence), then preventing drinking may have beneficial effects on cocaine use. However, during the past decade it has been discovered that disulfiram can significantly reduce cocaine use even in patients who do not have co-morbid alcohol abuse (Petrakis *et al.* 2000). An impressive RCT (Carroll *et al.* 1998) of patients who abused both alcohol and cocaine compared two types of psychotherapy – cognitive behavioural therapy (CBT) and 12-Step facilitation (TSF) – with ordinary clinical management (CM) with and without disulfiram. Disulfiram ingestion was monitored by a nurse twice weekly for the first month of treatment and weekly thereafter. 'The CBT/disulfiram group had the highest rate of retention (mean 8.8 weeks), followed by CM/disulfiram (8.4 weeks) and TSF/disulfiram (8.0 weeks). Subjects assigned to disulfiram treatment were retained significantly longer than those assigned to no medication (8.4 versus 5.8 weeks ($p<0.05$). No significant differences in retention by psychotherapy were found.'

They also found significant disulfiram effects on consecutive weeks of cocaine abstinence, alcohol abstinence and abstinence from both cocaine and alcohol. In contrast, the specific effect of the psychotherapies was rather modest. Whether or not the patients received either of the psychotherapies (CBT or TSF v. CM) was much less relevant to outcome than whether or not they received disulfiram. This is an important study, not only because it is further evidence for the effectiveness of supervised disulfiram, but also because retention in therapy is self-evidently desirable. Clinicians working in relapse prevention obviously need to spend enough therapeutic time with patients to help them to make positive cognitive and behavioural changes. Supervised disulfiram is clearly one of the most effective techniques for maximising treatment retention, but in 'pure' alcohol abuse the sobriety that it usually imposes also gives patients a better chance of dealing with ambivalence and denial and of learning and consolidating new coping skills and strategies.

I swear that I have not invented this rather impressive list of overwhelmingly positive studies, several of them published 15–20 years ago. The papers by Azrin and colleagues are often singled out for their exemplary methodology (Saunders 1985), and it is noteworthy that many of these studies were done largely by psychologists rather than by physicians. Yet in many units disulfiram is rarely prescribed, and some seem almost proud of never using it at all. In the two years up to September 2001 only one prescription for disulfiram was written at London's Kings College Hospital, an establishment which houses an internationally famous liver unit treating many alcoholic patients (T. Peters, personal communication).

Methadone

An earlier proposed title for a chapter in this book was 'Methadone maintenance: treatment or indulgence?' This would have neatly encapsulated one of the moral issues at the heart of methadone treatment. The main function of methadone is to prevent the emergence of the unpleasant opiate withdrawal symptoms and craving that occur when heroin levels fall below a certain point. Further doses of heroin will also prevent these withdrawal symptoms, and many people can actually function quite well if they can afford to keep their heroin intakes at a level which is high enough to prevent withdrawal symptoms but not so high that it makes them sleepy. (Though for quite a few addicts heroin has an energising rather than a soporific effect.) Many alcoholic patients also function quite well if they keep their blood alcohol levels sufficiently high by frequent topping up, but there is no need for formal alcohol maintenance programmes with compulsory counselling because alcoholics can buy their alcohol easily and comparatively cheaply from a large number of legitimate outlets. The problem with methadone maintenance, for some people, is that, looked at from one point of view, it *is* simply 'giving drugs to addicts', while from another perspective 'methadone is medicine', to quote one of the battle-cries of the pro-methadone lobby. Perhaps it would be more acceptable if it were realised that the principle behind it is very similar to that of nicotine replacement therapy (NRT) for smokers, especially now that it is apparent that for the best results NRT may need to be continued for months rather than weeks.

This is not an appropriate place to deal in detail with what I regard as the absurdity of the prohibition legislation, which has caused so many problems (and solved so few) since its introduction as a piece of emergency and temporary legislation during a 'moral panic' in the First World War (Hoare 1997). However, it is surely relevant to point out that before the criminalisation of opiates, hundreds of thousands of respectable citizens in Britain maintained themselves on laudanum (or, more rarely, on subcutaneous morphine or heroin) and, while no doubt many of them were annoyed that they had become dependent, I suspect that few of them felt much need for counselling, especially since laudanum – unlike alcohol – has negligible organ toxicity. Indeed, there was a debate in Victorian Britain about whether laudanum had a life-preserving effect (Berridge 1999).

Laudanum was comparatively cheap. So is methadone, and it would be even cheaper were it not for what seems an international conspiracy among pharmaceutical companies to keep its price high. Not long ago, I visited the sole methadone programme in Vilnius, the capital of Lithuania. The Baltic States have only recently started to recover from years of Soviet political and economic tyranny and average wages are relatively low. The Vilnius methadone programme has no limits on either dose or duration of treatment, but supervised daily consumption (including Sundays) is mandatory and the patients pay for their own methadone at more or less cost price. They can afford this because the pharmacy imports methadone powder at a cost of about US$1 per gram and makes up its own methadone mixture. This means that patients even on 200mg daily do not need to pay much more than the equivalent of £1 sterling per week (*c.* €1.50/$1.50) for their methadone. Since most British patients are spending four times that amount every day on cigarettes, it would not be much of a hardship if they followed the Victorian example and paid for their own opiates. Perhaps, as with the Carlisle Breweries during the First World War, this is a good argument for selective nationalisation.

Only moral (not to say moralistic) considerations seem to explain the consistent underdosing of most methadone patients for many years. It certainly can have nothing to do with science or evidence-based medicine. Dole and Nyswander (1965),who introduced the concept of methadone maintenance treatment (MMT), advised that some addicts needed doses well over 100 mg daily to prevent the emergence of withdrawal symptoms and craving. This advice was based on clinical observation rather than controlled trials but the first RCT (Newman and Whitehill 1979), which showed that methadone was vastly superior to a similar programme without methadone, used *an average* dose of 97 mg daily and a maximum of 130mg daily. Since the trial was done in Hong Kong, where the indigenous inhabitants tend to be smaller and lighter than their Western counterparts, this high average dose is particularly striking. Several other controlled trials of MMT have confirmed its effectiveness. Other studies (e.g. Caplehorn *et al.* 1994) indicate that a dosage range of 80–120mg daily should be regarded as fairly normal, while studies over the past decade on the differential metabolism of the two stereo isomers ('mirror image' molecules) of methadone explain why some patients with apparently very high blood methadone levels can have inadequate opiate activity. The explanation is that one can have a high level of the inactive d-isomer of methadone while simultaneously having a very low level of the active l-isomer (Eap *et al.* 1998). In many areas of medicine, therapeutic drug monitoring (TDM) is often used to optimise treatment. Because people can vary considerably in their absorption and metabolism of a particular drug, it may be necessary to measure blood levels to detect doses which are too low or too high. TDM is routine for anti-epileptic drugs, lithium, some antibiotics and many other drugs. It can certainly be helpful for some MMT patients. Yet few British methadone clinics examine blood methadone levels and virtually none do them routinely; and no British laboratory seems able to measure the differential isomer levels.

We need to ask ourselves why this impressive evidence base for MMT, going back over 20 years, was ignored for so long by influential figures in the British addiction establishment. The 1991 Department of Health guidelines on treatment barely mention MMT, implying that it is a rather exotic treatment suitable for only a small proportion of heroin addicts. The most recent guidelines, published in 1999, do belatedly recognise MMT as a routine and well-researched intervention but the evidence base was pretty strong in 1991, or indeed in 1981. The 1999 guidelines also accept that 60–120mg/day should be regarded as the normal dosage range for MMT and that some patients need more than this. Yet in a recent British survey the mean maintenance dose was only 52 mg/day, 71 per cent of patients received doses in the 30–60 mg/day range and only 23 per cent received doses of more than 60 mg/day (Gossop *et al.* 2001). This indicates serious underdosing on a national scale according to the Department's own published advice. Caplehorn (1995) suggests that a major factor in this widespread treatment inadequacy is the excessive adherence by certain leading British personalities in addiction to psychological theories of causation and treatment at the expense of pharmacological ones.

Furthermore, when it comes to methadone dosage the guidelines are almost certainly too conservative. In a recent study from Slovakia (Okruhlica *et al.* 2002) the *average* dose for MMT patients was 134 mg/day and there was evidence that patients who habitually injected heroin needed higher methadone doses than smokers. Doses were individually adjusted for each patient based on both objective and subjective data. The authors also compared methadone doses with methadone blood levels in all patients and the results are rather instructive.

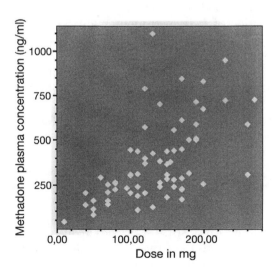

Figure 5.1: Relationship between methadone dose (mg/day) and blood level (ng/ml)
Source: Okruhlica *et al.* 2002.

Figure 5.1, showing the relationship of dose to blood level, shows that although there is a general correlation between methadone dose and methadone blood level there are numerous exceptions on both sides of the mean. The conventional wisdom is that the desirable range for adequate MMT lies between 200–600 ng/ml. Okruhlica *et al.* quote an important position statement by the American Society of Addiction Medicine (ASAM), that determination of methadone dosage by programme policy is inappropriate, and that dosage should be individually determined by well-trained clinicians based on subjective and objective data and be adequate for the individual patient in all cases. They note that the benefits of individualised methadone dosing are well documented. Yet despite the use of large doses by British standards, 17.4 per cent of their patients had blood methadone levels below the 200 ng/ml threshold, while slightly fewer – 15.9 per cent – had levels above the 600 ng/ml conventional upper limit. However, one patient taking 275 mg daily had a blood level of only 260 ng/ml, while two of the highest levels – 800 ng/ml and 1,200 ng/ml – were found in patients whose methadone doses were only 100–125 mg daily. As in Vilnius, methadone consumption was strictly supervised, with negligible take-home privileges, except at weekends. The authors say that recently patients have been allowed to collect methadone twice weekly, but only if they have been doing well in the programme for over a year.

Outcomes are impressive. The programme has an overall retention rate of 84 per cent at 12 months, compared with only 62 per cent in the survey by Gossop *et al.* (2001), which, ironically, stresses the importance of retaining patients in treatment for long enough to help them change. Furthermore, only 13 per cent of the Slovakian patients produce urines positive for heroin on random testing. Another recent paper reached similar conclusions. Following a relaxation of state methadone regulations in Illinois, Maxwell and Shinderman (2002) compared selected 'high-dose' (HD) patients with control (C) patients restricted to the previous state maximum of 100 mg/day. The HD group had significantly better retention and fewer 'dirty' urines than the C group. The *average* methadone dose for the HD group was 285 mg/day and the highest dose was 1,100 mg/day.

But where are the voices of social workers, probation officers, psychologists and counsellors clamouring for a fair deal for heroin addicts and adequate doses of methadone? That the clamour is conspicuous by its absence suggests to me that the social workers and psychologists are either ignorant of the scientific literature about methadone treatment or share the moralistic attitudes of many health professionals towards heroin addicts. Most probably, both factors are important. Indeed, the typical British methadone programme still insists on a steady reduction in dose, often over only a few months, despite the firm evidence that such forced reductions lead almost inevitably to the resumption of street heroin use.

Does this mean that patients on MMT are on it for life? Fortunately, that is not the case. First of all, the phenomenon of 'maturing out' ensures that a significant number of opiate-dependent patients spontaneously discontinue opiates for various reasons and in various ways, just as significant numbers of nicotine addicts manage to stop smoking. Some need maintaining for a few months, but many patients need maintaining for several years and some indefinitely. Studies (e.g. Gottheil *et al.* 1993) typically show that the longer patients stay in treatment the less likely they are to use illicit drugs. Consequently, in general, the longer patients stay in treatment the less likely they are to need counselling, because if they cease or considerably reduce their consumption of illicit drugs they will in most cases have fewer problems for which counselling would be appropriate.

Many counsellors seem to feel it is their duty to focus on the 'reasons' why a particular drug user started using drugs. In most cases the reasons are fairly – even blindingly – obvious. The first drug that most 'drug addicts' use (certainly the first one to which they become addicted) is nearly always nicotine. People use nicotine because at a certain stage of adolescence it becomes 'the thing to do' for quite a lot of adolescents, but by no means all. Few counsellors seem very interested in why their patients started smoking cigarettes. In part, this is probably because many counsellors and nurses working in addiction are themselves nicotine addicts. One reason heroin causes problems is that, although it is not quite as addictive as nicotine, it is nevertheless highly likely to cause physical dependence, but, unlike nicotine, the cost of a day's supply is extremely high. Cocaine causes problems in a minority of its users because of compulsive use which seems to have more to do with psychological than with physiological factors and because it too is relatively expensive. In the Andes, where whole populations consume it on a daily basis, cocaine is much less of a problem because it is cheap and available mainly in unconcentrated forms. This was once true of alcohol before the (Islamic) invention of distilling. For the same reason, cannabis poses relatively few problems even though, like alcohol, it can sometimes make its users do rather antisocial things and it may impair their employability.

Detoxification

Detoxification is a problem mainly for users of heroin and other opiates. Most alcohol abusers are not physically dependent on alcohol and the minority who are can usually be withdrawn from alcohol as outpatients or with no more than three or four days of inpatient treatment. (I leave it to readers to draw their own conclusion as to why private clinics so often advise that inpatient treatment is necessary and that alcoholics need at least a week or two to detoxify.) Although it may seem contrary to common sense, it is clear that the severity of withdrawal symptoms bears very little relationship to the amount of heroin or methadone consumed by individual users (Kosten *et al.* 1989). Mice can be selectively bred to have high or low withdrawal severity (Suzuki *et al.* 1987) and there is much evidence that the extreme variability of withdrawal symptoms in human beings is also to a large extent genetically determined. There are cases on record of non-identical twins born to opiate-dependent mothers but having very different neonatal withdrawal syndromes in terms of severity or duration. Certainly, patients taking quite small doses of opiates can have severe and prolonged withdrawal symptoms, while some patients taking very large doses seem to be able to stop with very little difficulty. Accordingly, withdrawal or detoxification programmes should reflect this diversity.

As with alcohol, a useful number of opiate users can be withdrawn on an outpatient basis and should be encouraged to do so. However, if they try and fail, or if they feel that the effort is very unlikely to succeed, inpatient or day-patient treatment should be offered. It is true that the failure rate of outpatient detoxification is somewhere between 50 and 80 per cent in many studies but it still represents a considerable number of people. The failure rate for conventional inpatient detoxification is typically somewhere between 30 and 70 per cent (Gossop *et al.* 1987; Gossling *et al.* 2001). One common reason for these high failure rates is that most units provide completely inadequate symptom relief. Opiate withdrawal is not always an agonising matter but it certainly can be for some patients. At its worst, it involves several days of vomiting, diarrhoea, shivering, sweating, muscular twitches and severe cramp-like pains in both the abdomen and the limbs. This is asking rather a lot of mere mortals to bear, especially as severe insomnia is the rule, so that there is no relief even at night. Yet many clinics offer little more than an aspirin or two. Drugs such as clonidine or lofexidine are useful (Gerra *et al.* 2001), but they are by no means universally effective and do nothing to shorten the duration of discomfort. Many clinics decline to offer sleeping tablets. Consequently, many addicts discharge themselves at an early stage. Some clinics conveniently ignore these early failures in calculating their success rates, but honesty requires that researchers assess effectiveness using an 'intention to treat' basis. To revert to our family planning analogy, a method of contraception which is theoretically very effective is not very effective in practice if most patients find it too uncomfortable to use.

Detoxification technology is being transformed in an increasing number of countries by the introduction of rapid opiate detoxification (ROD) techniques. Instead of discontinuing opiates abruptly or over a few days and allowing withdrawal symptoms to develop (a technique which adds the stress of anticipation to the actual pains of withdrawal), an alternative technique is to precipitate acute withdrawal over a space of three to four hours by administering opiate antagonists. These drive all opiates off the opiate receptors but also start the process of normalising the receptors so that the worst symptoms of withdrawal are over in two to three days rather than the two to three weeks which is typical in conventional programmes for most patients (Brewer 1997). Naltrexone is the usual opiate antagonist used. As well as being more efficient and humane, these techniques are also more cost-effective than conventional methods (Lahej *et al.* 2000; Carreno *et al.* 2002).

Naltrexone

As mentioned earlier, naltrexone was developed (in the 1960s) specifically as a reasonably long-acting oral opiate antagonist. It completely blocks the effects of heroin and other opiates, even in large doses, and the blockade can last up to three days after an oral dose of 150 mg, permitting thrice-weekly administration. It has low organ toxicity and, in particular, it is not toxic to the liver at the doses normally used in addiction treatment (Pini *et al.* 1991). It is important to distinguish between the *relapse-preventing* use of naltrexone and its ability to *precipitate and accelerate opiate withdrawal*, even though the latter is usually a necessary prelude to the former. Naltrexone cannot be given to patients who are physically dependent on opiates without special (though not necessarily very complicated) procedures.

Not surprisingly, controlled studies show that provided the administration of naltrexone is supervised (as with disulfiram) relapse rates are significantly reduced. The more quickly patients are transferred from methadone or heroin to naltrexone, the less opportunity they have to relapse at a particularly vulnerable time when relapse is otherwise common (Lahej *et al.* 2000). The ability of naltrexone to block the effects of heroin, or other opiates such as methadone, is not something that works only in a proportion of cases. It is clear that naltrexone will block street heroin habits of as much as 10 g daily and, although injecting 100 mg of pure heroin (diamorphine) would probably kill me several times over, I would willingly submit to such a dose if I were protected by a tablet of naltrexone. As with most disulfiram studies, all clinical trials of naltrexone where its administration was supervised have shown a positive effect. Naltrexone has a low incidence of side-effects and tolerance to the blockade does not develop. In a Singaporean study involving heroin-related offenders (not normally regarded as the most promising therapeutic material) success rates of intensive probation-linked treatment (including thrice-weekly urine testing, counselling and electronic tagging) were 25 per cent at one year but rose to 75 per cent when the identical programme was boosted by the addition of thrice-weekly supervised naltrexone (Chan 1996). Similar clinically and statistically significant benefits were achieved by an American probation-linked RCT and they were less impressive only because naltrexone was administered twice a week rather than three times (Cornish *et al.* 1997).

In effect, patients taking naltrexone cannot relapse to opiate addiction while adequate naltrexone is present in their blood. In the past three years, Drug Treatment and Testing Orders (DTTOs) have been introduced in England and Wales. They were supposed to offer drug-related offenders a range of treatments – medical and non-medical – within a probation framework. The specific benefits appear to have been modest and the cost benefits even lower (Ruben 2001). Yet despite the publication of the above two studies showing clear and considerable benefits from probation-linked naltrexone, it appears that only one DTTO offender has received naltrexone during the pilot study (M. Hough, personal communication). The increasing availability, use and popularity of naltrexone in implant form represents an important advance in compliance and effectiveness (Göltz and Partecke 2000; Hulse and O'Neill 2002; Brewer 2002; Foster *et al.* 2003).

Naltrexone also has useful effects in alcohol abuse. It does not block the effects of alcohol in the way that it blocks the effects of heroin. Neither does it produce an unpleasant reaction with alcohol, like disulfiram. In RCTs of detoxified alcohol abusers in abstinence-based programmes it does not increase the proportion of patients who remain abstinent, but if patients drink alcohol, then naltrexone (compared with a placebo) usefully increases the likelihood that such lapses will not become relapses. Acamprosate is another drug which reduces relapses (Besson *et al.* 1998). Controlled studies indicate that naltrexone is more effective than acamprosate but neither of them is anywhere near as effective as supervised disulfiram (Carroll *et al.* 1993; Brewer *et al.* 2000).

Residential rehabilitation

Almost by definition, patients receive treatment in residential rehabilitation centres (and, indeed, in any other inpatient or outpatient setting) because they find it difficult to resist the temptation to use heroin, alcohol or other drugs. If they did not find it difficult to resist these temptations they would not need treatment for drug problems. (Interestingly, the few RCTs that have addressed the issue all found little difference in outcome between fully residential programmes and much cheaper day-care programmes (Greenwood *et al.* 2001).) Not surprisingly, many patients (or clients or residents, if you prefer) find it difficult to abandon immediately and lastingly such well-established habits and therefore some of them continue to use their problem drug for varying periods after they have been admitted. Almost without exception, such use, even if isolated or sporadic, is viewed as a reason for expelling the patient. Isn't this just a tiny bit illogical? To expel patients from the rehab because they continue to do what brought them into the rehab in the first place is rather like – no, it is almost *exactly* like – throwing schizophrenics out of psychiatric hospitals because they have the cheek to continue to have delusions and hallucinations.

We normally help hospitalised schizophrenics to stop having these distressing symptoms by offering them appropriate medication in addition to the psychosocial and material supports provided by the hospital. We should surely help heroin addicts who find it difficult to stop using heroin, even in the supportive atmosphere of a rehabilitation centre, by offering to add naltrexone to their regime, not by throwing them out. Alternatively, given the unrivalled and well-documented ability of methadone to retain patients in treatment, we could offer them MMT as an inducement to stay and benefit from the potentially therapeutic atmosphere and structure of a good rehab. Rehabs certainly need all the help they can get to retain more than a small proportion of the addicts they admit.

In an RCT of outpatient MMT v. therapeutic communities (TCs), Bale *et al.* (1980) found that MMT had a significantly higher take-up (29.4 per cent v. 17.9 per cent). More importantly, while MMT retention was 74.5 per cent at one year, TCs had lost over 80 per cent of their residents at six months. The situation is no better in Britain. Keen *et al.* (2001) studied a series of admissions to Phoenix House, a fairly typical and well-regarded establishment. They noted 'overall low levels of programme completion and high levels of unplanned programme departure and eviction'. Only 25 per cent of residents stayed for more than 90 days and only 13 per cent were defined as 'successes'. It is likely that opening rehabs to patients on MMT or offering it to them as an alternative to compulsory detoxification would considerably improve these depressing figures. Once they had mastered or rediscovered a few rather basic social, psychological and employment skills, the residents could be discharged either on continued MMT or after withdrawal, with or without the protection of naltrexone. Similarly, relapsing alcoholic residents could be encouraged to stay and benefit, provided they demonstrated their commitment to treatment by taking disulfiram under the supervision of the staff. Surely this would be a sensible and evidence-based way of combining the benefits of both psychosocial and pharmacological components of treatment? Surely such a combination might be particularly relevant and helpful for a group of patients whose problems are often, by definition, at the more severe end of the scale? Yet I know of only two residential rehabilitation centres in Britain which, not without some hesitation, will consent to admit patients taking naltrexone or disulfiram, and not a single one that will take patients on MMT.

These and other irrational policies are likely to continue for as long as major decisions about management and funding are made by people who are actually profoundly ignorant of the possibilities and the literature of treatment and/or are afflicted with ideological tunnel vision. This sort of ignorance does not commonly exist among the staff of family planning clinics. It is time we stopped allowing and even facilitating its existence among those who work in addiction treatment centres.

Notes

1   Though not all. I once lectured at a semi-rural Irish hospital whose AA group had a rota to supervise the Antabuse taken by some of its members. Impressed by this combined socio-pharmacological approach, I telephoned AA HQ in Dublin to ask if it was a common pattern in Ireland. They were offended by my enquiry and suggested that the group in question couldn't have been a 'real' AA group. My attempts to establish a similar group in London received no support from AA HQ in Britain.

References

Alcoholics Anonymous (1975) *Living Sober* 60, London: Jupiter.
Andrews, G. (2001) 'Placebo Response in Depression: Bane of Research, Boon to Therapy', *British Journal of Psychiatry* 178: 192–4.

Azrin, N. H. (1976) 'Improvements in the Community-reinforcement Approach to Alcoholism', *Behaviour Research & Therapy* 14: 339–48.

Azrin, N. H., Sisson, R. W., Meyers, R. and Godley, M. (1982) 'Alcoholism Treatment by Disulfiram and Community Reinforcement Therapy', *Journal of Behaviour Therapy and Experimental Psychiatry* 13(2): 105–12.

Babow, I. (1975) 'The Treatment Monopoly in Alcoholism and Drug Dependence: A Sociological Critique', *Journal of Drug Issues* 5: 120–8.

Bale, R., Van Stone, W., Kuldau, J., Engelsing, T. M., Elashoff, R. M. and Zarcone, V. P., Jr (1980) 'Therapeutic Communities vs Methadone Maintenance. A Prospective Controlled Study of Narcotic Addiction Treatment: Design and One-year Follow-up', *Archives of General Psychiatry* 37: 179–93.

Berridge, V. (1999) *Opium and the People*, London: Free Association Books.

Besson, J., Aeby, F., Kasas, A., Lehert, P. and Potgieter, A. (1998) 'Combined Efficacy of Acamprosate and Disulfiram in the Treatment of Alcoholism: A Controlled Study', *Alcoholism – Clinical and Experimental Research* 22: 573–9.

Bourne, P. G., Alford, J. A. and Bowcock, J. Z. (1966) 'Treatment of Skid-row Alcoholics with Disulfiram', *Quarterly Journal of Studies on Alcohol* 27: 42–8.

Brewer, C. (1984) 'How Effective is the Standard Dose of Disulfiram?', *British Journal of Psychiatry* 144: 200–2.

Brewer, C. (1993) 'What the Textbooks Say about Disulfiram: A Review of Recent Publications', in C. Brewer (ed.) *Treatment Options in Addiction – Medical Management of Alcohol and Opiate Abuse*, London: Gaskell.

Brewer, C. (1997) 'Ultra-rapid, Antagonist-precipitated Opiate Detoxification under General Anaesthesia or Sedation', *Addiction Biology* 2: 291–302.

Brewer, C. (2002) 'Serum Naltrexone and 6-Beta-Naltrexol Levels from Naltrexone Implants Can Block Very Large Amounts of Heroin: A Report of Two Cases', *Addiction Biology* 7: 321–3.

Brewer, C. and Smith, J. (1983) 'Probation-linked Supervised Disulfiram in the Treatment of Habitual Drunken Offenders: Results of a Pilot Study', *British Medical Journal* 287: 1,282–3.

Brewer, C., Meyers, R. J. and Johnsen, J. (2000) 'Does Disulfiram Help to Prevent Relapse in Alcohol Abuse?', *CNS Drugs* 14(5): 329–41.

Brickman, B. (1988) 'Psychoanalysis and Substance Abuse: Toward a More Effective Approach', *Journal of the American Academy of Psychoanalysis* 16: 359–79.

Caplehorn, J. (1995) 'Methadone Maintenance Treatment: Britain Has Been Over-committed to Psychological Theories of Drug Dependence', *British Medical Journal* 310: 463.

Caplehorn, J., Dalton, S., Cluff, M. and Petrenas, A.-M. (1994) 'Retention in Methadone Maintenance and Heroin Addicts Risk of Death', *Addiction* 89: 203–7.

Carreno, J. E., Bobes, J., Brewer, C., Alvarez, C. E., San Narciso, G. I., Bascaran, M. T. and Sanchez del Rio, J. (2002) '24-Hour Opiate Detoxification and Antagonist Induction at Home – The "Asturian Method": A Report on 1368 Procedures', *Addiction Biology* 7: 243–50.

Carroll, K., Ziedonis, D., O'Malley, S., McCance-Katz, E., Gordon, L. and Rounsaville, B. (1993) 'Pharmacologic Interventions for Alcohol and Cocaine Abusing Individuals: A Pilot Study of Disulfiram vs Naltrexone', *American Journal of Addictions* 2: 77–9.

Carroll, K. M., Nich, C., Ball, S. A., McCance, E. and Rounsaville, B. J. (1998) 'Treatment of Cocaine and Alcohol Dependence with Psychotherapy and Disulfiram', *Addiction* 93(5): 713–28.

Chan, K. Y. (1996) 'The Singapore Naltrexone Community-based Project for Heroin Addicts Compared with Drugfree Community-based Program: The First Cohort', *Journal of Clinical Medicine* 3: 87–92.

Chick, J., Gough, K., Falkowski, W., Kershaw, P., Hore, B., Mehta, B., Ritson, B., Ropner, R. and Torley, D. (1992) 'Disulfiram Treatment of Alcoholism', *British Journal of Psychiatry* 161: 84–9.

Cornish, J. W., Metzger, D., Woody, G., Wilson, D., McLellan, A. T., Vandergrifft, B. and O'Brien, C. P. (1997) 'Naltrexone Pharmacotherapy for Opioid Dependent Federal Probationers', *Journal of Substance Abuse Treatment* 14: 529–34.

Davidson, K. (1993) 'Diagnosis of Depression in Alcohol Dependence: Changes in Prevalence with Drinking Status', *British Journal of Psychiatry* 166: 199–204.

Department of Health (1991, 1999) *Drug Misuse and Dependence: Guidelines on Clinical Management*, Norwich: HMSO.

Dole, M. and Nyswander, V. (1965) 'A Medical Treatment for Diacetylmorphine (Heroin) Addiction. A Clinical Trial with Methadone Hydrochloride', *Journal of the American Medical Association* 193: 646–50.

Durlak, J. (1979) 'Comparative Effectiveness of Professional and Paraprofessional Helpers', *Psychological Bulletin* 86: 80–92.

Eap, C. B., Bertschy, G., Baumann, P. (1998) 'High Interindividual Variability of Methadone Enantiomer Blood Levels to Dose Ratios', *Archives of General Psychiatry* 55: 89–90.

Edwards, G. (2000) *Alcohol: The Ambiguous Molecule*, Harmondsworth: Penguin.

Ernst, E. and White, A. (eds) (1999) *Acupuncture: A Scientific Appraisal*, London: Butterworth-Heinemann.

Foster, J., Brewer, C. and Steele, T. (2003) 'Naltrexone Implants Can Completely Prevent Early (One Month) Relapse after Opiate Detoxification. A Pilot Study of Two Cohorts Totalling 101 Patients with a Note on Naltrexone Blood Levels', *Addiction Biology* 8: 211–17.

Gallant, D. M., Bishop, M. P. Faulkner, M. A., Simpson, L., Cooper, A. Lathrop, D., Brisolara, A. M. and Bossetta, J. R. (1968) 'A Comparative Evaluation of Compulsory (Group Therapy and/or Antabuse) and Voluntary Treatment of the Chronic Alcoholic Municipal Court Offender', *Psychosomatics* 9: 306–10.

Gelder, M. G., Marks, I. and Wolff, H. H. (1967) 'Desensitisation and Psychotherapy in the Treatment of Phobic States: A Controlled Clinical Enquiry', *British Journal of Psychiatry* 113: 53–73.

Gerber, M., Joyce, C. R. B., Christen, A., Dudle, U., Duss, I., Widler, P. and Fisch, H. U. (1994) 'Disulfiram Administered by a Trustee Improves Quality of Life (QoL) in Alcoholic Outpatients', *European Psychiatry* 9: 184.

Gerra, G., Saimovic, A., Guisti, F.m Di Gennaro, C., Zambelli, U., Gardini, S. and Delsignore, R. (2001) 'Lofexidine vs Clonidine in Rapid Opiate Detoxification', *Journal of Substance Abuse Treatment* 21: 11–17.

Gerrein, J. R., Rosenberg, C. M. and Manohar, V. (1973) 'Disulfiram Maintenance in Outpatient Treatment of Alcoholism', *Archives of General Psychiatry* 28: 798–802.

Göltz, J. and Partecke, G. (2000) 'Katamnesticher Entwicklung opiatabhängiger nach naltrexon-induzierten Entzug unter Narcose, naltrexongestutzter Rückfallprophylaxe und ambulanter psychosozialer Nachsorge' [Catamnestic outcome of opiate addicts after rapid opiate detoxification under anesthesia, relapse-prophylaxis with naltrexone and psychosocial care], *Sücttherapie* 1: 166–72.

Gossling, H. W., Gunkel, S., Schneider, U. and Melles, W. (2001) [Frequency and causes of premature termination during in-patient opiate detoxification], *Fortschrift für Neurologie und Psychiatrie* 69: 474–81.

Gossop, M., Johns, A. and Green, L. (1987) 'Opiate Withdrawal: In-patient versus Out-patient Programmes and Preferred versus Random Assignment to Treatment', *British Medical Journal* 293: 103–4.

Gossop, M., Marsden, J., Stewart, D. and Treacy, S. (2001) 'Outcomes after Methadone Maintenance and Methadone Reduction Treatments: Two-year Follow-up Results from the National Treatment Outcome Research Study', *Drug & Alcohol Dependence* 62: 255–64.

Gottheil, E., Sterling, R. and Weinstein, S. (1993) 'Diminished Illicit Drug Use as a Consequence of Long-term Methdone Maintenance', *Journal of Addictive Diseases* 12: 45–57.

Greenwood, G., Woods, W., Guydish, J. and Bein, E. (2001) 'Relapse Outcomes in a Randomised Trial of Residential and Day Drug Abuse Treatment', *Journal of Substance Abuse Treatment* 20: 15–23.

Gunne, L. (1990) 'Politicians and Scientists in the Combat against Drug Abuse', *Drug and Alcohol Dependence* 25: 241–4.

Harris, P. (2001) 'Concrete Counselling – Ignoring Outcomes', *Druglink* (January/February): 10–13.

Harrison, L. (1992) 'Substance Misuse and Social Work Qualifying Training in the British Isles: A Survey of CQSW Courses', *British Journal of Addiction* 87: 635–42.

Haynes, S. N. (1973) 'Contingency Management in a Municipally Administered Antabuse Program for Alcoholics', *Journal of Behaviour Therapy and Experimental Psychiatry* 4: 31–2.

Hoare, P. (1997) *Wilde's Last Stand. Decadence, Conspiracy and the First World War*, London: Duckworth.

Hulse, G. K. and O'Neil, G. (2002) 'Using Naltrexone Implants in the Management of the Pregnant Heroin User', *Australian and New Zealand Journal of Obstetrics and Gynaecology* 42(5): 102–6.

Hunt, G. and Azrin, N. H. (1973) 'A Community Reinforcement Approach to Alcoholism', *Behaviour Research & Therapy* 11: 91–104.

Keane, T. M., Foy, D. W., Nunn, B. and Rychtarik, R. G. (1984) 'Spouse Contracting to Increase Antabuse Compliance in Alcoholic Veterans', *Journal of Clinical Psychology* 40: 340–4.

Keen, J., Oliver, P., Rowse, G. and Mathers, N. (2001) 'Residential Rehabilitation for Drug Users: A Review of 13 Months' Intake to a Therapeutic Community', *Family Practice* 16(5): 545–8.

Kosten, T. A., Jacobson, L. K. and Kosten, T. R. (1989) 'Severity of Precipitated Opiate Withdrawal Predicts Drug Dependence by DSM-111-R Criteria', *American Journal of Drug & Alcohol Abuse* 15: 237–50.

Lahej, R. J. F., Krabbe, P. F. M. and De Jong, C. A. J. (2000) 'Rapid Heroin Detoxification under General Anaesthesia', *Journal of the American Medical Association* 283: 1,143.

Liebson, I. and Faillace, L. A. (1971) 'The Pharmacological Reinforcement of Disulfiram – Maintenance in Chronic Alcoholism', *NIDA Research Monograph*: 1,266–73.

Liebson, I., Bigelow, G. and Flamer, R. (1973) 'Alcoholism among Methadone Patients: A Specific Treatment Method', *American Journal of Psychiatry* 130: 483–5.

Mcdonald, G., Sheldon, B. and Gillespie, J. (1992) 'Contemporary Studies of the Effectiveness of Social Work', *British Journal of Social Work* 22: 615–43.

McIntosh, C. and Ritson, B. (2001) 'Treating Depression Complicated by Substance Misuse', *Advances in Psychiatric Treatment* 7: 357–64.

Mathew, R. J., Georgi, J. and Nagy, P. (1994) 'Substance Abuse Treatment: Beyond the Minnesota Model', *North Carolina Medical Journal* 55: 224–6.

Maxwell, S. and Shinderman, M. (2002) 'Optimising Long-term Response to Methadone Maintenance Treatment: A 152-week Follow-up Using Higher-dose Methadone', *Journal of Addictive Diseases* 21(3): 1–12.

Miller, W. and Hester, R. (1986) 'In-patient Alcoholism Treatments: Who Benefits?', *American Psychologist* 41: 794–805.

Najavitz, L. and Weiss, R. (1994) 'Variations in Therapist Effectiveness in the Treatment of Patients with Substance Use Disorders: An Empiricial Review', *Addiction* 89: 679–88.

Newman, R. and Whitehill, W. (1979) 'Double-blind Comparison of Methadone and Placebo Maintenance Treatments of Narcotic Addicts in Hong Kong', *Lancet* 2: 485–8.

Petrakis, I. L., Carroll, K. M., Nich, C., Gordon, L. T., McCance-Katz, E. F., Frankforter, T. and Rounsaville, B. J. (2000) 'Disulfiram Treatment for Cocaine Dependence in Methadone-maintained Opioid Addicts', *Addiction* 95: 219–28.

Pini, L., Ferretti, C., Trenti, T., Ferrari, A. and Sternieri, E. (1991) 'Effects of Long Term Treatment with Naltrexone on Hepatic Enzyme Activity', *Drug Metabolism and Drug Interactions* 9: 161–74.

Prioleau, L., Murdock, M. and Brody, N. (1983) 'An Analysis of Psychotherapy versus Placebo Studies', *Behavioural and Brain Sciences* 6: 275–310.

Robichaud, C., Strickler, D., Bigelow, G. and Liebson, I. (1979) 'Disulfiram Maintenance Employee Alcoholism Treatment: A Three-phase Evaluation', *Behaviour Research & Therapy* 14: 618–21.

Ruben, S. (2001) 'Drug Treatment and Testing Orders: The New Answer to Drug Problems? A Personal View', *Royal College of Psychiatrists Substance Misuse Faculty Newsletter* (June): 4.

Saunders, B. (1985) 'Treatment Does Not Work: Some Criteria of Failure', in N. Heather, I. Robertson and P. Davies (eds) *The Misuse of Alcohol: Crucial Issues in Dependence, Treatment & Prevention*, London: Croom Helm.

Sereny, G., Sharma, V., Holt, J. and Gordis, E. (1986) 'Mandatory Supervised Antabuse Therapy in an Out-patient Alcoholism Program: A Study', *Alcoholism: Clinical and Experimental Research* 10: 290–2.

Shuckit, M. A. (1994) 'Alcohol and Depression: A Clinical Perspective', *Acta Psychiatrica Scandinavica* (Suppl.) 377: 28–32.

Sloane, R., Staples, F., Cristol, A. and Yorkston, N. J. (1975) *Psychotherapy versus Behaviour Therapy*, Cambridge, MA: Harvard University Press.

Strupp, H. and Hadley, S. (1979) 'Specific versus Non-specific Factors in Psychotherapy: A Controlled Study of Outcome', *Archives of General Psychiatry* 36: 1,125–36.

Sun, F., Tsuritani, I. and Yamada, Y. (2002) 'Contribution of genetic polymorphisms in ethanol-metabolising enzymes to problem drinking behaviour in middle-aged Japanese men', *Behaviour Genetics* 32(4): 229–36.

Suzuki, T., Koikey, Y., Yanaura, S., George, F. and Meisch, R. (1987) 'Genetic Differences in the Development of Physical Dependence on Pentobarbital in Four Inbred Strains of Rats', *Japanese Journal of Pharmacology* 45: 479–86.

Tønnesen, H., Rosenberg, J., Nielsen, H., Rasmussen, V., Hauge, C., Pedersen, I. K. and Kehlet, H. (1999) 'Effect of Preoperative Abstinence on Poor Postoperative Outcome in Alcohol Misusers: Randomised Controlled Trial', *British Medical Journal* 318: 1,311–16.

Tu, G.-C., Cao, Q.-N. and Israel, Y. (1995) 'Inhibition of Gene Expression by Triple Helix Formation in Hepatoma Cells', *Journal of Biological Chemistry* (24 November) 270(47): 28,042–7.

6 Coerced treatment for drug-using criminal offenders

Douglas Longshore, Michael L. Prendergast and David Farabee

Coerced treatment for drug-using criminal offenders

Use of coerced treatment for drug-using offenders is based on three assumptions. The first is that drug use is highly correlated with criminal activity other than drug use, such that a reduction in drug use among offenders will be accompanied by a significant reduction in nondrug crime. A second assumption is that being in treatment can be beneficial even for persons not there voluntarily. A third assumption pertains to the person's perception of problems arising from drug use. Although it is widely believed that drug users must "hit bottom" before they can benefit from treatment, reliance on coercion presupposes that treatment can be effective with persons who perceive the adverse consequences of their drug use to be minimal or acceptable.

The empirical literature on coerced treatment offers support for all three of these assumptions. Drug users are responsible for a high proportion of crime, and the frequency of their criminal activity tends to rise and fall in direct relation with their drug use (Anglin and Perrochet 1998; M. R. Chaiken 1986; J. M. Chaiken and Chaiken 1982, 1990; Fagan 1990; McBride and McCoy 1993; White and Gorman 2000). Moreover, coerced treatment is known to be at least modestly effective in reducing both drug use and criminal recidivism (Farabee *et al.* 1998; Leukefeld and Tims 1988; Marlowe *et al.* 2001). Finally, drug users who do not initially believe that their drug use is causing serious problems can nonetheless be engaged in treatment and benefit from it (Biernacki 1986; Nurco *et al.* 1995; Sia *et al.* 2000).

The literature remains inconclusive, however, with respect to several questions, each explored in this chapter. First, what are the important dimensions of coerced treatment? Second, how shall we think critically about effects of coerced treatment as documented in the empirical literature? Third, are there moderating conditions under which coerced treatment is more, or less, effective? Finally, what is the process by which clients entering treatment involuntarily later become actively engaged in it.

We have organized this chapter in the form of a path model: dimensions of coerced treatment on the left side (input), its possible outcomes on the right, moderating factors that might strengthen or weaken the direct path from coercion to outcomes, and the process of treatment engagement as a factor at least partially mediating the outcomes of coerced treatment (see Figure 6.1). By arranging questions about coerced treatment in this model, we seek to represent their interrelatedness and to identify implications for future research in a unified way.

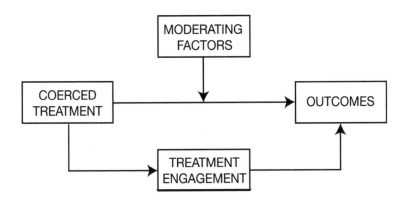

Figure 6.1: Path model of coerced treatment

Dimensions of coerced treatment

The left side of the model in Figure 6.1 shows coerced treatment as input. Traditionally, coerced treatment has been understood in simple terms. Drug-using offenders are "coerced" if they are under criminal justice supervision at treatment entry (Simpson and Friend 1988) or have been referred to treatment by a criminal justice agency (Collins and Allison 1983). But coercion appears to be a continuous variable, not simply a dichotomous one. In addition, people may be pressed into treatment by sources other than criminal justice. Finally, coercion is a matter of perception as well as objective events or conditions. In short, coercion is multidimensional, and this must be taken into account if we are understand its input function.

Coercion as a continuous variable

Coercion is not experienced in the same way by each and every client referred to treatment by criminal justice. Rather, there are varying degrees of coercion, which may be defined by the amount of control exerted over the referred client by various criminal justice agencies. In a study of criminal justice referrals among the sample of treatment clients enrolled in the US Drug Abuse Treatment Outcome Study, Farabee, Prendergast, and Anglin (1998) found that 23.3 percent had been referred by criminal justice to a treatment program without an explicit, formal order to enroll in it and without being required to submit to periodic drug testing while enrolled (low coercion); 22 percent had been formally ordered to treatment but had no drug testing imposed (moderate coercion); and 54.6 percent had been ordered to enter treatment and to undergo drug testing (high coercion). Additional studies using this three-step typology of coercion as a single index have shown that greater coercion is associated with longer retention in treatment and more favorable outcomes (Anglin *et al.* 1989; Anglin and Hser 1990; Hiller *et al.* 1998).

Source of coercion

The majority of studies on coerced treatment have focused on criminal justice as the source of coercion. This is probably the combined result of ease of measurement (information on referral source is routinely collected during the admission process) and obvious relevance for policy. But criminal justice does not account for all coerced treatment admissions. Moreover, even for drug users entering treatment under criminal justice pressure, the threat of adverse legal consequences is not necessarily the most salient reason to remain in and complete treatment. In a study of persons admitted to a community-based outpatient cocaine treatment program, Marlowe *et al.* (1996) found that approximately one-third reported some level of coercion. However, financial, social, and family concerns were the primary sources of coercion, even if the referral itself had been made by criminal justice. Similarly, in a study of clients entering alcohol treatment more than 40 percent reported having been pressed to enter treatment by one or more sources (Polcin and Weisner 1999). Family, not criminal justice, was the source most commonly cited (59 percent). Among the other sources cited were criminal justice (21 percent) and healthcare professionals (15 percent).

Perceived coercion

Many studies have defined coercion according to objective indicators of criminal justice status and referral source (Farabee *et al.* 1998). The assumption in these studies was that persons entering treatment through the criminal justice system did so against their will. This assumption fails to take into account three important considerations. First, legal status can change during a person's course of treatment. In fact, there is evidence that people who show significant improvement early in treatment are more likely to transition to voluntary status than those who do not (Cuffel 1992). Second, many people classed as "voluntary" may have been subject to coercion had they not entered treatment on their own. Third, the presence of an objective indicator of coercion does not mean the person was actually reluctant to enter treatment. As part of a study of drug-using parolees in treatment, Farabee, Shen, and Sanchez (2002) conducted a factor analysis of survey items regarding reasons for being in treatment. The items loaded on two distinguishable factors – perceived coercion and perceived need for treatment – and the correlation between factors was not statistically significant. Thus, drug users who feel coerced into treatment do not necessarily believe they have no need for it. In a study of male prison inmates (Farabee 1995), 50 percent expressed interest in participating in treatment while incarcerated. Among those with an interest in treatment, approximately 50 percent reported a willingness to participate *even if it meant extending their stay in prison for three months.*

In short, the literature on coercion indicates that persons referred to treatment through the criminal justice system should not be assumed to be under greater coercion than others. In fact, the criminal justice system may serve to facilitate voluntary entry into treatment. Finally, those who are coerced into treatment are not necessarily uninterested in being there.

Outcomes of coerced treatment

We now turn to the outcomes side of the model in Figure 6.1. A full understanding of the outcomes of coerced treatment requires consideration of two issues, often neglected. First, it is important to be quite specific regarding the comparison condition. Second is the issue of appropriate outcomes.

Comparison condition

It is often assumed that the appropriate comparison is between clients coerced into treatment and those in treatment voluntarily. In many studies the two classes of treatment client show equivalent outcomes (or, in statistical terms, no significant difference is seen between groups) (Anglin and Hser 1990; Hubbard *et al.* 1989). The straightforward conclusions are that coerced treatment is effective and that it is worthwhile to order people into treatment since their outcomes will be (roughly) the same as those for people who enter treatment on their own.

A second comparison is defensible, however, and is suggested by researchers and policy-makers with a particular belief about the nature of addiction and recovery. That belief is often expressed as "an addict has to hit bottom before he can recover" or "an addict has to want to change if treatment is to be effective." If either of these assumptions is true, then forcing people into treatment is largely futile unless they have "hit bottom" or "want to change" when the coercion takes place. On the other hand, under this logic coerced treatment looks good if it is more effective than no treatment, even though it may not be as effective as voluntary treatment. Returning to the first comparison, one might ask why the justification for coerced treatment should depend on whether it produces outcomes equivalent to those for voluntary treatment. Should it not suffice that offenders coerced into treatment have significantly better outcomes than those who receive no treatment at all?

Outcomes

Apart from the choice of comparison condition, a second issue arises with regard to the outcomes being compared – what outcomes are important and when they should be assessed. Research indicates that treatment retention (length of time in treatment) is strongly related to post-treatment success (Simpson *et al.* 1997). Treatment retention or completion is accordingly employed as an outcome measure in many studies of coerced treatment. Exposure to treatment is considered beneficial in itself and is taken as a proxy for post-treatment outcomes.

One crucial problem is that research on the relationship between retention and post-treatment success is nonexperimental and thus liable to self-selection bias. People who remain in treatment longer may have come into treatment with a stronger commitment to recovery; those who complete treatment even more so. Thus, people who stay longer or complete treatment might have done quite well *after* treatment even if their time in treatment had, for whatever reason, been shorter than it actually was. There is no substantial body of experimental research (e.g. randomized trials comparing treatments that differ only in planned duration) to buttress the claim that the relationship between treatment retention and post-treatment outcomes is causal.

This problem looms even larger in studies of coerced treatment. Because of the threat of sanctions for leaving treatment prematurely, coerced clients may be compliant with treatment without becoming engaged in it in any meaningful sense. That is, they may present themselves; obey program rules; participate in group counseling sessions minimally, if at all; and produce negative drug tests most of the time. But in merely going through the motions such clients resist becoming actively engaged in the treatment process, and their behavior is unlikely to change. Treatment retention or completion is clearly not a reliable indicator of success for such clients. For these reasons, measuring the effectiveness of coerced treatment probably requires assessments of drug use, criminal activity, psychosocial status, and other outcomes *after* treatment. (Of course, practical constraints on research design often mean that outcomes will be assessed only at the end of treatment – the date of treatment completion for clients who "stay the course" and the date of treatment withdrawal for those who do not.)

Moderating factors

Outcomes of coerced treatment may depend on person factors such as demographic characteristics, life history, drug of choice, or prior experience in treatment. Similarly, program factors such as modality, treatment protocol, staging, or adjunct services might moderate outcomes of coerced treatment. This possibility is represented as an arrow from moderating factors to the input–outcomes path in Figure 6.1.

There has been no accumulation of research sufficient to identify client or program factors that moderate outcomes of coerced treatment. The potential importance of moderating factors can be illustrated, however, by means of one example. This pertains to a person factor commonly called motivation for treatment or internal motivation.

People enter treatment for a variety of reasons, some internal (e.g. "I really want to stop using") and some external (e.g. "I came to treatment because someone else says I have a problem"). The internal part of the mix is often conceptualized and measured as treatment motivation, entirely independent of any coercive pressures that may also be in play. But the person's own motivation and the coercion imposed upon him may interact in either of two ways. First, motivation may have less bearing on treatment outcomes when coercive pressure is strong enough to hold a person in treatment (Simpson and Joe 1993). Second, the combination of internal motivation and external coercion may lead to outcomes better than those produced by either factor alone (De Leon *et al.* 1994; Simpson and Joe 1993). Indirect evidence on this latter possibility emerged in a study by De Leon *et al.* (1993). Motivation predicted treatment retention best for African-Americans and least for whites in their sample. In addition, African-Americans were significantly more likely to be in treatment involuntarily. In other words, internal motives had more influence on retention among persons experiencing stronger external pressure for treatment. More direct evidence of internal/external interaction has emerged in two other studies. Ryan *et al.* (1995) found that treatment retention was highest among alcoholics scoring high on both internal and external motives. Ryan and his colleagues concluded that these users had "internalized" the external pressure that pushed them into treatment. In a study by Marin (1995) treatment retention was unrelated either to external pressure or to internal motivation. However, Marin also tested the possibility of interaction between these two predictors. Retention was significantly higher for clients whose external and internal scores were both high.

How might external pressure lead to increased internal motivation for treatment? The experience of a criminal justice sanction may be precisely the crisis experience that causes drug users to "hit bottom" (De Leon and Jainchill 1986; Waldorf *et al.* 1991). However, for many people sufficient internal motivation may be generated by pressure short of actual coercion, by events not viewed as crises, or by positive events such as marriage or a religious experience (Kiecolt 1994; Klingemann 1991; Rosenbaum 1982; Waldorf *et al.* 1991). Thus the effect of external pressure on treatment motivation does not seem to hinge on the adversity or severity of the pressure. Recent theoretical work suggests that this effect may depend instead on whether people see external pressure as a consequence of their own behavior or merely as a nuisance imposed from outside (Cullari 1996; Deci and Ryan 1985, 1991; Kiecolt 1994; Marlowe 2001; Shaver and Drown 1986). That is, external and internal motives may jointly affect treatment success when external pressure is internalized or "transformed" by the person into an internal motive ("someone saw that I have a problem and has forced me to a place where I may be able to do something about it, even if I didn't want to be here at first"). In research on recovery from heroin and cocaine use, Biernacki (1986), Nurco *et al.* (1995), Shaffer and Jones (1989), and Waldorf *et al.* (1991) have documented the ways in which drug users may internalize external pressure.

Treatment engagement

The degree to which coerced clients become actively engaged in treatment may help to explain its outcomes. This possibility is represented as the mediated path in Figure 6.1. We have already suggested that coerced clients may remain in treatment longer than they otherwise would if the coercion is internalized or transformed into internal motivation. We now turn to studies indicating how treatment might be delivered so as to promote the internalization process and thus raise the person's treatment motivation. These studies fall into three domains: motivational intervention, contingency management, and procedural justice.

Motivational intervention

Research based on the transtheoretical model of behavior change (Prochaska *et al.* 1992; Prochaska and Norcross 1994) has identified five discrete stages of change: precontemplation, contemplation, preparation, action, and maintenance. Transtheoretical research has also focused on *how* people change, i.e. what they think, feel, and do as they move through these stages. Are particular cognitions, emotions, and behaviors more salient in some stage transitions than in others? The answer is yes. Change processes known as consciousness-raising, dramatic relief, and environmental re-evaluation are associated with moving from precontemplation to contemplation. These processes all involve raising one's awareness of a problem and assessing its impact on oneself and others. At later stages change processes appear to be more behavioral, e.g. reinforcement management, counterconditioning, and stimulus control. Such processes are geared toward actively managing one's environment in order to facilitate and maintain the change one has started to make.

Findings from transtheoretical research have been applied in the development of motivational interventions that assess a person's stage of change and apply counseling techniques likely to trigger the processes that move a person forward in the stage sequence (Miller and Rollnick 1991). Such interventions, delivered one on one or in small-group formats, rely on five techniques:

- expressing empathy (counselor accepts clients' feelings without judging, criticizing, or blaming;
- developing discrepancy (counselor leads clients to see the discrepancy between their values/concerns and current behavior;
- avoiding argument (clients are not directly confronted about negative aspects of their behavior;
- rolling with resistance (counselor uses the clients' own words to guide them to appropriate insights and decisions);
- supporting self-efficacy (counselor encourages clients to take steps which they view as achievable).

Longshore and Grills (2000) tested a motivational intervention to promote recovery among drug-using African-Americans recruited from street settings. Because most study participants were expected to be at the precontemplation and contemplation stages of change, counselors were trained to work on the change processes (e.g. consciousness-raising and dramatic relief) most relevant at those early stages. Accordingly, counselors used the participants' own words to trigger new insights and decisions and sought to develop discrepancies between their stated values/concerns and their substance use. Counselors also expressed empathy and, especially with persons in the contemplation stage, supported self-efficacy for taking initial steps toward recovery. Study participants were randomized to one session of motivational intervention or one session of generic counseling. Those in the motivational intervention were, by self-report and counselor rating taken immediately after the intervention, more engaged in the session – more active, more willing to self-disclose, and more motivated to change (Longshore *et al.* 1999). At a one-year follow-up those in the motivational intervention were also more likely to be drug abstinent as indicated by self-report and urine test results (Longshore and Grills 2000; see also Dansereau *et al.* 1996; Simpson *et al.* 1993). Blankenship *et al.* (1999) and Sia *et al.* (2000) have described a motivational intervention delivered during treatment to drug-using offenders attending treatment under criminal justice mandate. The intervention has shown favorable effects on indicators of treatment engagement. Its effects on drug use or other post-treatment outcomes have not yet been reported.

Contingency management

A large body of empirical literature supports the use of positive reinforcement schedules to promote desirable behavior among treatment clients (Higgins and Silverman 1999). As behavioral contingencies shift, clients may become more engaged in the treatment process. Contingency management may be particularly effective with persons coerced into treatment inasmuch as the threat of punishment implicit in various forms of coercion may not, by itself, lead people to become engaged in treatment and may even promote resistance.

Procedural justice

When people are referred to treatment by criminal justice their perception of the level of coercion and their reaction to it may depend on whether they believe they were treated fairly and given an opportunity to tell their side of the story. That is, outcomes of coerced treatment may be mediated by aspects of "procedural" or "restorative" justice (Braithwaite 1999; Kurki 1999; Monahan *et al.* 1995). Drug court is a newly emerging example of criminal justice coercion in which the case processing and disposition are meant to be manifestly more therapeutic than punitive (Hora *et al.* 1999; Longshore *et al.* 2001). Offenders in drug court are ordered to treatment and their progress through treatment is monitored closely. Their engagement in treatment may be greater if initial case processing (prior to treatment) and ongoing monitoring (during treatment) proceed under principles of procedural justice.

Conclusion

We offer this summary of issues reviewed in this chapter and implications for future work. First, the field must move beyond the simple binary question of whether coerced treatment is or is not effective. This is because coercion is a multidimensional phenomenon. Coercion can be studied as an objective condition or as the person's perception of it. One important topic for future research is, in fact, the relationship between objective and perceived coercion and the conditions under which objective indicators such as a criminal justice order and a person's perception of coercion are either convergent or divergent. In addition, future research on coerced treatment must account for the fact that coercion or pressure can arise from sources other than criminal justice and may be the primary reason for entering treatment even for persons under criminal justice supervision. It is particularly important to recognize that internal motivation for treatment is not necessarily low among people entering treatment under external pressure. Finally, effectiveness itself is a complex phenomenon. The behavior of coerced clients during treatment and their status at treatment discharge may be unreliable indicators of their likely post-treatment behavior. Future studies of coerced treatment should include outcome assessments at some point after treatment and/or should measure the degree to which coerced clients are actively engaged in, rather than merely compliant with, the demands placed upon them in treatment.

Second, research is needed on factors that may moderate the outcomes of coerced treatment. We cited treatment motivation as an example of a person factor that might moderate the effect of (interact with) coercion. Anglin and Hser (1991) cited several program factors that may enhance the effectiveness of coerced treatment. Among these were degree of program structure, planned duration of treatment, and provision of aftercare. There is, as we have noted, no accumulation of research on person or program factors as possible moderators of coerced treatment outcomes. We must also note that none of the coerced treatment studies known to us was conducted outside the United States. Thus, nation or multi-nation region, perhaps as a proxy for cultural or socioeconomic context, might well be added to the list of moderating factors to be investigated. Because moderator effects are liable to arise serendipitously, investigation of these effects should be the rule, not the exception, in research on coerced treatment. Only then will it be possible to identify factors with reliable and robust moderating effects.

Third, apart from its importance as a proxy for post-treatment outcomes, treatment engagement needs to be better understood as a dynamic process. How does external pressure become internalized, and how can this process be facilitated during treatment? Motivational intervention and contingency management are two methods known to raise engagement in treatment and post-treatment outcomes. However, there has been no accumulation of research documenting their effects among clients coerced into treatment by criminal justice or other sources. Similarly, while the drug court movement is based on (among other things) the concept of procedural justice, little is known about the impact of drug courts on post-treatment behavior of drug-using offenders (Belenko 2001) or about whether the client's perception of procedural justice mediates that impact.

References

Anglin, M. D. and Hser, Y. (1990) "Treatment of Drug Abuse," in M. Tonry and J. Q. Wilson (eds.) *Crime and Justice: Annual Review of Research*, vol. 13: *Drugs and Crime*, Chicago: University of Chicago Press .

Anglin, M. D. and Hser, Y. (1991) "Criminal Justice and the Drug-abusing Offender: Policy Issues of Coerced Treatment," *Behavioral Sciences and the Law* 9: 243–67.

Anglin, M. D. and Perrochet, B. (1998) "Drug Use and Crime: A Historical Review of Research Conducted by the UCLA Drug Abuse Research Center," *Substance Use and Misuse* 33(9): 1,871–914.

Anglin, M. D., Brecht, M., and Maddahian, E. (1989) "Pretreatment Characteristics and Treatment Performance of Legally Coerced versus Voluntary Methadone Maintenance Admissions," *Criminology* 27(3): 537–57.

Belenko, S. (2001) *Research on Drug Courts: A Critical Review 2001 Update*, Alexandria, VA: National Drug Court Institute.

Biernacki, P. (1986) *Pathways from Heroin Addiction: Recovery without Treatment*, Philadelphia: Temple University Press.

Blankenship, J., Dansereau, D. F., and Simpson, D. W. (1999) "Cognitive Enhancements of Readiness for Corrections-based Treatment for Drug Abuse," *Prison Journal* 79(4): 431–45.

Braithwaite, J. (1999) "Restorative Justice: Assessing Optimistic and Pessimistic Accounts," in M. Tonry (ed.) *Crime and Justice: A Review of Research*, Chicago: University of Chicago Press.

Chaiken, J. M. and Chaiken, M. R. (1982) *Varieties of Criminal Behavior* (R-2814-NIJ), Santa Monica, CA: RAND.

Chaiken, J. M. and Chaiken. M. R. (1990) "Drugs and Predatory Crime," in M. Tonry and J. Q. Wilson (eds.) *Drugs and Crime: Crime and Justice, A Review of Research*, vol. 13, Chicago: University of Chicago Press.

Chaiken, M. R. (1986) "Crime Rates and Substance Abuse among Types of Offenders," in B. D. Johnson and E. Wish (eds.) *Crime Rates among Drug-abusing Offenders: Final Report to the National Institute of Justice*, New York: Narcotic and Drug Research, Inc.

Collins, J. J. and Allison, M. A. (1983) "Legal Coercion and Retention in Drug Abuse Treatment," *Hospital and Community Psychiatry* 34(12): 1,145–9.

Cuffel, B. (1992) "Characteristics Associated with Legal Status Change among Psychiatric Patients," *Community Mental Health Journal* 28(6): 471–82.

Cullari, S. (1996) "Treatment Resistance, A Guide for Practitioners." Boston, MA: Allyn and Bacon.

Dansereau, D. F., Joe, G. W., Dees, S. M., and Simpson, D. D. (1996) "Ethnicity and the Effects of Mapping-enhanced Drug Abuse Counseling," *Addictive Behaviors* 21: 363–76.

Deci, I. L. and Ryan, R. M. (1985) *Intrinsic Motivation and Self-determination in Human Behavior*, New York: Plenum.

Deci, I. L. and Ryan, R. M. (1991) "A Motivational Approach to Self: Integration in Personality," in R. Dienstbier (ed.) *Nebraska Symposium on Motivation*, vol. 38: *Perspectives on Motivation*, Lincoln, NE: University of Nebraska Press.

De Leon, G. and Jainchill, N. (1986) "Circumstance, Motivation, Readiness and Suitability as Correlates of Treatment Tenure," *Journal of Psychoactive Drugs* 18(3): 203–8.

De Leon, G., Melnick, G., Schoket, D., and Jainchill, N. (1993) "Is the Therapeutic Community Culturally Relevant? Findings on Race/Ethnic Differences in Retention in Treatment," *Journal of Psychoactive Drugs* 25(1): 77–86.

De Leon, G., Melnick, G., Kressel, D., and Jainchill, N. (1994) "Circumstances, Motivation, Readiness, and Suitability (the CMRS Scales): Predicting Retention in Therapeutic Community Treatment," *American Journal of Drug and Alcohol Abuse* 20(4): 495–515.

Fagan, J. (1990) "Intoxication and Aggression," in M. Tonry and J. Q. Wilson (eds.) *Drugs and Crime: Crime and Justice, A Review of Research*, vol. 13, Chicago: University of Chicago Press.

Farabee, D. (1995) *Substance Use among Male Inmates Entering the Texas Department of Criminal Justice – Institutional Division, 1993*, Austin, TX: Texas Commission of Alcohol and Drug Abuse.

Farabee, D., Prendergast, M., and Anglin, D. (1998) "The Effectiveness of Coerced Treatment for Drug-abusing Offenders," *Federal Probation* 62(1): 3–10.

Farabee, D., Shen, H. and Sanchez, S. (2002) "Perceived Coercion and Treatment Need among Mentally Ill Parolees," *Criminal Justice and Behavior* 29(1): 76–86.

Higgins, S. T. and Silverman, K. (eds.) (1999) *Motivating Behavior Change among Illicit Drug Abusers: Research on Contingency Management Interventions*, Washington, DC: American Psychological Association.

Hiller, M. L., Knight, K., Broome, K. M., and Simpson, D. D. (1998) "Legal Pressure and Treatment Retention in a National Sample of Long-term Residential Programs," *Criminal Justice and Behavior* 25(4): 463–81.

Hora, P. F., Schma, W. G., and Rosenthal, J. T. A. (1999) "Therapeutic Jurisprudence and the Drug Treatment Court Movement: Revolutionizing the Criminal Justice System's Response to Drug Abuse and Crime in America," *Notre Dame Law Review* 74: 439–538.

Hubbard, R. L., Marsden, M. E., Rachal, J. V., Harwood, H. J., Cavanaugh, E. R., and Ginzburg, H. M. (1989) *Drug Abuse Treatment: A National Study of Effectiveness*, Chapel Hill, NC: University of North Carolina Press.

Kiecolt, K. J. (1994) "Stress and the Decision to Change Oneself: A Theoretical Model," *Social Psychology Quarterly* 57(1): 49–63.

Klingemann, H. (1991) "The Motivation for Change from Problem Alcohol and Heroin Use," *British Journal of Addiction* 86: 727–44.

Kurki, L. (1999) *Incorporating Restorative and Community Justice into American Sentencing and Corrections*, NCJ 175723, Washington, DC: National Institute of Justice.

Leukefeld, C. G. and Tims, F. M. (eds.) (1988) *Compulsory Treatment of Drug Abuse: Research and Clinical Practice*, NIDA Research Monograph 86, DHHS Publication No. ADM 89–1578, Washington, DC: US Government Press.

Longshore, D. and Grills, G. (2000) "Motivating Recovery from Illegal Drug Use: Evidence for a Culturally Congruent Intervention," *Journal of Black Psychology* 26: 288–301.

Longshore, D., Grills, C., and Annon, K. (1999) "Effects of a Culturally Congruent Intervention on Cognitive Factors Related to Recovery," *Substance Use and Misuse* 34(9): 1,223–41.

Longshore, D., Turner, S., Wenzel, S., Morral, A., Harrell, A., McBride, D., Deschenes, E., and Iguchi, M. (2001) "Drug Courts: A Conceptual Framework," *Journal of Drug Issues* 31(1): 7–26.

McBride, D. C. and McCoy, C. B. (1993) "The Drugs–Crime Relationship: An Analytic Framework," *Prison Journal* 73(3–4): 257–78.

Marin, M. E. (1995) "Motivation for Drug Abuse Treatment and Retention Rates in Standard and Enhanced Methadone Maintenance Programs," doctoral dissertation, Department of Education, University of California, Los Angeles.

Marlowe, D. B. (2001) "Coercive Treatment of Substance Abusing Criminal Offenders," *Journal of Forensic Psychology Practice* 1(1): 65–73.

Marlowe, D. B., Kirby, K. C., Bonieskie, L. M., Glass, D. J., Dodds, L. D., Husband, S. D., Platt, J. J., and Festinger, D. S. (1996) "Assessment of coercive and Noncoercive Pressures to Enter Drug Abuse Treatment," *Drug and Alcohol Dependence* 42(2): 77–84.

Marlowe, D. B., Glass, D. J., Merikle, E. P., Festinger, D. S., DeMatteo, D. S., Marczyk, G. R., and Platt, J. J. (2001) "Efficacy of Coercion in Substance Abuse Treatment," in F. M. Tims, C. G. Leukefeld, and J. J. Platt (eds.) *Relapse and Recovery in Addictions*, New Haven, CT: Yale University Press.

Miller, W. R. and Rollnick, S. (1991) *Motivational Interviewing: Preparing People to Change Addictive Behavior*, New York: Guilford Press.

Monahan, J., Hoge, S. K., Lidz, C., Roth, L. H., Bennett, N., Gardner, W., and Mulvey, E. (1995) "Coercion and Commitment: Understanding Involuntary Mental Hospital Admission," *International Journal of Law and Psychiatry* 18(3): 249–63.

Nurco, D. N., Primm, B. J., Lerner, M., Stephenson, P., Brown, L. S., and Ajuluchukwu, D. C. (1995) "Changes in Locus-of-control Attitudes about Drug Misuse in a Self-help Group in a Methadone Maintenance Clinic," *International Journal of the Addictions* 30(6): 765–78.

Polcin, D. L. and Weisner, C. (1999) "Factors Associated with Coercion in Entering Treatment for Alcohol Problems," *Drug and Alcohol Dependence* 54: 63–8.

Prochaska, J. O. and Norcross, J. C. (1994) *Systems of Psychotherapy: A Transtheoretical Analysis*, 3rd edition, Pacific Grove, CA: Brooks/Cole.

Prochaska, J. O., DiClemente, C. C., and Norcross, J. C. (1992) "In Search of How People Change: Applications to Addictive Behavior," *American Psychologist* 47(9): 1,102–14.

Rosenbaum, M. (1982) "Getting on Methadone: The Experience of the Woman Addict," *Contemporary Drug Problems* 11: 113–43.

Ryan, R. M., Plant, R. W., and O'Malley, S. (1995) "Initial Motivations for Alcohol Treatment: Relations with Patient Characteristics, Treatment Involvement, and Dropout," *Addictive Behaviors* 20(3): 279–97.

Shaffer, H. J. and Jones, S. B. (1989) *Quitting Cocaine: The Struggle Against Impulse*, Lexington, MA: Lexington Books.

Shaver, K. G. and Drown, D. (1986) "On Causality, Responsibility, and Self-blame: A Theoretical Note," *Journal of Personality and Social Psychology* 50(4): 697–702.

Sia, T. L., Dansereau, D. F., and Czuchry, M. L. (2000) "Treatment Readiness Training and Probationers' Evaluation of Substance Abuse Treatment in a Criminal Justice Setting," *Journal of Substance Abuse Treatment* 19(4): 459–67.

Simpson, D. D. and Friend, H. J. (1988) "Legal Status and Long-term Outcomes for Addicts in the DARP Follow Up Project," in C. G. Leukefeld and F. M. Tims (eds.) *Compulsory Treatment of Drug Abuse: Research and Clinical Practice*, NIDA Research Monograph 86, DHHS number (ADM)89–1578, Washington, DC: US Government Press.

Simpson, D. D. and Joe, G. W. (1993) "Motivation as a Predictor of Early Dropout from Drug Abuse Treatment," *Psychotherapy* 30(2): 357–68.

Simpson, D. D., Chatham, L. R., and Joe, G. W. (1993) "Cognitive Enhancements to Treatment in DATAR: Drug Abuse Treatment for AIDS Risk Reduction," in J. A. Inciardi, F. M. Tims, and B. W. Fletcher (eds.) *Innovative Approaches in the Treatment of Drug Abuse: Program Models and Strategies*, Westport, CT: Greenwood.

Simpson, D. D., Joe, G., and Brown, B. (1997) "Treatment Retention and Follow-up Outcomes in the Drug Abuse Treatment Outcomes Study (DATOS)," *Psychology of Addictive Behaviors* 11(4): 294–307.

Waldorf, D., Reinarman, C., and Murphy, S. (1991) *Cocaine Changes: The Experience of and Quitting*, Philadelphia: Temple University Press.

White, H. R. and Gorman, D. M. (2000) "Dynamics of the Drug–Crime Relationship," in E. Jefferis and J. Munsterman, (eds.) *Crime and Justice 2000*, vol. 1: *The Nature of Crime: Continuity and Change*, Washington, DC: National Institute of Justice, US Department of Justice.

7 Treating patients with comorbidities

Nicholas Seivewright, Muhammad Z. Iqbal and Helen Bourne

Relatively few drug misusers are entirely free from other physical or mental health problems. Many such problems represent direct consequences, even of so-called 'recreational' drug use: mood disturbances after 'ecstasy', psychotic episodes in stimulant use and respiratory disease due to cannabis are frequent examples. Drug injecting brings a further range of complications, from minor skin problems to fatal blood-borne virus infections, while dependent users suffer physical and psychological withdrawal effects, and frequently the various forms of mental distress associated with a disrupted lifestyle and social decline. Furthermore, it is not a random cross-section of the population who elect to use illicit drugs, with such individuals often having pre-existing psychological difficulties, perhaps arising from childhood disturbance and being manifest as personality disorder, depression or related conditions.

Often it can be expected that treatment of a drug problem itself, for instance by way of drug counselling, detoxification programmes or methadone maintenance, will alleviate the associated consequences, while to a degree the more intensive approaches such as long-term residential rehabilitation also aim to resolve characteristic underlying personal difficulties. However, some additional disorders are sufficiently severe or specific for the users concerned to in effect be seen as special needs cases, requiring a dual approach in terms of clinical management. Prominent among these groups are individuals who have both severe mental illness and drug misuse, and indeed the term 'dual diagnosis' is increasingly used to denote such cases specifically. This particular combination is encountered extensively now that patients with schizophrenia and other severe psychiatric illnesses tend to be managed in the community rather than in long-stay hospitals, and the general exposure to drug misuse poses many problems in treatment, not least since various drugs can directly worsen psychoses despite offering short-term subjective relief.

There is now a reasonably substantial literature on management of individuals with dual diagnosis, including from units which specialise in this area clinically and offer intensive treatment approaches. In this chapter we will review that work and the evidence for effectiveness of a range of methods, also indicating the general principles of such treatment, as most clinicians do not have access to highly specialist facilities. Service issues are indeed likely to be the subject of much debate in the forthcoming years, and to place these aspects into context we will first examine the main associations between psychiatric disorders and drug misuse, and the extent to which combined problems have been found in various settings. Although we cannot review physical comorbidity in detail, the final section considers those serious infectious complications which, as well as being important clinically, have also had a particular impact on drug misuse treatment policies.

Comorbidity with psychiatric disorders

Main associations

One of the main reference points regarding the co-existence of substance misuse and psychiatric disorders is the Epidemiologic Catchment Area study (Regier *et al.* 1990), undertaken in the USA, in which lay interviewers rated the presence of both types of disorders in a large random sample of the population using a basic diagnostic instrument. In the overall figures, it was found that of individuals diagnosed as having any mental disorder 29 per cent had had substance abuse or dependence at some time in their life, with that figure rising to 47 per cent of those with schizophrenia. Looking at the situation the other way round, 53 per cent of those with substance abuse or dependence had had another mental disorder at some stage. These figures are high, and again it is necessary to immediately acknowledge the general associations between drug or alcohol misuse and various psychiatric symptoms which may or may not reflect truly separate disorders. Therefore features of depression occur in stimulant withdrawal, anxiety in withdrawal from tranquillisers or alcohol, and a range of disturbances including psychosis are produced in states of intoxication – and a degree of tautologous rating can never be fully ruled out. However, smaller-scale studies using more clinically based ratings have also typically found at least 50 per cent, and up to 90 per cent, of drug misusers to have additional psychiatric conditions (Rounsaville *et al.* 1982; Musselman and Kell 1995; Kokkevi and Stefanis 1995; Mason *et al.* 1998), with one relevant consideration there being that relatively high rates are probably likely among the more severe users found in treatment settings. The most common psychiatric disorders detected in drug misusers in systematic studies are:

- personality disorder
- depression
- anxiety
- psychosexual dysfunction
- psychotic disorders.

Of particular interest in the context of this chapter is a study by Menezes *et al.* (1996), in which rates of substance misuse in the previous year were established in a population of patients attending psychiatric services in an area of South London who had definite 'functional' psychotic disorders such as schizophrenia. Of these individuals 36 per cent had a substance misuse problem on formal rating, with alcohol more common than drugs and the rate generally much higher in young males. Those with dual diagnosis had required more hospitalisation than other patients, which accords with many similar findings of generally worse outcomes in both psychiatric and drug misuse treatments, a theme which will be explored further below (pp. 000–00). Most of our discussion is specifically about treatment of patients with severe mental illness who abuse substances, but brief consideration will first be given to three diagnoses commonly made in drug misusers which also have very important clinical implications.

Personality disorder

Personality disorders of various kinds, but predominantly antisocial, are undoubtedly very frequent precursors of drug misuse, often following on from conduct disturbances in adolescence. Once again, prevalence rates of well over 50 per cent are found in many studies (Verheul *et al.* 1995), and the additional presence of personality disorder has been shown to adversely affect outcome across a range of drug misuse treatments, as indeed it leads to worsened progress when associated with other psychiatric disorders (Reich and Vasile 1993). One of us has previously reviewed these various aspects with a colleague in detail (Seivewright and Daly 1997), and only two main points will be reinforced here.

The first is that personality disorder is the classic example of a condition whose features can easily be confused with the behavioural aspects of drug misuse itself. Thus the diagnosis of antisocial personality disorder relies strongly on features such as aggressiveness, irresponsible behaviours and impulsivity, and so the potential tautology can readily be seen, especially when in some classifications acquisitive crime or the tendency to substance misuse itself may be used as a personality disorder criterion. Many rating instruments do not clearly make the distinction between so-called 'primary' and 'secondary' antisocial behaviours, but, importantly, when methods are used to improve this separation the category of antisocial personality disorder still emerges as probably the most common underlying type in substance misusers, with the borderline category also very frequent (Seivewright and Daly 1997; Trull *et al.* 2000).

In relation to treatment of drug misuse, it is notable that the generally adverse effect of the additional presence of personality disorder does not apply to outcomes in methadone maintenance treatment as much as it does in treatments aimed at full detoxification (Gill *et al.* 1992; Darke *et al.* 1994). It is reasonable to observe that detoxifying fully or undergoing an abstinence-based rehabilitation programme demands more in terms of personality resources than relying on a substitute opioid, but also the very stabilising effect of methadone, psychologically as well as physically, may be directly beneficial for some individuals with personality disorder, as indeed it probably is in some cases of psychosis (Brizer *et al.* 1985).

Depression

Depressed mood is a recognised feature of personality disorder itself, even in the absence of superimposed depressive illness. Depressive feelings are also undoubtedly common as a response to social and lifestyle problems, and these two considerations probably account for a large proportion of depression among drug misusers and instances of lack of response to antidepressants (where non-compliance is also frequent). However, true clinical depression can clearly also occur, and it is very important to be able to recognise this, given generally high rates of self-harm and suicide in drug-takers (Davoli *et al.* 1993; Kokkevi and Stefanis 1995; Oyefeso *et al.* 1999).

The so-called 'biological' symptoms of depression are relatively unhelpful as a diagnostic aid, since once again features such as insomnia, loss of appetite or diurnal variation of mood are often directly produced by drug misuse. Some authorities consider that suicidal ideation is among the best indicators of an actual depressive illness (just as phobic symptoms strongly suggest a true anxiety disorder), while satisfactory responses to antidepressant medications have been demonstrated in studies of drug misusers employing standard diagnostic criteria (e.g. Nunes *et al.* 1998; McDowell *et al.* 2000). Oyefeso *et al.* (1999) found antidepressant drug overdosage to be a relatively common suicide method, and stressed the importance of careful prescribing in relation to both diagnosis and limiting supplies.

Drug-induced psychosis

This is crucially relevant to the consideration of dual diagnosis cases, as it represents the other side of the coin to the development of substance misuse in individuals with established psychotic conditions. Of course the distinction between the two situations is far from clear cut, in that various drugs of abuse can worsen psychoses as well as newly cause such symptoms, while it is extremely common in practice to see a condition of which the aetiology is uncertain, with drugs seemingly playing some role in an individual who anyway has a psychotic vulnerability.

It is very important to know the drugs which can produce an outright drug-induced psychosis, as it is the same range of substances which can worsen pre-existing conditions or cause other 'pathoplastic' reactions (Poole and Brabbins 1996; Boutros and Bowers 1996). Importantly, opiates do not have this capacity, with the main candidates being the stimulants amphetamine, cocaine, and 'ecstasy' (MDMA, methylenedioxymethamphetamine), plus hallucinogens such as LSD and other rarer drugs, including the anti-emetic cyclizine, which may be abused by injection. In general the hallucinogens produce more visual symptoms of a typically 'organic' nature, both acutely and as 'flashback' experiences, while the stimulants can lead to paranoid delusional states symptomatically indistinguishable from schizophrenia. There has been much debate as to whether cannabis alone can result in psychosis, with the strongest evidence being that it can at least produce brief symptoms or worsen existing conditions (Hall 1998; Johns 2001). The sedative/hypnotics – most commonly now benzodiazepines – and alcohol are more likely to produce psychotic symptoms in severe withdrawal states, rather than as actual drug effects. These and some other fundamental points regarding drug-induced psychosis are summarised as follows:

- It can be produced by stimulants, hallucinogens, cyclizine, cannabis, and sedative/hypnotics (in withdrawal).
- Evidence for lasting psychosis, as opposed to chronic hallucinosis, caused by drugs is weak.
- Drug use may be incidental in an individual developing functional psychosis.
- Symptoms should subside if drug use is eliminated.
- Antipsychotic drug treatment resembles that in functional psychosis but can be ineffective if drug use continues.

The difficult area of correctly establishing a diagnosis of drug-induced psychosis has been well considered by Poole and Brabbins (1996). In particular, they reinforced the original findings of Connell (1958) in his seminal work on amphetamine psychosis, that psychotic conditions caused by drugs are relatively short lived, and if symptoms persist in the face of evidence of abstinence (e.g. from urine tests), then a diagnosis of true functional psychosis increasingly has to be considered. Unfortunately there is no exact answer as to what such a time cut-off point should be, while clearly the diagnosis of drug-induced psychosis can be 'allowed' for longer after cessation of heavy regular usage than after a single instance of drug-taking. Along similar lines, it is also important to recognise that, since drug misuse is now so common in many areas, even the finding of drugs in a test may sometimes be incidental, in a case where an underlying psychiatric disorder is present. This may particularly be brought about by a temptation to use drugs in the early distressing stages of a psychotic illness.

The prescribing of antipsychotic medications in drug-induced psychosis, where necessary, can usually be very short term, as opposed to the continued treatment often required in schizophrenia or bipolar affective disorder. As yet, there are no indications that the actual selection of medication should be different, and so this will usually be based on the prominent symptoms, including whether sedation is required, and avoidance of adverse effects as in general psychiatric practice. There is some evidence that psychotic reactions to 'ecstasy' may be particularly resistant to treatment (Solowij 1993), with some observers making the link with the cerebral neurotoxicity which this drug can produce.

The term 'dual diagnosis'

This term is somewhat unsatisfactory in at least two ways. First, it could mean the combination of any two diagnoses of any kind, including physical conditions. Second, even if it denotes psychiatric disorder and substance misuse, such individuals can often have more than two diagnoses: for instance drug misuse, alcohol dependence and schizophrenia; or drug misuse, personality disorder and depression. However, the usage in relation to psychiatric disorder has become quite firmly established, with dual diagnosis usually taken to mean *severe* psychiatric *illness* plus substance misuse. When 'dual diagnosis workers' are attached to clinical services the idea is not usually that they see the cases who have somewhat more severe neurotic or personality problems than others, but rather that they address the issue of patients with severe illnesses such as schizophrenia who abuse substances. This usage of the term is the one applied in much of the literature, and will be used here.

Treatment of dual diagnosis patients

Particular complications

One reasonably well-developed aspect of the literature on dual diagnosis is that relating to the complications, in terms of clinical presentation and management, which are more prevalent in dual diagnosis cases than in individuals who solely have a psychotic condition (Dixon 1999). The following main problems are identified as particularly prevalent in dual diagnosis cases:

- violence (Cuffell *et al.* 1994; Scott *et al.* 1998);
- non-compliance with treatment (Bebbington 1995; Dixon 1999; Swofford *et al.* 2000);
- poor prognosis (Drake and Wallach 1989; Swofford *et al.* 1996);
- erratic service usage (Bartels *et al.* 1993; McCrone *et al.* 2000);
- family problems (Lehman *et al.* 1993).

Some of these studies are from case notes, or otherwise various kinds of prospective investigations. Relatively high rates of violence and hostile behaviour in dual diagnosis cases are well established, and Scott *et al.* (1998) found that the effect also extended to criminal offending. Non-compliance with treatment may involve missed clinic appointments or failure to take antipsychotic medication, and this area has been examined in detail by Bebbington (1995). It appears somewhat characteristic that routine outpatient appointments are missed, with then higher rates of emergency presentations and inpatient treatment, involving greater costs (McCrone *et al.* 2000).

In general, prognosis has been found to be worsened by the additional presence of substance misuse in psychotic patients, in aspects including frequency of relapses and severity of psychiatric symptoms. The behavioural consequences can also be more severe, as indicated above (pp. 000–00), but a 'paradox' has been noted in which, although there are greater disturbances of that kind, social competence is better preserved in the dually diagnosed (Penk *et al.* 2000). Possible explanations for such a finding include the direct effects of substances actually counteracting the negative symptoms of schizophrenia or, more likely, a diagnostic issue whereby cases akin to drug-induced psychosis have been included in the psychotic cohorts. Although social skills may broadly be more intact, high rates of overt lifestyle and family problems have been found in the dually diagnosed, relating mostly to drug misuse (Lehmann *et al.* 1993).

Principles of treatment

Much work has been published on the subject of managing dual diagnosis patients by Drake and his colleagues (e.g. Drake *et al.* 1993; Drake and Mueser 2000) relating to treatment in a specialised unit in New Hampshire, USA. The earlier paper described some fundamental principles of such management, which could apply not only in specialist settings but in general psychiatric casework with dually diagnosed individuals. These largely self-explanatory principles comprised assertive outreach, close monitoring, integration of services, comprehensive approach, attention to stable living situation, treatment flexibility, stage-wise treatment, a longitudinal perspective and therapeutic optimism, and they have been examined in more detail in a previous review (Seivewright 2000a).

The experienced clinicians in that group clearly feel the need to acknowledge that treatment in dual diagnosis may be very long term, given the chronic relapsing nature of both psychotic disorders and substance misuse, and also to counter the demoralisation which can sometimes occur in relation to this patient group. This is supported by the work of Goldsmith (2000), who found that removal of input for patients can lead to a rapid decline in function. The other fundamental aspects relate to service provision, guarding against the worst scenario whereby a drug service may not feel able to address mental health issues while the psychiatric service is reluctant to accept drug misusers, with the patient potentially falling in between. 'Integration' therefore refers to, at the very least, close liaison between general psychiatric and substance misuse services, but often the same team of clinicians managing both aspects. Clearly a number of models of joint- or single-service working are possible in dual diagnosis (Hoffman *et al.* 1993; Johnson 1997; Crome 1999; Drake and Mueser 2000), and service issues are discussed further below (pp. 000–00). In terms of the principles, however, 'comprehensiveness' relates to the ability to tackle very practical aspects as well as providing actual therapies, while 'flexibility' indicates the need to tailor treatment to particular situations, for instance not requiring individuals with acute paranoid schizophrenia to attend group addiction counselling. Although the use of medications is predominant in many cases of opiate dependence, counselling of various kinds represents the mainstay of management of non-opiate misuse, and so the need for flexibility within this for individuals with compromised intellectual functioning is readily apparent. Some specific approaches used in dual diagnosis cases will now be outlined, with evidence for effectiveness where this is available from systematic studies.

Methods and outcomes

A basic objective in dual diagnosis management is to ensure that appropriate evidence-based treatments are deployed for both the drug misuse and psychiatric illness, respectively. Broadly, the main non-medical approaches in drug misuse are systematic drug counselling, motivational interviewing (Noonan and Moyers 1997) and group therapy, which may be used in a variety of community and residential settings. These methods can be applicable across all forms of substance misuse, while most of the proven medications are for management of opiate dependence specifically. These include clonidine or lofexidine in detoxification (Carnwath and Hardman 1998; Strang *et al.* 1999), methadone and buprenorphine in either detoxification or maintenance therapy (Bertschy 1995; Marsch 1998; Ling *et al.* 1998), and the competitive antagonist naltrexone after opiate withdrawal (Farren 1997; Seivewright 2000b). Symptomatic medications are sometimes given in withdrawal from stimulant use but the evidence base for this is modest (Seivewright 2000c), while there are established methods in benzodiazepine dependence, mainly comprising supported gradual withdrawal of the drug (Mant and Walsh 1997). In terms of severe mental illness (Cunningham Owens and Johnstone 2000), in addition to psychosocial management, which may notably include cognitive therapy, social skills training and family interventions, antipsychotic medication in oral or depot form is frequently required in schizophrenia, schizoaffective disorder or bipolar disorder, with the mood stabilisers lithium and carbamazepine also used in the latter condition.

To a large extent, the indications for each of these treatments with subsequent monitoring of progress need to be considered independently, but in practice it will often be hoped that improvements in one area will also lead to better outcomes in the associated condition. Thus a patient whose symptoms are significantly reduced on antipsychotic medication may feel less desire to use drugs, especially if there has been an element of 'self-medica-tion' (Khantzian 1997); or an individual rendered free of drug-induced varying mood states and withdrawal distress, by stabilisation on methadone or achieving a drug-free state, may well experience general psychological improvement. Some evidence relating to the former situation comes from studies showing reduced alcohol, smoking and cocaine use in schizophrenics prescribed the antipsychotic medication clozapine (Buckley 1998; Zimmet *et al.* 2000), although olanzapine is also an attractive antipsychotic treat-ment option because of a low rate of adverse effects (Glazer 1997). In terms of drug misuse treatments, methadone maintenance is of particular interest, not only because it has been demonstrated to improve overall psychological well-being in opiate addicts (Musselmann and Kell 1995), possibly even to the point of reducing psychotic symptoms (Brizer *et al.* 1985), but also because by its nature it has a very marked effect on retention in treatment. In patients who have complied poorly with general psychiatric care it might therefore appear tempting to have early recourse to methadone both for its own utility and to ensure sufficient engagement to deploy all the required psychiatric treatments. Against that proposition, however, is the evidence that dual diagnosis patients tend in general to be less dependent on opiates than individuals who present without psychiatric complications (Drake and Mueser 2000), and so as a treatment usually for severe dependence methadone might actually be less indicated. On balance, it appears at this stage that the indications for the various treatments in opiate misuse should be considered similar for dual diagnosis and other patients, although quick detoxification methods often rely substantially on associated drug coun-selling to address motivational aspects (Seivewright 2000d), which, along with other counselling approaches, may be more demanding in psychiatri-cally ill individuals.

Treatment of dual diagnosis cases can clearly take place in a very wide variety of situations and clinical settings. Approaches specifically devised for such treatment which have been demonstrated to be effective in systematic studies are as follows:

- case management (Drake and Mueser 2000);
- educational approaches (Ziedonis and Trudeau 1997);
- modified substance misuse treatments (Drake *et al.* 1998);
- relapse-prevention group therapy (Nigam *et al.* 1992);
- therapeutic community techniques (Westreich *et al.* 1996).

The rather non-specific term 'case management' has become a familiar one in the dual diagnosis literature. It has mainly been used to describe the basic integrated approach of Drake and colleagues in their specialised service, where treatments for psychiatric illness and drug misuse are deployed by the same team of clinicians. Multidisciplinary case management embodies the general principles referred to above (Drake *et al.* 1993), so that allocated case workers see small numbers of patients each and attend carefully to practical issues, housing and personal support, as well as to specific treatments. Developing a team to do this work is seen as a maturational process, with established services having been found to achieve impressive results in terms of reduced substance use and remissions in psychiatric disorders (Drake and Meuser 2000). An ability to involve patients in decisions about their treatment is considered crucial, and in general service quality issues appear to be important in relation to outcomes (Jerrell and Ridgely 1999). In such specialised programmes substance misuse treatment methods are adjusted to the needs of this particular patient group, which can apply to individual, group or family formats. Clear motivation on the part of patients to stop using all substances appears relatively rare, and various studies have suggested benefits from an educational rather than direct treatment approach in the early stages (Drake *et al.* 1993; Ziedonis and Trudeau 1997). The use of the set '12-step' methods of Alcoholics Anonymous (AA) and Narcotics Anonymous (NA) is somewhat controversial in dual diagnosis (Laudet *et al.* 2000), with the obvious risk that individuals with severe mental illness might be unable to tolerate the group therapy or would disrupt it for others. However, in relation to AA Pristach and Smith (1999) found that among a sample of inpatients with schizophrenia and other disorders most were comfortable with the basic tenets and 37 per cent had regularly attended in the past.

Most case management is undertaken in outpatients, with inpatient care mainly reserved for initial assessment, stabilisation and treatment planning (Drake and Meuser 2000). However, Moggi *et al.* (1999a) devised a four-month integrated inpatient programme for dual diagnosis patients and studied outcomes at one year. Significant improvements were demonstrated in psychiatric symptoms and general social functioning but not in frequency of substance use, and the authors considered that further controlled studies were indicated. In the outpatient setting one-year outcomes were investigated in 118 consecutive individuals in a dual disorders programme in Seattle, with this being a wider patient group including cases of major depression and post-traumatic stress disorder (Sloan and Rowe 1998). Pharmacotherapy and substance misuse treatment, initially based on support and education, were provided together with crisis intervention, and patients engaged in the treatment for a median of 217 days. In 60 per cent of the patients all the regular urine drug tests were negative when the treatment was in progress, and a substantial reduction in the requirement for inpatient treatment was demonstrated. In an overall factor analysis study of 981 male dual diagnosis patients in treatment, Moggi *et al.* (1999b) found that those in programmes with a stronger dual diagnosis orientation showed better psychiatric improvement than patients in less targeted programmes, and also that individuals with less severe psychiatric illness responded better than the more severely ill within the specialised approaches. Again, quite a high rate of abstinence (39 per cent) was found at one year in the group as a whole.

A detailed description of group therapy aimed at relapse prevention in dual diagnosis patients has been provided by Nigam *et al.* (1992). In this small study, patients with schizophrenia or affective psychoses and with prolonged histories of drug misuse progressed well in weekly therapy focusing on precipitants of substance abuse, principles of recovery and relapse prevention strategies. At the more intensive end of the group approach spectrum are residential therapeutic communities, and such techniques were studied in dual diagnosis by Westreich *et al.* (1996). Only one-third of patients stayed for the full six months and progressed to the follow-on accommodation in the community, but those subjects had mainly avoided alcohol and drugs completely. A history of criminal offending has been found not to adversely affect progress in this treatment modality (Taylor *et al.* 1997), as indeed the case management approach has produced positive results within the criminal justice system. In a six-month outcome study of the latter intervention Godley *et al.* (2000) demonstrated reductions for dual diagnosis subjects in offending and psychiatric symptoms, and improved general functioning. Furthermore, various of the approaches described here have been successfully incorporated in a comprehensive service in New York catering for dual diagnosis cases with high rates of violence, offending, homelessness and crack cocaine abuse (Galanter *et al.* 1994). The often severely disturbed individuals are treated either as inpatients, day patients or in a 'halfway house', with educational and '12-step' groups, peer leadership and a rewards system for compliance. In a discussion of the severe problems which can be caused by comorbidity the authors point out that such cases are typically found presenting to emergency services and general medical facilities, as well as in planned treatment.

Service issues

Inferences can be drawn from the studies in this review regarding desirable settings for the provision of dual diagnosis treatment. Beyond the specific findings, a major policy issue has been whether treatment should be provided by ultra-specialist teams who have the requisite experience in managing dual diagnosis, or whether in practice most developments will rely on liaison and joint working between existing services. The highly influential group of Drake and his colleagues are quite forthright in asserting that integrated (one-team) treatment is necessary, with 'traditional' psychiatric and drug misuse services having let this patient group down in the past (Drake and Meuser 2000). Some of the problems of services oriented towards one group failing to successfully manage dual diagnosis relate to specific aspects such as health insurance cover, and so they may perhaps be less relevant in countries such as the UK than in the USA.

This theme has been developed by Johnson (1997), who pointed out some traditional strengths in the UK, including close links between psychiatric services and primary care, which could be compromised by referring dual diagnosis cases to highly specialised units only. That author suggested that most developments for dual diagnosis treatment could take place in the first instance within community mental health teams, which is indeed likely in view of the high prevalence of comorbidity and the lack of feasibility of setting up many new services covering larger areas. A practice is now emerging in this country of identifying dual diagnosis worker posts within teams and providing substantial training resources in the field, with a general emphasis on the principles of a case management approach, as described earlier (pp. 128-9).

Given the focus on severe mental illness it is inevitable that inpatient as well as community care will sometimes be required, and a pragmatic approach to joint working is often necessary in practice whereby general psychiatric and drug misuse services provide their own specific treatments, with the respective degrees of involvement relating to needs at any one point. The required liaison is perhaps likely to work best where the drug service is itself psychiatric by discipline, but dual diagnosis workers with small caseloads and operating along outreach lines ought to be able to form links with a wide variety of statutory and non-statutory services. In drug projects which are not psychiatrically based, training in dual diagnosis issues may be provided, just as psychiatric services can require additional training in drug misuse (Hall and Farrell 1997). The relevant training and service development needs have also been considered in a comprehensive review of comorbidity by Crome (1999).

Comorbidity with specific physical disorders

Brief consideration will be given to two conditions which are currently of major concern for drug misuse services, HIV and hepatitis C.

HIV

Injected drug misuse is one of the main ways in which the human immunodeficiency virus (HIV) and the subsequent clinical disease acquired immunodeficiency syndrome (AIDS) can be contracted. In Western countries the first 'wave' of HIV infection was among male homosexuals, but then mainly in the 1980s it became apparent that drug misusers were not only at high risk themselves but also posed a major route of spread to the broader heterosexual community. As indicated in various policy reports (e.g. Advisory Council on the Misuse of Drugs 1988), this led to a substantial change in emphasis in drug misuse treatment, from purely addressing the addiction of individuals to using treatments as HIV-preventive measures. The most direct of the 'harm reduction' approaches was to give clean injecting equipment in organised schemes, but also prominent was the encouragement of methadone maintenance treatment, on the grounds that this is the simplest way to quickly reduce drug users' injecting behaviours. Drug workers were also required to consider sexual risk behaviours of their patients, and in general there was a great emphasis on retention in treatment as opposed to discharge for breach of contract, with therefore less stringent requirements attached to methadone therapy. The concept of 'harm reduction' prescribing grew up (Buning *et al.* 1990; Klingemann 1996), whereby fairly modest doses of methadone could be provided with no real requirement on the addict to abstain from other drug use, except that much advice was given on 'safe' methods of usage. In individuals for whom full detoxification in the short term is unrealistic, alternative substitute medications to methadone can also be given (Seivewright 2000e), but following decades of use overall the evidence base for methadone is strongest (Bertschy 1995; Marsch 1998).

The kinds of guidance given around the late 1980s applied to both HIV prevention and the treatment of drug misusers who had acquired HIV and AIDS (Advisory Council on the Misuse of Drugs 1988, 1989). Some of the general principles are similar, including the strong emphasis on avoiding injecting wherever possible, but if not, then adopting safe practices. As well as deploying psychological interventions to reduce risk behaviours (Baker *et al.* 1993), opiate addicts with HIV are often given relatively high maintenance doses of methadone in comparison with other cases to try and better limit other drug use, with ongoing drug misuse seemingly a 'co-factor' increasing the progression of the disease. Some clinicians are tempted to use injectable methadone for those individuals who find it particularly difficult to stop injected illicit use (Strang *et al.* 1996), but, while injecting methadone may be less harmful than injecting heroin, stabilisation on oral medication is highly preferable in HIV cases. Once again, the risks of ongoing injecting can be viewed in terms of both the individual's health and potential transmission to others.

As with psychiatric comorbidity, it is essential that adequate treatment for both the drug misuse and HIV/AIDS is provided, with linking between services where necessary. The results of treatment for AIDS have improved greatly in recent years with the use of antiretroviral medications, and survival times are now much better than was feared when the disease first affected drug misusers. In terms of the associations discussed in this chapter, it is notable that individuals with severe mental illness have been shown to be at increased risk of HIV infection, largely through sexual behaviours, irrespective of involvement in drug misuse (Checkley *et al.* 1996; Carey *et al.* 1997).

Hepatitis C

This is now attracting more attention in terms of management of drug misusers than hepatitis B, although the latter is very important as a preventive vaccination can be given (Farrell *et al.* 1990; Mast *et al.* 1999). The remarkable aspect of hepatitis C is its sheer prevalence, commonly 60–90 per cent among populations of injecting drug misusers (Alter and Moyer 1998). Like HIV it can be transmitted by injection, sexually or through vertical transmission from mother to baby (Gillett *et al.* 1996), and it is particularly infective by blood transmission through sharing injecting equipment. Indeed, it appears that much of the advice that was given by needle exchange schemes in relation to HIV transmission was inadequate in terms of avoiding hepatitis C, which could in effect be caught more easily.

Hepatitis C is a chronic liver disease which progresses to cirrhosis and sometimes liver carcinoma (Alter 1999). It is well recognised that heavy use of alcohol adversely affects prognosis, and drug misusers must be advised against this, with specific treatments for alcohol misuse given if necessary. Abnormal liver function as detected on blood testing may affect the ability to give the relevant medications, and this can also cause problems for the use of naltrexone in its indication as an antagonist given after opiate detoxification (Farren 1997), as this drug is known to sometimes cause raised liver enzymes. If an opiate misuser has reached the stage of naltrexone treatment by detoxifying, however, it will often be considered preferable to provide this with regular monitoring rather than risk relapse into drug use and injecting. As with HIV patients, much effort must be put into the avoidance of injecting wherever possible, with again a substantial role for methadone and related treatments. Reasonable results of treatment of hepatitis C with antiviral medication are now being achieved (Jowett *et al.* 2001), but with both HIV and hepatitis C many liver specialists will only consider direct treatment justified for individuals who have stopped injecting drugs.

References

Advisory Council on the Misuse of Drugs (1988) *AIDS and Drug Misuse, Part 1*, Department of Health, London: Her Majesty's Stationery Office.

Advisory Council on the Misuse of Drugs (1989) *AIDS and Drug Misuse, Part 2*, Department of Health, London: Her Majesty's Stationery Office.

Alter, M. J. (1999) 'Hepatitis C Virus Infection in the United States', *Journal of Hepatology* 31 (Suppl. 1): 88–91.

Alter, M. J. and Moyer, L. A. (1998) 'The Importance of Preventing Hepatitis C Virus Infection among Injection Drug Users in the United States', *Journal of Acquired Immune Deficiency Syndromes and Human Retrovirology* 18 (Suppl. 1): 6–10.

Baker, A., Heather, N., Wodak, A., Dixon, J. and Holt, P. (1993) 'Evaluation of a Cognitive Behavioural Intervention for HIV Prevention among Injecting Drug Users', *AIDS* 7: 247–56.

Bartels, S. J., Teague, G. B., Drake, R. E., Clarke, R. E., Bush, P. W. and Noordsy, D. L. (1993) 'Service Utilisation and Costs Associated with Substance Use Disorder among Severely Mentally Ill Patients', *Journal of Nervous and Mental Disease* 181: 227–32.

Bebbington, P. E. (1995) 'The Content and Context of Compliance', *International Clinical Psychopharmacology* 9 (supplement 5): 41–50.

Bertschy, G. (1995) 'Methadone Maintenance Treatment: An Update', *European Archives of Psychiatry and Clinical Neuroscience* 245: 114–24.

Boutros, N. N. and Bowers, M. B. Jnr (1996) 'Chronic Substance-induced Psychotic Disorders: State of the Literature', *Journal of Neuropsychiatry and Clinical Neuroscience* 8: 262–9.

Brizer, D. A., Hartman, N., Sweeney, J. and Millman, R. B. (1985) 'Effect of Methadone Plus Neuroleptics on Treatment-resistant Chronic Paranoid Schizophrenia', *American Journal of Psychiatry* 142: 1,106–7.

Buckley, P. F. (1998) 'Substance Abuse in Schizophrenia: A Review', *Journal of Clinical Psychiatry* 59 (supplement 3): 26–30.

Buning, E. C., van Brussel, G. H. A., van Santen, M. D. and van Santen, G. (1990) 'The "Methadone by Bus" Project in Amsterdam', *British Journal of Addiction* 85: 1,247–50.

Carey, M. P., Carey, K. B., Weinhardt, L. S. and Gordon, C. M. (1997) 'Behavioural Risk for HIV Infection among Adults with a Severe and Persistent Mental Illness: Patterns and Psychological Antecedents', *Community Mental Health Journal* 33: 133–42.

Carnwath, T. and Hardman, J. (1998) 'Randomised Double-blind Comparison of Lofexidine and Clonidine in the Outpatient Treatment of Opiate Withdrawal', *Drug & Alcohol Dependence* 50: 251–4.

Checkley, G. E., Thompson, S. C., Crofts, N., Mijch, A. M. and Judd, F. K. (1996) 'HIV in the Mentally Ill', *Australian and New Zealand Journal of Psychiatry* 30: 184–94.

Connell, P. H. (1958) *Amphetamine Psychosis*, Institute of Psychiatry Maudsley Monograph No. 5, London: Oxford University Press.

Crome, I. B. (1999) 'Substance Misuse and Psychiatric Comorbidity: Towards Improved Service Provision', *Drugs, Education, Prevention and Policy* 6: 151–74.

Cuffell, B. J., Shumway, M., Chouljian, T. L. and MacDonald, T. (1994) 'A Longitudinal Study of Substance Use and Community Violence in Schizophrenia', *Journal of Nervous and Mental Disease* 182: 704–8.

Cunningham Owens, D. G. and Johnstone, E. C. (2000) 'Treatment and Management of Schizophrenia', in M. G. Gelder, J. J. Lopez-Ibor Jnr and N. C. Andreasen (eds) *New Oxford Textbook of Psychiatry*, Oxford: Oxford University Press.

Darke, S., Hall, W. and Swift, W. (1994) 'Prevalence, Symptoms and Correlates of Antisocial Personality Disorder among Methadone Maintenance Clients', *Drug and Alcohol Dependence* 34: 253–7.

Davoli, M., Perucci, C. A., Forastiere, F., Doyle, P., Rapiti, E., Zaccarelli, M. and Abeni, D. D. (1993) 'Risk Factors for Overdose Mortality: A Case Control Study within a Cohort of Intravenous Drug Users', *International Journal of Epidemiology* 22: 273–7.

Dixon, L. (1999) 'Dual Diagnosis of Substance Abuse in Schizophrenia: Prevalence and Impact on Outcomes', *Schizophrenia Research* 35 (supplement): 93–100.

Drake, R. E. and Mueser, K. T. (2000) 'Psychosocial Approaches to Dual Diagnosis', *Schizophrenia Bulletin* 26: 105–18.

Drake, R. E. and Wallach, M. A. (1989) 'Substance Abuse among the Chronically Mentally Ill', *Hospital and Community Psychiatry* 40: 1,041–6.

Drake, R. E., Bartels, S. J., Teagues, G. B., Noordsy, D.L. and Clark, R. E. (1993) 'Treatment of Substance Abuse in Severely Mentally Ill Patients', *Journal of Nervous and Mental Disease* 181: 606–11.

Drake, R. E., McHugo, G. M., Clark, R. E., Teague, G. B., Ackerson, T., Xie, H. and Miles, K. M. (1998) 'A Clinical Trial of Assertive Community Treatment for Patients with Co-occurring Severe Mental Illness and Substance Use Disorder', *American Journal of Orthopsychiatry* 68: 201–15.

Farrell, M., Battersby, M. and Strang, J. (1990) 'Screening for Hepatitis B and Vaccination of Injecting Drug Users in the NHS Drug Treatment Services', *British Journal of Addiction* 85: 1,657–9.

Farren, C. K. (1997) 'The Use of Naltrexone, an Opiate Antagonist, in the Treatment of Opiate Addiction', *Irish Journal of Psychological Medicine* 14: 26–31.

Galanter, M., Egelko, S., Edwards, H. and Vergaray, M. (1994) 'A Treatment System for Combined Psychiatric and Addictive Illness', *Addiction* 89: 1,227–35.

Gill, K., Nolimal, D. and Crowley, T. J. (1992) 'Antisocial Personality Disorder, HIV Risk Behaviour and Retention in Methadone Maintenance Therapy', *Drug and Alcohol Dependence* 30: 247–52.

Gillett, P., Hallam, N. and Mok, J. (1996) 'Vertical Transmission of Hepatitis C Virus Infection', *Scandinavian Journal of Infectious Diseases* 28: 549–52.

Glazer, W. M. (1997) 'Olanzapine and the New Generation of Antipsychotic Agents: Patterns of Use', *Journal of Clinical Psychiatry* 58: 18–21.

Godley, S. H., Finsh, M., Dougan, L., McDonnell, M., McDermeit, M. and Carey, A. (2000) 'Case Management for Dually Diagnosed Individuals Involved in the Criminal Justice System', *Journal of Substance Abuse Treatment* 18: 137–48.

Goldsmith, R. J. (2000) 'Overview of Psychiatric Comorbidity: Practical and Theoretical Considerations', *Addictive Disorders* 22: 331–49.

Hall, W. (1998) 'Cannabis and Psychosis', *Drug and Alcohol Review* 17: 433–44.

Hall, W. and Farrell, M. (1997) 'Comorbidity of Mental Disorders with Substance Misuse', *British Journal of Psychiatry* 171: 4–5.

Hoffman, G. W. Jnr, Dirito, D., McGill, E. (1993) 'Three-month Follow-up of 28 Dual Diagnosis Inpatients', *American Journal of Drug and Alcohol Abuse* 19: 79–88.

Jerrell, J. M. and Ridgely, M. S. (1999) 'Impact of Robustness of Program Implementation on Outcomes of Clients in Dual Diagnosis Programs', *Psychiatric Services* 50: 109–12.

Johns, A. (2001) 'Psychiatric Effects of Cannabis', *British Journal of Psychiatry* 178: 116–22.

Johnson, S. (1997) 'Dual Diagnosis of Severe Mental Illness and Substance Misuse: A Case for Specialist Services?', *British Journal of Psychiatry* 171: 205–8.

Jowett, S. L., Agarwal, K., Smith, B. C., Craig, W., Hewett, M., Bassendine, D. R., Gilvary, E., Burt, A. D., Bassendine, M. F. (2001) 'Managing Chronic Hepatitis C Acquired through Intravenous Drug Use', *Quarterly Journal of Medicine* 94: 153–8.

Khantzian, E. J. (1997) 'The Self-medication Hypothesis of Substance Use Disorders: A Reconsideration and Recent Applications', *Harvard Review of Psychiatry* 4: 231–44.

Klingemann, H. K. H. (1996) 'Drug Treatment in Switzerland: Harm Reduction, Decentralisation and Community Response', *Addiction* 91: 723–36.

Kokkevi, A. and Stefanis, C. (1995) 'Drug Abuse and Psychiatric Comorbidity', *Comprehensive Psychiatry* 36: 329–37.

Laudet, A. B., Magura, S., Vogel, H. S. and Knight, E. (2000) 'Recovery Challenges among Dually Diagnosed Individuals', *Journal of Substance Abuse Treatment* 18: 321–9.

Lehman, A. F., Myers, C. P., Thompson, J. W. and Corty, E. (1993) 'Implications of Mental and Substance Use Disorders: A Comparison of Single and Dual Diagnosis Patients', *Journal of Nervous and Mental Disease* 181: 365–70.

Ling, W., Charuvastra, C., Collins, J. F., Batki, S., Brown, L. S., Kintaudi, P., Wesson, D. R., McNicholas, L., Tusel, D. J., Malkerneker, U., Renner, J. A. Jnr, Santos, E., Casadonte, P., Fye, C., Stine, S., Wang, R. I., Segal, D. (1998) 'Buprenorphine Maintenance Treatment of Opiate Dependence: A Multicenter, Randomized Clinical Trial', *Addiction* 93: 472–86.

McCrone, P., Menezes, P. R., Johnson, S., Scott, H., Thornicroft, G., Marshall, J., Bebbington, P. and Kuipers, E. (2000) 'Service Use and Costs of People with Dual Diagnosis in South London', *Acta Psychiatrica Scandinavica* 101: 464–72.

McDowell, D. M., Levin, F. R., Seracini, A. M., Nunes, E. V. (2000) 'Venlafaxine Treatment of Cocaine Abusers with Depressive Disorders', *American Journal of Drug and Alcohol Abuse* 26: 25–31.

Mant, A. and Walsh, R. A. (1997) 'Reducing Benzodiazepine Use', *Drug and Alcohol Review* 16: 77–84.

Marsch, L. A. (1998) 'The Efficacy of Methadone Maintenance Interventions in Reducing Illicit Opiate Use, HIV Risk Behaviour and Criminality: A Meta-analysis', *Addiction* 93: 515–32.

Mason, B. J., Kocsis, J. H., Melia, D., Khuri, E. T., Sweeney, J., Wells, A., Borg, L., Millman, R. B. and Kreek, M. J. (1998) 'Psychiatric Comorbidity in Methadone Maintained Patients', *Journal of Addictive Diseases* 17: 75–89.

Mast, E. E., Alter, M. J. and Margolis, H. S. (1999) 'Strategies to Prevent and Control Hepatitis B and C Virus Infections: A Global Perspective', *Vaccine* 17: 1,730–3.

Menezes, P. R., Johnson, S., Thornicroft, G., Marshall, J., Prosser, D., Bebbington, P. and Kuipers, E. (1996) 'Drug and Alcohol Problems among Individuals with Severe Mental Illness in South London', *British Journal of Psychiatry* 168: 612–19.

Moggi, F., Hirsbrunner, H. P., Brodbeck, J. and Bachmann, K. M. (1999a) 'One-year Outcome of an Integrative Inpatient Treatment for Dual Diagnosis Patients', *Addictive Behaviors* 24: 589–92.

Moggi, F., Ouimette, P. C., Finney, J. W. and Moos, R. H. (1999b) 'Effectiveness of Treatment for Substance Abuse and Dependence for Dual Diagnosis Patients: A Model of Treatment Factors Associated with One-year Outcomes', *Journal of Studies on Alcohol* 60: 856–66.

Musselman, D. L. and Kell, M. J. (1995) 'Prevalence and Improvement in Psychopathology in Opioid Dependent Patients Participating in Methadone Maintenance', *Journal of Addictive Diseases* 14: 67–82.

Nigam, R., Schottenfeld, R. and Kosten, T. R. (1992) 'Treatment of Dual Diagnosis Patients: A Relapse Prevention Group Approach', *Journal of Substance Abuse Treatment* 9: 305–9.

Noonan, W. C. and Moyers, T. B. (1997) 'Motivational Interviewing', *Journal of Substance Misuse* 2: 8–16.

Nunes, E. V., Quitkin, F. M., Donovan, S. J., Delivannides, D., Ocepek-Welikson, K., Koenig, T., Brady, R., McGrath, P. J. and Woody, G. (1998) 'Imipramine Treatment of Opiate-dependent Patients with Depressive Disorders. A Placebo-controlled Trial', *Archives of General Psychiatry* 55: 153–60.

Oyefeso, A., Ghodse, H., Clancy, C. and Corkery, J. M. (1999) 'Suicide among Drug Addicts in the UK', *British Journal of Psychiatry* 175: 277–82.

Penk, W. E., Flannery, R. B. Jr, Irvin, E., Geller, J., Fisher, W. and Hanson, M. A. (2000) 'Characteristics of Substance-abusing Persons with Schizophrenia: The Paradox of the Dually Diagnosed', *Journal of Addictive Diseases* 19: 23–30.

Poole, R. and Brabbins, C. (1996) 'Drug Induced Psychosis', *British Journal of Psychiatry* 168: 135–8.

Pristach, C. A. and Smith, C. M. (1999) 'Attitudes Towards Alcoholics Anonymous by Dually Diagnosed Psychiatric Inpatients', *Journal of Addictive Diseases* 18: 69–76.

Regier, D. A., Farmer, M. E., Rae, D. S., Locke, B. Z., Keith, S. J., Judd, L. L. and Goodwin, F. K. (1990) 'Comorbidity of Mental Disorders with Alcohol and Other Drug Abuse', *Journal of the American Medical Association* 264: 2,511–18.

Reich, J. H. and Vasile, R. G. (1993) 'Effect of Personality Disorders on the Treatment Outcome of Axis I Conditions: An Update', *Journal of Nervous and Mental Disease* 181: 475–83.

Rounsaville, B. J., Weissman, M. M., Klever, H. and Wilber, C. (1982) 'Heterogeneity of Psychiatric Diagnosis in Treated Opiate Addicts', *Archives of General Psychiatry* 39: 161–6.

Scott, H., Johnson, S., Menezes, P., Thornicroft, G., Marshall, J., Bindman, J., Bebbington, P. and Kuipers, E. (1998) 'Substance Misuse and Risk of Aggression and Offending among the Severely Mentally Ill', *British Journal of Psychiatry* 172: 345–50.

Seivewright, N. (2000a) 'Dual Diagnosis – Drug Misuse and Psychiatric Disorder', in *Community Treatment of Drug Misuse: More than Methadone*, Cambridge: Cambridge University Press.

Seivewright, N. (2000b) 'Achieving Detoxification and Abstinence – Naltrexone', in *Community Treatment of Drug Misuse: More than Methadone*, Cambridge: Cambridge University Press.

Seivewright, N. (2000c) 'Treatment of Non-opiate Misuse – Cocaine and Amphetamine', in *Community Treatment of Drug Misuse: More than Methadone*, Cambridge: Cambridge University Press.

Seivewright, N. (2000d) 'Achieving Detoxification and Abstinence – Quick Detoxifications from Heroin', in *Community Treatment of Drug Misuse: More than Methadone*, Cambridge: Cambridge University Press.

Seivewright, N. (2000e) 'More than Methadone? The Case for Other Substitute Drugs', in *Community Treatment of Drug Misuse: More than Methadone*, Cambridge: Cambridge University Press.

Seivewright, N. and Daly, C. (1997) 'Personality Disorder and Drug Use: A Review', *Drug and Alcohol Review* 16: 235–50.

Sloan, K. L. and Rowe, G. (1998) 'Substance Abuse and Psychiatric Illness: Treatment Experience', *American Journal of Drug and Alcohol Abuse* 24: 589–601.

Solowij, N. (1993) 'Ecstasy (3,4-Methylenedioxymethamphetamine)', *Current Opinion in Psychiatry* 6: 411–15.

Strang, J., Sheridan, J. and Barber, N. (1996) 'Prescribing Injectable and Oral Methadone to Opiate Addicts: Results from the 1995 National Postal Survey of Community Pharmacies in England and Wales', *British Medical Journal* 313: 270–2.

Strang, J., Bearn, J. and Gossop, M. (1999) 'Lofexidine for Opiate Detoxification: Review of Recent Randomised and Open Controlled Trials', *American Journal on Addictions* 8: 337–48.

Swofford, C. D., Kasckow, J. W., Scheller-Gilkey, G. and Inderbitzin, L. B. (1996) 'Substance Use: A Powerful Predictor of Relapse in Schizophrenia', *Schizophrenia Research* 20: 145–51.

Swofford, C. D., Scheller-Gilkey, G., Miller, A. H., Woolmine, B. and Mance, R. (2000) 'Double Jeopardy: Schizophrenia and Substance Use', *American Journal of Drug and Alcohol Abuse* 26: 343–53.

Taylor, S. M., Galanter, M., Dermatis, H., Spivack, N. and Egelko, S. (1997) 'Dual Diagnosis Patients in the Modified Therapeutic Community: Does a Criminal History Hinder Adjustment to Treatment?', *Journal of Addictive Diseases* 16: 31–8.

Trull, T. J., Sher, K. J. and Minks-Brown, C. (2000) 'Borderline Personality Disorder and Substance Use Disorders: A Review and Integration', *Clinical Psychology Review* 20: 235–53.

Verheul, R., van den Brink, W. and Hartgers, C. (1995) 'Prevalence of Personality Disorders among Alcoholics and Drug Addicts: An Overview', *European Addiction Research* 1: 166–77.

Westreich, L., Galanter, M., Lifshutz, H., Metzger, E. J. and Silberstein, C. (1996) 'A Modified Therapeutic Community for the Dually Diagnosed: Greenhouse Program at Bellevue Hospital', *Journal of Substance Abuse Treatment* 13: 533–6.

Ziedonis, D. M. and Trudeau, K. (1997) 'Motivation to Quit Using Substances among Individuals with Schizophrenia: Implications for a Motivation-based Treatment Model', *Schizophrenia Bulletin* 23: 229–38.

Zimmet, S. V., Strous, R. D., Burgess, E. S., Kohnstamm, S. and Green, A. I. (2000) 'Effects of Clozapine on Substance Use in Patients with Schizophrenia and Schizoaffective Disorder: A Retrospective Survey', *Journal of Clinical Psychopharmacology* 20: 94–8.

8 Drug testing

A necessary prerequisite for treatment and for crime control

John A. Carver

Abstract

Substance abuse continues to be a major problem facing the United States and many other countries. It strains law enforcement and public health resources, disrupts families and is closely associated with criminal behavior. Indeed, it is now known that substance abuse is a "multiplier" of criminal behavior.

Strategies for reducing overall drug use and thereby reducing crime have begun to demonstrate effectiveness. Particularly promising is the use of criminal justice leverage to change behavior among that segment of the drug-using population that is most heavily involved in crime: heavy users who are already under some form of nominal criminal justice control. Drug testing coupled with sanctions is an essential component of this approach. Drug testing is quick. It is accurate. It is becoming cheaper. It quickly cuts through the denial associated with addiction. And it has great potential to change behaviors when used within a context of accountability, with immediate consequences for drug use. Yet as part of a comprehensive national strategy to reduce drug use, drug testing has yet to achieve anything close to its real potential.

This chapter begins by briefly reviewing the nature of addiction and the drug–crime connection. The case for using the criminal justice system as a key component in a national drug control policy is set forth. Despite numerous calls for adopting such an approach over the last decade, and promising results at the program level, system-level change has simply not occurred. The reasons for this inertia are explored as a means of understanding what must be done if criminal justice drug testing is to achieve its potential value as a key element of an effective national policy of drug control.

I Drug testing: a necessary prerequisite for treatment and for crime control

Introduction

It has been a decade and a half since the crack cocaine epidemic burst onto the scene, reeking havoc on neighborhoods, stretching law enforcement, overwhelming social service agencies, clogging the courts, impacting the healthcare system and even affecting the educational system. Although drug use patterns are constantly changing, drugs and drug-related crime continue as major – some would say intractable – problems facing the justice system and society at large. The resource burden attributable to drug use is enormous. During the 1980s and 1990s state correctional costs soared, draining resources from other segments of public spending.

Since the heroin epidemic of the 1970s our understanding of the nature of addiction has grown. The connection between drug use and crime is better understood. Instruments for assessing the severity of addiction and delivering effective interventions have advanced. Within the criminal justice system, jurisdictions have experimented with various techniques for improving treatment outcomes, the most notable of which can be seen with the advent and rapid expansion of specialized drug treatment courts.[1]

Drug courts rely on frequent drug testing, rapid sanctions, and rewards to increase participation in treatment (US Department of Justice 1997). Drug courts have come to understand the value of frequent testing, backed up by systems of swift consequences and rewards. The drug test is the objective measure of how the participant is doing. It cuts through the denial and dishonesty that is so much a part of addiction. When the test is negative or "clean" it is a small victory for the drug user, one more drug-free day on the step-by-step road to a clean and sober lifestyle. A series of clean tests is noted with praise, as the participant moves through the various phases of the process. On the other hand, when the test is positive or "dirty" the participant knows the consequences and eventually comes to understand that it was his or her own behavior (rather than the eloquence of his or her attorney, or which judge is covering the calendar, or some other external reason) that landed him or her in jail for a few days. Drug testing is the foundation of an approach that promotes personal responsibility and pro-social values. Although drug courts have expanded almost exponentially, they still reach only a small percentage of drug-dependent individuals within the criminal justice system. It is not the position of this chapter that every courtroom should be a drug court. Rather, there are behavior-changing practices pioneered by drug courts that could be applied throughout the criminal justice system. Implementing these practices on a broad scale will be neither easy nor inexpensive, but the benefits will far outweigh the costs.

The tools available to detect and monitor drug use have advanced along with the improvements in our understanding of how best to use drug testing. Drug testing methodologies have become easier to use, more reliable and cheaper as the market for testing services has expanded. Advancements in the science of drug testing have opened up new methods for detecting prior drug use by sampling not just blood or urine, but also hair, saliva, breath, and even perspiration. These methods each have their own detection windows, level of invasiveness, advantages and disadvantages, but together they offer a range of possibilities appropriate for detecting past drug use in a variety of settings and for a variety of purposes.[2] Other advances have been made in the development of non-laboratory or point-of-contact testing methodologies. Finally, improvements have been made in the marriage of computerized lab management software and drug testing technologies.

Despite the scientific advances in testing methodologies, the criminal justice and treatment communities do not make effective use of these advances. Drug testing, though increasingly common, has simply not been implemented in ways most likely to produce the kinds of results that one should expect. To the contrary, it is often done in ways that are positively harmful. For example, many individuals with known drug abuse histories are not tested at all. Some supervision programs test only infrequently, and then on regularly scheduled reporting days. Some drug testing programs have so few internal controls that offenders find it easy to avoid detection through any number of techniques. Even if a probationer tests positive, the most likely response will be nothing but a warning from the probation officer at the next reporting date, which could be a month after the test was taken. If the violation does come before the judge, the hearing is likely to be months after the fact.[3] And finally, judges are likely to do one of two things. They may revoke probation and impose the remainder of the sentence in prison. Or they may admonish the person not to use drugs again. In summary, we have a system where there is a low rate of detection for drugs; there is a low rate of enforcement for violations; there may be high punishment severity *if punishment is actually applied*. If one set out to design a system to produce failure, it is hard to imagine a better one.

In short, we have seen major advances in our understanding of drug addiction, treatment interventions and tools to detect and monitor drug use. At the same time that testing options have expanded and reliability has increased, costs have been coming down. We have not made progress in using that knowledge to reduce drug use in that segment of society – criminal offenders – who are most troublesome and over whom we have the greatest leverage. Why do we have such difficulty in moving from success at the individual or program level to reform at the system level?

It is the thesis of this chapter that drug testing is a necessary prerequisite for effective treatment and as a crime control strategy. Drug testing alone is not sufficient. To achieve optimal effectiveness, it should be one element of a comprehensive strategy that takes into account what we know about addiction and what we know about criminal justice pressure to reduce drug use and reduce crime. To be effective, it must be done frequently, reliably, and – this is key – within a framework of real accountability. If we are to change drug-using behaviors there must be immediate consequences for relapse as well as acknowledgments of progress. With a few notable exceptions (namely some drug courts), the criminal justice system is not even close to using this tool effectively. Though drug testing is becoming ubiquitous throughout the criminal justice system, much of it occurs on an *ad hoc* basis, with no coherent policy framework on how best to use it, and without a clear understanding of what could be accomplished. As a result, criminal justice drug testing often wastes precious resources. Worse, if done without immediate responses to drug-positive results it can be counterproductive, sending unintended messages to drug abusers that there are no consequences for use, reinforcing their denial that is a part of addiction.

This chapter begins with a brief overview of what we know about addiction, the drug–crime connection, and the effectiveness of criminal justice pressure to reduce drug use and criminal behavior. With this as the foundation, the elements of a strategy for getting the most out of drug testing will be set forth, along with the current evidence of effectiveness. Finally, the impediments which must be overcome to implement this strategy on a broad scale will be discussed.

II Addiction, the drug–crime connection and criminal justice pressure

Addiction

Drug addiction is now understood to be a complex illness associated with compulsive and sometimes uncontrollable cravings for drugs. Dr. Alan Leshner, former director of the National Institute on Drug Abuse (NIDA), notes that

> [while] the onset of addiction begins with the voluntary act of taking drugs, the continued repetition of "voluntary" drug taking begins to change into "involuntary" drug taking, ultimately to the point where the behavior is driven by compulsive craving for the drug. This compulsion results from a combination of factors, including in large part dramatic changes in brain function produced by prolonged drug use. This is why addiction is considered a brain disease – one with embedded behavioral and social context aspects. Once addicted, it is almost impossible for most people to stop the spiraling cycle of addiction on their own without treatment.
>
> (Leshner 1999: 1314)

The cravings experienced by addicts can persist even in the face of extremely adverse consequences such as loss of one's job, one's family or one's liberty. Drug addiction often becomes a chronic condition, characterized by relapses that can occur even after years of treatment and struggle for sobriety. In fact, addiction is recognized and defined as a chronic and relapsing condition.

The reason addiction is such a chronic and long-term condition is because the ingestion of drugs produces reward by stimulating the brain's pleasure centers. It is now understood that mind-altering substances have the ability to elevate the level of a substance known as dopamine in the brain, which produces a sense of intense pleasure. The brain is programmed to repeat pleasurable experiences and avoid unpleasant ones.

Addiction is characterized by dishonesty and denial. So pleasurable is the ingestion of drugs that users often stubbornly insist that they have their use under control, and that it is not really a problem. They believe that they can use alcohol or other drugs without causing harm to themselves or to others.

As a result of the effect on the brain produced by drugs, the compulsion to repeat intensely pleasurable experiences, and the inherent denial of addicts that their drug use is causing problems, the lives of drug abusers tend to spiral out of control. Eventually they may reach the point where they "hit bottom" and realize that they cannot continue on their self-destructive path. This point may come with an ultimatum from their family, the loss of a job, or an arrest. An arrest presents an opportunity for society, through the criminal justice system, to begin establishing a framework of honesty and accountability by which the process of recovery can begin.

The drugs–crime connection

The relationship between drug use and crime has been the subject of considerable research interest and debate for at least a century.[4] The interrelationship between drug use, drug policy, and crime continues to this day to be a topic of some controversy. Is there a causal connection between drug use and criminal behavior? Is addiction a form of deviancy associated with individuals already predisposed to committing crimes? Or does criminal behavior follow addiction as a necessary means of supporting one's habit?

Somewhat related to the question of causality are questions relating to the effect of drugs (and drug enforcement policies) on criminal behavior. Is it the pharmacology of particular drugs that lowers inhibitions, encourages reckless or aggressive behaviors, and leads people to commit crimes that they would otherwise not consider? Or is criminal behavior primarily related to the economics of drug dealing, and the public corruption and violence over turf to protect lucrative black markets made valuable precisely because of drug prohibition and enforcement? Or are most drug-related crimes simply fueled by the need for money to support one's drug habit?

The popular and scientific literature is extensive.[5] Aside from the fact that no scientific consensus has emerged on some of these questions, the precise relationships between criminal and drug-abusing behaviors need not be determined in order to formulate and implement effective crime-reduction strategies. As noted by David Boyum and Mark A. R. Kleiman, attempting to nail down answers to these questions may simply "highlight differences where, from a policy perspective, it may not matter." They go on to say:

> Consider the evidence that drug users commit more crime during periods of heavy addiction, less during periods of abstinence or reduced use. Is this because heavy drug use increases the economic motivation to commit crimes, or is the heightened criminal activity the product of the intoxicating and dehumanizing effects of some patterns of drug use? For certain policy decisions, the answer may be irrelevant. Either explanation implicitly endorses policies that reduce drug use, for a reduction in drug use will, other things being equal, reduce crime. For policy purposes, it is often sufficient to know whether depressing the brake or accelerator makes the car go slower or faster. Arguing about why can sometimes distract us from learning how to drive.
>
> (Boyum and Kleiman 1995: 303)

For purposes of this policy discussion, just three principal research findings are relevant. First, drug users are concentrated among criminal justice populations. Second, drug-involved offenders commit serious crimes with much greater frequency than offenders who do not use drugs. Stated another way, "among predatory offenders, the ones who are *high*-frequency drug users are also very likely to be *high*-rate predators and to commit many different types of crimes, including violent crimes, and to use many different types of drugs" (Chaiken and Chaiken 1990: 212). Third, among drug-abusing offenders under criminal justice control, periods of relative abstinence or reduced drug use are associated with periods of reduced criminality. In other words, interventions that reduce drug use reduce crime. The scientific evidence for each of these three findings is summarized below.

There are many indicators that lend support to the first proposition that as a segment of society drug abusers – especially hardcore drug abusers – are concentrated in the criminal justice system and thus are already subject to supervision. Looking first at overall consumption of illegal drugs, it is estimated that in the United States 6.3 percent of the population age 12 and older are current illicit drug users, meaning that they used drugs within the past month (US Department of Health and Human Services 2000). Within the drug-using segment of the population is a smaller group of "hardcore" drug users, generally defined as weekly users of illicit drugs. Research indicates that this group of hardcore drug users consumes the bulk of illicit drugs. Looking specifically at cocaine consumption, researchers from RAND analyzed cocaine consumption patterns for both light users and heavy users (Rydell and Everingham 1994). Noting that the total number of cocaine users was in slight decline from its peak in the early 1980s, the authors point out that "the downward trend in the total number of users is misleading, because a decline in the number of light users has masked an increase in the number of heavy users" (ibid.). The report determined that heavy users consumed cocaine at eight times the rate of light users. The report went on to explore various policy alternatives to reducing cocaine consumption, concluding that it is more cost effective to treat heavy users than it is to fund alternative strategies, including interdiction of drugs, source-country control, and domestic enforcement.

From this RAND study we know that hardcore users consume a disproportionate amount of the total drugs consumed in the country. What is the evidence that these heavy users of drugs are likely to be found in criminal justice populations? There are a number of data sources that all point to the concentration of drug users within various criminal justice populations.

One way to visualize the flow of criminal cases through the justice system is to think of a funnel – wide at the mouth, narrowing at each stage as cases progress to disposition and sentencing. The first step in the process, and the widest part of the funnel, occurs at the point of arrest. After arrest the flow narrows somewhat as prosecutors review cases and decide to drop some. The remaining cases are set for trial. Between arraignment and trial additional charges fall by the wayside as a result of plea bargains, evidentiary issues, or other reasons. Most criminal defendants plead guilty and proceed to sentencing, although a relative few go to trial. At sentencing, the flow of cases to prison narrows again, as most convicted defendants are sentenced to probation.

Data regarding drug use is available at each step in the process and shows high prevalence rates for drugs within each criminal justice population or subgroup. Some of the best data has been gathered where the criminal justice funnel is at its widest – the point immediately after arrest. This data, gathered quarterly in dozens of cities since the mid-1980s, does not rely solely on self-reports, but consists of both anonymous interview data and, more importantly, urine sample results. In city after city, quarter after quarter, one finding has held constant: a majority of new arrestees are drug positive at the point of arrest. While the type of drugs detected varies from place to place, and the prevalence rate fluctuates by city and over time, the fact that arrestees are saturated with drugs is beyond question.[6] Since this data is based on a combination of self-reports and actual test results, and since it samples those coming in the "front door" of the justice system – the wide end of the funnel – one would expect to find similar drug-prevalence rates in the various "downstream" populations – pretrial detainees, pretrial releasees, probationers, prison inmates, and parolees.

As expected, the high rates of drug use detected in recent arrestees are confirmed by numerous other indicators among discrete segments of the criminal justice population. For example, the 1998 Annual Survey of Jails, conducted by the Bureau of Justice Statistics, sampled over 800 jails and concluded that 70 percent of all inmates in local facilities had committed a drug offense or used drugs regularly (US Department of Justice 2000). Turning to the much larger correctional population, the Bureau of Justice Statistics and the Center on Addiction and Substance Abuse (CASA) estimate that from 60 percent to 83 percent of this population have used drugs at some point in their lives (Office of National Drug Control Policy 2001). Similarly, within state correctional systems it is estimated that 73.6 percent of female inmates and 69.3 percent of male inmates had previously used drugs regularly (US Department of Justice 1999). Other surveys, using different methodologies and covering different time periods, yield similar results.

It is one thing to observe that criminal justice populations contain a very high percentage of drug users. But does that mean that most drug users end up in the criminal justice system? Various studies exploring this question have pointed out that there are many kinds of offenders, including successful offenders who are rarely apprehended and inept or emotionally disturbed offenders who are arrested frequently. That said, it has been established that heavy drug users of multiple drugs who commit predatory crimes at high rates are frequently caught because of both the frequency of the crimes and the opportunistic nature of their behavior (Chaiken and Chaiken 1990: 215). One recent estimate concluded that 60 percent of all cocaine consumed in the United States in any given year is consumed by the subset of users who are also arrested within the same year (Kleiman 1997). Although the *percentage* of high-rate drug users already under criminal justice control can only be estimated, for purposes of this discussion it does not matter. What matters is that there is a large concentration of known drug users causing a great deal of trouble for the community. While we have the legal power to do something about this, we are using that authority ineffectively, for reasons that will be discussed later.

The second important research finding supporting the policy thesis of this chapter is that drug-involved offenders commit serious crimes with much greater frequency than offenders who do not use drugs. Heavy users of drugs or users of multiple drugs commit crimes with greater frequency than do occasional drug users. The evidence for this finding is unequivocal, and is supported by a number of classic, long-term studies of heroin addicts in California,[7] Miami (Inciardi 1986; also see Inciardi *et al.* 1996), and Baltimore (Ball *et al.* 1983). This research has consistently shown that narcotics addicts engage in a great amount of criminal activity. During periods of heavy use addicts commit crimes on a daily basis and as a result sometimes commit hundreds, even thousands, of offences per individual during their addiction careers (Ball *et al.* 1983). These offences go beyond illegal transactions to procure drugs. Extensive research of drug abusers in Miami has shown that drug-related crime is at times far more violent than had been generally understood. While violent crime is proportionately a small percentage of crimes committed by addicts, since they commit so many crimes the number of violent offences is substantial (Inciardi 1986; also see Inciardi *et al.* 1996).

To summarize a large body of research, drugs drive crime. Leaving aside questions of cause and effect, or which came first – criminal or drug-using behavior – drug use tends to intensify over time and perpetuate criminal careers. Drug use has been characterized as a multiplier of criminal behavior. Thus, any strategy that can reduce drug use holds great promise for reducing crime.

Finally, the third finding supporting the position of this chapter holds that among drug-abusing offenders under criminal justice control periods of relative abstinence or reduced drug use are associated with periods of reduced criminality. A corollary finding is that coerced abstinence is effective in lowering criminal activity. Many long-term studies of addicts have shown a cyclical pattern to their drug use. Often drug users become deeply involved in a drug-using lifestyle before engaging in treatment. However, the drug use frequently escalates to the point where they are forced into treatment, sometimes only after coming to the attention of the criminal justice system. Because of either incarceration or pressure from family or criminal justice heavy drug users tend to have periods of abstinence, or at least relative abstinence. Their addiction careers may be marked by multiple treatment episodes. Periods of relative abstinence are often followed by relapse to drugs.

By following individual addicts through these cyclical periods of addiction and relative abstinence, researchers have been able to compare rates of crime during periods of drug use and compare them with rates of crime when the same addicts are in the community but not using drugs. One of the most rigorous studies using this longitudinal approach was conducted with a sample of narcotics addicts in Baltimore.[8] By comparing crime rates during timeframes categorized as periods of addiction and periods of abstinence, the study found that the number of crime-days[9] per year-at-risk averaged 248 during periods of active addiction, and only 41 during periods of nonaddiction. In other words, there was a *sixfold increase* in criminality during periods of active drug use compared with periods of relative abstinence. Hence the conclusion that drugs fuel crime, or act as a multiplier of criminal behavior.

If more drug-free days translate directly into more crime-free days, what strategies can be employed to increase the number of drug-free days? Accepting the fact that addiction is a chronic and relapsing condition, how can the problem of addiction be managed to lengthen the time between relapses, increasing the percentage of drug-free days? One way is to keep people locked up. Another way is to keep them engaged in the treatment process.

There is now a large body of literature that supports the proposition that treatment not only works but is cost effective. A 1997 RAND study looked at the relative benefits of spending an additional $1 million to cut drug consumption and related drug crime via different policy interventions. Researchers concluded that spending funds to reduce drug consumption *through treatment* rather than incarceration would reduce serious crimes 15 times more effectively (Caulkins *et al.* 1997). A California study reported savings from treatment of $1.5 billion over 18 months, with the largest savings coming from reductions in crime. The study estimated that for every $1 spent on treatment approximately $7 could be gained in future savings (Gerstein *et al.* 1994). Treatment, then, is cost effective. Keeping people in treatment increases the benefit, since there is also a body of literature that establishes that the longer an addict remains in treatment the better the treatment outcomes.

Despite the accumulation of evidence that drug treatment works, historically there has been less agreement – especially among treatment professionals – about the conditions under which addicts can benefit from treatment. For years the conventional wisdom was that addicts had to recognize their own need for treatment. Only when they came to the realization that they had hit "rock bottom" and needed outside help could treatment be beneficial. Without such insight on the part of the addict, treatment providers often concluded that individuals were not "amenable" to treatment. Forcing people into treatment before they were ready simply meant that the people who wanted and could benefit from treatment would be short-changed. There was a strong sense that criminal justice pressure was not effective as a motivator for treatment. We now know that the opposite is true. There is considerable evidence not only that compulsory or coerced treatment works, but that it may even be more effective than voluntary treatment.

There is also new evidence that frequent drug testing coupled with sanctions is effective in reducing drug use and subsequent arrests. A major evaluation by the Urban Institute of the District of Columbia Superior Court Drug Intervention Programs studied the impact of different approaches in the design of drug courts.[10] Drug-involved defendants were randomly assigned to one of three dockets: a standard docket with twice-weekly testing and routine judicial monitoring; a treatment docket, consisting of enrollment in a comprehensive court-based outpatient drug treatment program; and a sanctions docket, consisting of twice-weekly drug testing with swift and certain sanctions, with available but not mandated treatment. The study examined the impact of each approach on defendants' drug use, criminal activity, social and economic functioning, as well as costs and benefits.

Both of the experimental groups (treatment program participants and sanctions program participants) were substantially more likely to be drug free in the month prior to sentencing than the defendants on the standard docket. Sanctions program participants were significantly less likely to be arrested in the year following sentencing than standard docket participants.

Among the strongest findings of the study were the long-term effects achieved by combining graduated sanctions with voluntary participation in 12-step programs. That subgroup had a much lower likelihood of cocaine or heroine use in the year after sentencing.

Finally, the study underscored the "importance of getting the defendants' up-front commitment to the rules":

> In the focus group, sanction program participants said they agreed in advance to the sanctions and the rules for applying penalties because it gave them a feeling of control and a sense they were treated fairly. These defendants knew they could avoid penalties by not using drugs, and it was their responsibility to show the judge they were clean through drug test results. This "contingency contract" between the judge and defendant clearly differentiates these sanctions from imposed penalties using poorly understood or inconsistently enforced rules.
>
> (Harrell *et al.* 2000: 11)

Taken together, these studies suggest a direction for the future. We have learned a great deal over the past few decades. We have a pretty good idea of which approaches are most promising. The challenge is to take key elements of the best programs and make them the foundation for the entire system.

III Six steps to more effective use of drug testing

From the previous review of what we know about addiction, the relationship between drugs and crime, and the value of reducing drug use to cut crime, we turn now to propose elements of a strategy for an effective criminal justice and treatment approach toward common goals. The fact that the criminal justice system is swamped with drug use, drug users, and drug-related crime presents both a challenge and an opportunity. The challenges are seen every day in any courtroom, where the devastating impact of drugs can be seen on the faces of defendants, probationers, victims, and the families of each. The challenges take the form of enormous numbers of people and cases that bog down the system until it is little more than an assembly line process, with no hope for anything good coming from all this churning effort. The opportunity comes from the same factors. Nowhere is the *potential* for improvement so immediate and so clear. In the criminal justice system there are large concentrations of drug users. Many of them are heavy drug users. Many of them are responsible for a great number of crimes. We can – if we choose – quickly figure out who is using drugs. We can further determine who among drug users is using multiple drugs. We can – if we choose – decide to *use* the power of the justice system to intervene in the cycle of drug use and crime. After all, we know (or certainly should know) who the drug users are, where they live, and whether they are abiding by our solemn orders to stay away from drugs as a condition of release. Pressure, effectively applied, will reduce drug use and cut crime.

There are six elements to the proposed strategy. All of them are straightforward. Some may wonder why these commonsense proposals are not already routine features of the justice system. Many will recognize elements of the proposed strategy as common features in drug treatment courts. There are similarities, but the intent is to move beyond specialized programs to reform of the entire system. There are substantial barriers to implementing these proposals, which will be more fully discussed. All of the elements are interdependent. The strategy cannot succeed if any component is missing. The basic elements of the strategy are as follows:

1   Drug users should be identified through testing at the earliest possible point in the process.
2   Regardless of legal status, conditions of release regarding drug use and consequences for violations should be spelled out clearly in the form of a simple contract.
3   A range of graduated sanctions for drug use should be developed.
4   Sanctions for drug use should be applied swiftly and with certainty.
5   Criminal justice systems and treatment systems should form alliances to develop a range of drug treatment modalities.
6   The period of drug intervention and risk management should be long, from the point of arrest to the completion of sentence.

Element 1: drug users should be identified through testing at the earliest possible point in the process

Every arrestee charged with a criminal offense should be given a routine drug test prior to his or her first appearance before a judicial officer. At this stage of a criminal proceeding, judges must make a two-part assessment of the defendant's likelihood to appear for trial and the threat to community safety if released. To assist the court in making this judgment, the judicial officer in most jurisdictions is provided with information on the defendant's background – employment status, ties to the community, stability of residence, educational level, prior criminal record, etc. Equally important, but rarely provided, is current information on drug use. This information can only be ascertained reliably through drug testing, and only one major jurisdiction in the country – Washington, DC – provides this service on a routine basis. Whether (and how many) drugs are present in a defendant's system is important for two reasons: first, it is a highly useful piece of information to assess risk; second, it suggests the kinds of release conditions that could be imposed to manage the risk. Both of these reasons go to the heart of the pretrial release decision-making process.[11] Making release or detention decisions without all the relevant and readily obtainable information is a disservice to the community and the defendant alike.

Element 2: regardless of legal status, conditions of release regarding drug use and consequences for violations should be spelled out clearly in the form of a simple contract

An important lesson learned from drug courts is the therapeutic value of operating in an environment where the drug offender can exercise some control over the outcome. In drug courts the enrollment process generally begins with a discussion between the drug court participant and the judge. The dialogue covers expectations regarding frequency of drug testing, referral for assessment and/or treatment, and consequences of failure to abide by the terms of the contract. The deal is sealed when the judge and the participant sign the contract. In some courtrooms the seriousness of the agreement is reinforced by the judge leaving the bench, walking down to the well of the courtroom, looking the participant in the eye, and shaking hands on the agreement. The judge may even say something to the effect that the defendant is now in complete control over whether he or she goes back to jail or not. Though simple, this is in marked contrast to the rapid-fire, assembly line nature of justice dispensed in many high-volume courtrooms.

This system of contracts and accountability only works if there is no room for subjective interpretation or ambiguity. There must be predictability in the enforcement of the contract. Experience shows that sanctions schemes are most likely to be followed if the sanctions are short. A sanctions schedule viewed as too harsh simply invites the search for reasons to deviate from the policy. Once that door is opened the integrity of the entire process is undermined. Defendants/offenders are encouraged to plead for exceptions. The focus shifts from drug-using behavior to finding the best excuse. Simple is best. Formulaic sanctions, consistently applied, teach personal responsibility for one's behavior – an important lesson on the road to recovery.

Element 3: a range of graduated sanctions for drug use should be developed

For a number of reasons discussed later in this chapter (pp. 162), jurisdictions have difficulty moving from the "all or nothing" sanctions approach to a graduated sanctions approach. Those responsible for devising and implementing graduated sanctions should have a clear idea of what constitutes a sanction. A sanction is a punishment. It is designed to reinforce societal messages of what is acceptable and what is unacceptable behavior. It should be sufficiently disagreeable that the person will seek to avoid it. It should involve a restriction on one's freedom of movement. Short periods of detention are certainly sanctions, but are not the only means of delivering meaningful consequences. Examples of sanctions that do not require a jail cell include a three-day observation period in drug court, a seven-day admission to a residential detox program, a return to a halfway house (in the case of a parolees), or admission to a drug-treatment-oriented residential sanctions center. While these kinds of non-jail sanctions can be effective, there must be the capacity to move quickly to jail-based sanctions for those who continue to violate their contracts.

Element 4: sanctions for drug use should be applied swiftly and with certainty

Rapid and predictable enforcement of release conditions is difficult to achieve but critically important if the criminal justice system is serious about maximizing its potential to change behavior and cut crime.

Swift action is key. Ideally, drug offenders are tested and, if drugs are detected, sanctioned on the spot. Less than ideal but still effective is a system where the sanctioning process occurs within a day or two of the detected violation. Setting such a performance standard raises all kinds of logistical and legal issues, but it can be done. To the extent that lawyers, judges, monitoring staff, and courtroom support staff are required, as they certainly would be during implementation of such an ambitious initiative, scheduling conflicts would be the norm and pressure to defer action immense.

Predictability or certainty in the delivery of sanctions is as important as quick action. Consequences should be clearly spelled out in advance, and delivered consistent with the contract. Deviations from the pre-agreed-upon consequences should be the rare exception.

Element 5: criminal justice systems and treatment systems should form alliances to develop a range of drug treatment modalities

Once real criminal justice pressure to stay off drugs begins to kick in, the demand for treatment will go up. Some drug users will want to avoid the disruption to their lives of repeated sanctions, and will come to understand that enrollment in a treatment program gives them their best opportunity.

There should be a broad range of jail-based, prison-based, and community treatment programs. Short-term detox programs can be especially useful as an early consequence of drug use, and as a first step in a long treatment process. Ideally, all major treatment modalities will be present, permitting drug offenders to seek that which works best for them. Long-term aftercare must be available. Self-help programs or 12-step meetings (Alcoholics Anonymous or Narcotics Anonymous) are valuable components of long-term strategies for maintaining sobriety.

Element 6: the period of drug intervention and risk management should be long, from the point of arrest to the completion of sentence

Criminal justice supervision of drug users is often fragmented and ineffective. One of the reasons for this fragmentation is that the legal system tends to focus on cases rather than individuals. While this approach may address court management goals, it neither serves the needs of drug offenders nor advances the broad public safety goals of society. As individuals pass through the system, different entities assume responsibility for the supervision of the individual or the processing of the case. Criminal justice supervision agencies (pretrial services, community corrections, probation or parole) are primarily concerned about what happens when the individual is under their direct supervision. A pretrial program, for example, may measure recidivism only in terms of crimes committed while on pretrial release. A crime committed a week after the defendant is sentenced and placed on probation, though regrettable, is simply not within the scope of responsibility of the pretrial services agency. Similarly, courts are mostly concerned about their dockets and the time it takes to process a case from filing to disposition. After that, the individual becomes the responsibility of another part of the government.

While there are good reasons for courts to track cases and measure success in terms of timely case disposition, what does this approach mean for a drug-using individual who finds himself in trouble with the law? From the offender's point of view, each step along the way can be a "fresh start," where the past is forgotten, and with little or no continuity in the management of one's drug addiction. As a pretrial defendant, the individual may have been drug tested, referred for treatment, clinically assessed, and assigned to a particular treatment modality or program. But, if sentenced to probation, the process starts over. It is rare that the probation officer has independent access to any of this historical information, including how a person fared in a particular program. From the point of view of a drug offender in denial, who is constantly looking for ways to beat the system, this scenario is ideal. But from the public policy vantage point, resources are wasted; time is lost; personal responsibility is undermined; opportunities to build upon treatment experiences are squandered.

Even within supervision agencies, funding constraints often create powerful incentives to reduce or eliminate monitoring functions. The frequency of drug testing is scaled back, sometimes after only a matter of weeks of "clean" tests. These resource-driven policies fail to take into account the nature of addiction as a chronic and relapsing condition. They ignore the fact that many drug users need the structure of regular testing to maintain sobriety.

Within the same jurisdiction, different supervision agencies may have different capabilities, organizational philosophies, or policies. From the drug offender's point of view, the system is inconsistent and fragmented – not an environment conducive to recovery.

All of the organizations and institutions responsible for handling criminal cases (judges, pretrial services, probation, corrections, parole boards, parole supervision) should seek a consistent approach in the supervision of drug offenders by negotiating a set of principles that recognize the long-term nature of the recovery process. Contracts should be encouraged at all release points. The contracts should spell out in clear terms the consequences for violations or breaches of the contract. The parties should strive for consistency in monitoring and enforcement capabilities. System-wide goals should be established to ensure that consequences for drug use occur quickly, preferably within a day or two. While sanctions need not be identical in all circumstances,[12] there should be consistency in the enforcement of contracts. Finally, there should be a presumption that supervision information moves with the individual from one legal status to the next.[13]

Using criminal justice leverage: a brief history

Of a commonsense proposal

The idea of using criminal justice leverage to reduce drug use and thereby reduce criminal activity is not new. It has been proposed before. It has only recently begun to pick up support. Nevertheless, it remains the exception, not the rule. A brief history of this idea is in order if we are ever to overcome our current state of paralysis and inertia and begin moving toward more rational and cost-effective crime control policies.

A quarter of a century ago, the first director of the National Institute on Drug Abuse, Dr. Robert L. DuPont, proposed a major new initiative to refocus national efforts on heroin addiction in the criminal justice system. Known as Operation Tripwire, the proposal called for universal drug testing of offenders, with clean results as a condition for remaining in the community.[14] The plan envisioned drug screening for all parolees and probationers, regardless of their conviction offense or their record of drug abuse. Drug offenders would be subject to regular urine monitoring, with clean urines being a requirement to remain in the community.

Foreshadowing drug courts by two decades, the plan called for escalating responses for each positive drug test. Offenders testing positive for heroin would initially be subject to closer supervision, with "weekly or more frequent urine tests" (Dupont and Wish 1992: 99). A second positive test would require that the offender enter a treatment program, with the modality of treatment selected by the offender. Subsequent or repeated failures would lead to "prompt reincarceration" of three to six months, followed by re-release to the community under intensive supervision with frequent unannounced tests. The cost of the initial pilot phase of Operation Tripwire was set at $12–14 million per year.

Controversial from the outset, Operation Tripwire never got off the ground. There was simply no consensus regarding the three key features of the proposal – that heroin use was linked to crime; that close supervision with strict consequences could reduce heroin use; and that reducing heroin use would lead to reduced criminal activity. So intense was the opposition to Operation Tripwire that the proponent of the idea credits it with the loss of his job as first NIDA director.[15] Operation Tripwire was an idea before its time, and many years would pass before the key features of the proposal would find wider acceptance.

Little by little, support for some of the concepts in Dr. DuPont's proposal grew – at least in public policy circles, if not among criminal justice or drug treatment professionals. Research studies documenting the association between drug use and crime began accumulating.

In 1988, amidst great public concern surrounding the crack cocaine epidemic, a piece of omnibus Federal drug legislation was passed by Congress and signed into law.[16] Under this legislation, an Office of National Drug Control Policy was created within the White House, and William J. Bennett was appointed director or "drug czar." In September 1989 the first National Drug Control Strategy was issued. The very first sentence in the document reads "no strategy designed to combat illegal drug use can succeed if it fails to recognize the crucial role of criminal justice" (White House 1989: 17). As one of its criminal justice priorities, the strategy called for "adoption by the States of drug-testing programs throughout their criminal justice systems: for arrestees, prisoners, parolees and those out on bail" (ibid.: 16). To prod the states into action, the strategy made receipt of Federal criminal justice block grant funds conditional on the development of such programs (White House 1989: 16).

Despite this unequivocal language, the idea was not developed in the strategy document beyond general statements on the need to establish offender accountability by exploring alternative sanctions. However, the idea of making federal funding conditional on the existence of system-wide drug testing provoked a firestorm of criticism. Various professional associations representing State and local criminal justice disciplines quickly figured out that the costs of implementing drug testing would far exceed the federal grant funding at issue. Thus, there was no grant-related incentive to implement the idea. Rather than explore the merits of the proposal or take up implementation issues, a great deal of intellectual energy was spent attacking the proposal. Although the grant application process did incorporate the idea, it was really a triumph of form over substance. There was little real progress toward a system of drug testing, with accountability, throughout the criminal justice system.

When the second National Drug Control Strategy was issued the following year, the notion of using criminal justice drug testing as a keystone of national policy came into slightly better focus:

Drug testing through urinalysis is the only reliable and practical method currently available for determining whether someone in custody or under correctional supervision has been using illegal drugs. Testing within the criminal justice system can serve as an "early warning system" that provides another method of keeping offenders in check while they are on pretrial or post-conviction release. Moreover, random, mandatory drug tests, coupled with certain penalties, create a powerful incentive for those under correctional supervision – a high risk group – to get off and stay off drugs.

(White House 1990: 25–6)

Specifics were still lacking, although a few well-known voices in the drug policy world began to sketch out more detailed proposals regarding the best use of criminal justice drug testing. Writing for the opinion page of the *New York Times* on July 25, 1992, Mark A. R. Kleiman – then an associate professor of public policy at Harvard's Kennedy School of Government – called for a big-city field trial of drug testing (Kleiman 1992: 21). Echoing themes that had cost Dr. DuPont his job a decade and a half earlier, Kleiman wrote that

drug-using offenders are often arrested, convicted and released on proba- tion or, after some time in prison, on parole. Unfortunately, we have no way to keep them off drugs when they aren't behind bars. The key to changing their life style is to make abstinence, verified by regular tests, a condition of staying out of jail.

(Kleiman 1992)

Kleiman proposed testing felony offenders, especially robbers, burglars, and drug dealers, reasoning that this group accounts for the majority of the nation's hard-drug consumption and is responsible for more than one-third of its serious crime. "Penalties for missed or failed tests," wrote Kleiman in the *New York Times*, "need not be drastic but must be immediate and auto- matic. The certainty of spending a few days in jail is a better disincentive to drug use than a small probability of being sent back to prison for years" (ibid.). Citing data on a handful of programs already using immediate, short-term jail-based sanctions, Kleiman concluded that for a cost of about $3,500 per offender per year a program based on frequent testing and auto- matic sanctions would more than pay for itself, even if only half of its subjects stayed away from crime and out of prison.

In the late 1980s and early 1990s the first fledgling drug treatment courts began to spring up around the country. These early specialized courts were often started by innovative judicial leaders, frustrated by the futility of endlessly processing drug cases to no apparent effect, and willing to take a chance by experimenting with ways to get at the drug-abusing behavior underlying so many of the cases on their calendars. The courts were, in large part, a reaction to the failings of the traditional offender supervision mechanisms to address the problem of addiction and its effect on the courts.

Throughout the 1990s drug courts continued to proliferate, aided both by federal assistance in the form of hundreds of planning and implementation grants[17] and by a growing consensus among judges, prosecutors, and others that traditional case processing practices did nothing to address the underlying factor of addiction that is responsible for bringing so many individuals to court in the first place. Yet, for all the enthusiasm generated by drug courts, they remained specialized programs within larger systems that continued to function as they always had. Many operate as diversion options, which almost by definition exclude defendants charged with more serious offenses.[18] As programs, their reach is necessarily limited by eligibility criteria, judicial resources, and treatment capacity. Federal funding itself imposed eligibility limitations on local grantees.[19]

Although early claims of drug court successes have been questioned due to the lack of methodological rigor in some program evaluations,[20] the practices adopted by these new programs represent a significant departure from business as usual. First, there is real supervision, consisting of frequent drug testing, regular appearances before the court, quick admission to treatment, and systems of immediate sanctions and rewards.

As fundamental as most of these functions may seem in a rational system of community corrections, they are more the exception than the rule. The contrast between drug court monitoring and probation supervision, for example, is striking. Despite the fact that more than two-thirds of probationers have a history of drug abuse,[21] only 25 percent of probationers reported that they were required to undergo any urinalysis testing (Bonczar 1997). The urinalysis testing that does occur is often conducted infrequently during regularly scheduled appointments, with little or no consistency regarding consequences for failures. Fully one-quarter of felony probationers in a 1995 survey reported no contact whatsoever with their probation officer during the previous month. Thus, separate and apart from the unique features of drug courts,[22] they all served to fill the supervision vacuum that had developed over time as pretrial, probation and parole caseloads exploded throughout the 1980s and 1990s. But they only provide supervision and treatment for those fortunate enough to find themselves in a drug court. The rest – those coming out of prison, those already on probation, those who don't meet the eligibility criteria for drug court, or those who simply fall between the cracks – are subject to normal "supervision," which is likely to be no supervision at all.

In summary, drug courts are small programs within much larger systems. They target individuals with certain offense, prior record, and drug abuse characteristics. Utilizing frequent drug testing, they create a unique courtroom and treatment environment with incentives and disincentives designed to keep their participants in treatment for the long haul. By design, they reach only a tiny fraction of the drug-dependent individuals under criminal justice supervision. By design, they require substantial judicial resources to provide the regular review of test results and treatment progress, along with appropriate rewards or sanctions. As drug courts have evolved and demonstrated the success of their approach, larger policy questions remain. What lessons from the drug court experience can be applied to the much larger population of drug-dependent individuals already under nominal criminal justice control? If frequent drug testing coupled with quick sanctions is effective in the courtroom, might not a variation of these techniques produce similar results throughout correctional populations? Can the system itself be changed? Or must we be content with small but innovative programs operating within a broken system? What are the barriers to system change? How can those barriers be overcome?

Throughout the 1990s a few lone voices continued to press for system-wide change, calling for more effective use of drug testing as a drug control strategy. The National Institute of Justice (NIJ) launched an ambitious program in several cities known as "Break the Cycle," which called for system-wide drug screening, referral to treatment for those testing positive, frequent monitoring through urine testing, and immediate sanctions for positive tests. The State of Maryland launched its own "Break the Cycle" program, closely modeled after the NIJ initiative. For a number of reasons discussed later (pp. 162), all of these programs had difficulty achieving the lofty goals of their proponents.

As the decade came to a close, a small but growing number of leaders among criminal justice practitioners began to embrace what had once been a controversial idea – widespread criminal justice drug testing to hold offenders accountable. In October of 1999, State of New York Chief Judge Judith S. Kay created a commission[23] to study the impact of drug cases on New York State courts. When their report was issued the following June, it summarized the emerging evidence of success of drug courts, documented the shortcomings of the probation system,[24] and described the steep price of underfunding probation. Among the conclusions of the commission was the notion that "coerced" drug treatment reduces crime, saves money, and alleviates the impact of drug cases on the court. Successful treatment programs, reasoned the commission, incorporate efficient drug testing, effective rewards, and sanctions, with sanctions that are rational, well understood, and, most important, certain and immediate.

At about the same time, a handful of practitioners in the probation field began to come to the same conclusions as their court system colleagues in New York. In August of 1999, a hard-hitting report was released by the Center for Civic Innovation at the Manhattan Institute, which characterized probation as the "most troubled" part of America's criminal justice system (Center for Civic Innovation 1999). Significantly, the report was written largely by leaders within the probation field itself, including the National Association of Probation Executives (NAPE) and the American Probation and Parole Association (APPA), and unveiled at the association's annual meeting. In a painfully accurate self-assessment, the authors acknowledged the validity of many of the harshest criticisms of their field. They forthrightly acknowledged that inadequate funding is not the only cause of probation's failure, citing a list of commonplace and ineffective probation practices such as drug testing that is scheduled in advance, on an infrequent basis, with results provided weeks after the test. The report was especially critical of the lack of accountability within probation supervision: "Probationers often realize they may expect two or more 'free ones' when it comes to dirty urine samples.... *For probation to be effective, this permissive practice must be abandoned*" (ibid.: 1). The central theme of the report is that probation has the potential – if it can reform itself – to be a driving force in a strategy to reduce crime: "Either probation will be at the political and intellectual core of future policy-oriented efforts to promote public safety and offender rehabilitation in America, or it will continue to be widely marginalized, mischaracterized and underfunded" (ibid.: 1)

By 2002, even elected officials were beginning to grasp the nuances of probation program operations, appreciate the funding dilemma, and call for reforms. On June 12, 2002, Senator John Edwards of North Carolina gave a speech on the floor of the Senate describing the probation/parole/supervised-release system as "overburdened, understaffed, inconsistent, and almost completely unsuccessful."[25] He laid out three principles, starting with accountability based on a "simple bargain – obey the law, or suffer the consequences." In describing the lack of accountability that exists now, he said:

> We need real punishments for people who commit real violations of probation and parole. Today we have the opposite. We have a system where at one extreme, people can violate probation or parole ten times before anything actually happens to them. Nearly half the people in the probation system have violated the terms of probation, but only one in five get sent back to jail for doing it. At the other extreme we have some people who miss an appointment and go back to jail for years. It just doesn't make sense.
>
> Let me give an example. We know that many people commit crimes to feed their drug habits. Almost half of the crimes in many big cities are committed by drug users. So if we are going to cut crime, we have to get people on probation and parole off of drugs.
>
> Now, it's true that right now, we say you have to remain drug-free while you're on probation or parole. But too often, that requirement only exists on paper. Drug tests are few and far between – maybe once a month and maybe less, so if a guy is using, he can hide it. If he does get caught, his parole officer has to negotiate a bureaucracy to get the guy punished, so a lot of the time the officer doesn't bother. And if he does

bother, the judge may choose not to impose the only punishment that's available, which may be years in jail.

The result of all this is that drug users on probation or parole know they're not likely to get caught, and so they use again and again and again. As they return to addiction, they commit more crimes.

We can do better. A rational probation and parole system would deter crime before it happens, using two basic elements. First, we'd have strict supervision focused on the conduct that leads to crime. Instead of just rules against drug use, we'd have frequent drug testing, like twice-a-week testing. Second – and this is critical – we'd have automatic punishments for people who break the rules. Those punishments would be swift and certain and graduated. You test positive for drugs, you get punished. You test positive a second time, you get punished more severely. Automatic, no exceptions; simple, swift punishment. Here in the District of Columbia, the system is moving in this direction, and research shows that it is helping in the fight against crime. It's time for more places to do the same.

> (John Edwards, http://www.senate.gov/edwards/
> statements/20020612—parole.html)

Frequent drug testing of offenders; swift but measured punishments for violations: the same basic ideas as those proposed by NIDA director Dr. Robert L. DuPont 25 years earlier. Once considered controversial, even outlandish, the elements of this commonsense strategy have picked up steam, gaining empirical support and backers among practitioners, academics, and politicians. Yet, except for the District of Columbia, there has been very little impetus to make fundamental changes in offender super-vision, especially as it relates to drug testing.

Obstacles and myths impeding implementation of an effective crime control policy

> Arguments about crime control tend to focus on how to change the behavior of crim-inals. In some ways, that's the easy part; criminals respond when their behavior has immediate and predictable consequences. The hard part is changing the behavior of officials to make those things happen.
>
> (Kleiman 2002: Blueprint Online Magazine.)

The foregoing has set forth the case that drug testing, *when implemented within a system of true offender accountability*, is essential both for optimizing successful outcomes within a treatment context and for achieving larger public safety goals. To recap, focusing our efforts on drug-using offenders is particularly useful. Why? Because most crime, especially serious or violent crime, is committed by repeat offenders. Many repeat offenders are already under criminal justice "control." Most offenders – by some estimates as many as 80 percent – have current or recent histories of substance abuse. Effective interventions to curb drug use translate directly into reduced crime rates. Coerced treatment is effective. Frequent drug testing, conducted in a context of real accountability, is the best way to use criminal justice pressure either to encourage people to get off drugs or to let criminal justice authorities know who cannot safely continue in the community. If we are going to have a system of supervised release, why not make it mean something?

As we have seen, the technology of drug testing has advanced to the point where it is now cheap, reliable, and readily available for a variety of different samples. As a tool of offender supervision, it is the *only* thing that permits the monitoring of behavior over the course of several days, rather than just during the few minutes of an office visit. Yet much of the drug testing currently being conducted is done on a perfunctory basis, with no real framework of accountability. When done poorly, drug testing is not only a waste of money but may actually hinder recovery. When court orders are not enforced the unintended message being conveyed to the offender is that there are no real consequences to drug use.

Why, then, does the criminal justice system continue to employ drug testing in such an unproductive – indeed counterproductive – way? What will it take to move the system forward, taking into account all we have learned about the nature of addiction, the relationship between drugs and crime, the benefits of coerced abstinence, and the importance of frequent drug testing and offender accountability?

Structural imbalance in correctional spending

One reason we have not used drug testing effectively is because we have failed to invest in community corrections at all, let alone a drug testing component within community corrections. There is a structural imbalance in correctional spending. Briefly stated, there are two sides to our correctional system – the institutional side and the community side. Despite the fact that two-thirds of individuals under correctional supervision are in the community, the institutional side absorbs nine out of every ten correctional dollars. This imbalance in correctional resource allocation seems to be a peculiarly American phenomenon. Canada, for example, spends a much higher proportion of its correctional dollar on those being supervised in the community. The average annual cost of supervising an offender on parole or statutory release during 1998/9 in Canada was $13,000 per offender (Solicitor General of Canada 1999). By contrast, many jurisdictions in the United States spend barely $200 per year per probationer for supervision (Petersilia 1997).

This funding imbalance has only worsened over the past two decades. On the institutional side, the country has engaged in a massive prison construction effort to house the burgeoning number of sentenced offenders, many of whom were convicted of drug or drug-related offenses and were subject to increasingly tough sentencing laws.[26] As the number of prisoners increased, so too did the funding needed to build and run the prisons to house them. At the same time, the opposite was occurring on the community side of corrections. Probation and parole caseloads were also rising dramatically during the same time period. But budgetary support for probation and parole remained static or declined. Exacerbating the problem was the fact that more and more individuals in statistically higher-risk categories were being sentenced to probation. In many jurisdictions, probation or parole officers were (and still are) responsible for supervising caseloads in excess of 200 persons, and are being asked to perform additional functions as well. It is little wonder, then, that offender supervision has deteriorated over the past few decades to the point where it now consists of little more than infrequent and perfunctory office visits for the more "responsible" offenders. The "less responsible" offenders – the drug users, the chronic offenders, the persons about whom the public should be most concerned – often simply stop reporting. By failing to report as required, they fall into a catchall category known as "absconders." As absconders they are generally written off, removed from the active caseload, with the result that there is almost no chance that anyone will come looking for them. Although warrants are generally requested and eventually issued, they often join thousands of other warrants, creating a backlog of impossible proportions. Many of these so-called absconders have never left their neighborhoods and are eventually apprehended in the commission of new crimes, often when their relapse to drugs has gone unchecked. If their new crime is particularly noteworthy, the resulting adverse publicity further undermines the already discredited and under-funded agency responsible for their supervision. And so the cycle continues.

There are, then, deep structural imbalances which make it very difficult to expect much in the way of effective monitoring from probation or parole agencies. Inadequate resources *are* a problem, but by no means the only barrier to moving ahead with more effective supervision techniques such as drug testing. It is important to keep in mind that drug testing is one of the very few tools at the disposal of supervision agencies that can provide an accurate window on at least one aspect of an offender's behavior over the span of several days. Drug use is one of the best early warning indicators of criminal behavior, and thus one of the most important signs to monitor carefully. No other tool in the supervision officer's toolbox is as useful as drug testing. Despite the inadequate level of funding for most probation or supervised-release agencies, drug testing has become commonplace. So why is it not used more effectively? This is an important question, for without an accurate diagnosis of the ailment it will be difficult to prescribe the remedy.

Poor coordination between criminal justice and treatment

There are a number of models by which the criminal justice system manages drug offenders. Some justice agencies operate their own in-house treatment programs. Many more make referrals to the public health system with the expectation that there will be regular exchanges of information on the treatment status of the individual. Some jurisdictions expect the treatment program to conduct drug testing as it sees fit. Others require the individual to continue to report to the justice agency (pretrial services, probation or parole) for regular testing, at least as long as the individual is in an outpatient program.

Historically there has been a wide cultural gulf between the justice and the treatment communities. Coming from different academic disciplines, the two professions often regarded each other with deep-seated mistrust or even hostility. Treatment program administrators often found justice-mandated clients to be more troublesome than their walk-in patients, and looked for ways to limit intake of court referrals. Judges were often frustrated by eligibility criteria they did not understand or a tendency to discharge from treatment those who committed minor infractions, such as showing up late for appointments. The information flow between treatment programs and supervising agencies often was and still is exceedingly slow. In an account of relations between New York treatment and criminal justice that could be applied to many cities, a Vera Institute of Justice publication stated:

> communication between the mandating agent and treatment staff about the status of a criminal justice client was nearly always informal and often unreliable. Treatment providers hid relapse, because they viewed criminal justice agents as adversaries who would respond inflexibly. Weeks might pass before a probation or parole officer would learn that someone had dropped out or been expelled from treatment.
>
> (Trone and Young 1996: 15)

Judicial responses to treatment failures often did little to overcome perceptions that courts do not understand the needs of treatment programs or their patients. Large probation caseloads and crowded court dockets often result in an "all or nothing" approach to drug relapse. On the one hand, systems are often so swamped that nothing happens except in high-profile cases. Even if violations get to court, they can be dropped for any number of reasons – shoddy record keeping, no one present to resolve factual discrepancies between the offender and the program, an 11th-hour re-enrollment in another treatment program, etc. Judges may believe that the only option for holding someone accountable for a violation is the ultimate punishment – revocation of probation. Some may resist this option as too harsh and give the drug offender "one more chance." Other judges may take a different approach, revoking probation at the first violation. Inconsistent responses to identical behavior undermine the integrity of the justice system, reinforce the perceptions of treatment professionals that judges do not understand the recovery process, and, perhaps worst of all, teach drug offenders that they are not responsible for their behavior.

This historic tension between the treatment and the criminal justice communities has been an obstacle to the formulation of policies that could enhance the effectiveness of both systems. Only recently, with the advent of drug treatment courts, have we begun to see a concerted effort to work together to advance the goals of both disciplines.

The mistaken belief that "nothing works" in rehabilitation programs

For about two decades beginning in the mid-1970s, prison-based or correctional drug treatment programs were given very low funding priority based on the widespread popular belief that "nothing works" in the field of rehabilitation. This anti-rehabilitation view was not only in keeping with the prevailing correctional philosophy of the day, but seemed to be supported by empirical research. A review of 30 years of rehabilitative efforts for criminal offenders, published in 1975, came to the conclusion that "the field of corrections has not as yet found satisfactory ways to reduce recidivism by significant amounts" (Lipton *et al.* 1975: 627). A summary of this scholarly review of treatment studies stated that "with few and isolated exceptions, rehabilitative efforts that have been reported so far have no appreciable effect on recidivism" (ibid.: 25).

Further research eventually began to show that rehabilitative programs do indeed work.[27] Even the original study left open the possibility that treatment programs could attain rehabilitative goals. The authors of the original study eventually revised their conclusions, distancing themselves from the "nothing works" sound bite that emerged from their earlier work. Yet many accepted as fact the notion that recidivism cannot be reduced, embracing instead the idea of selective incapacitation as the only effective criminal justice strategy for enhancing public safety. Lacking an underlying belief in the value of treatment, it is perhaps not surprising that little thought was given to the question of how drug testing might best be used to keep people engaged in the treatment process.

The myth that drug testing is useless without treatment

By the mid-1980s the District of Columbia Pretrial Services Agency had established routine and comprehensive drug testing of all arrestees – a program that continues to this day and is still the only big-city program doing universal drug testing as part of the intake process. The pre-arraignment drug testing is used as a quick risk-screening mechanism to determine drug use. For those testing positive, the Agency recommends conditions of release (generally ongoing testing and referral to treatment) designed to reduce the risk posed by the release of drug abusers to the community.[28]

As the first jurisdiction to implement such a broad testing program, it attracted considerable national attention, especially with the onset of the crack cocaine epidemic. A frequently voiced concern was the idea that drug testing was pointless without treatment. Why identify drug users, the argument went, if we know there are long waiting lines for scarce treatment slots?

There are a number of practical considerations that refute this argument. First, judges must make a release decision in any event, and the better the background information available on the defendant, the more informed will be the decision. Second, without comprehensive criminal justice drug testing, how will communities ever determine how many treatment slots are really needed? Third and even more significant, long-term experience with drug testing in the District of Columbia has demonstrated that testing is an effective way to allocate scarce treatment resources, since some individuals can abstain from drugs simply with regular testing and the certainty of quick, short sanctions for drug use. It is a myth that testing without enough treatment is a waste of time.

It is precisely because good treatment programs are in short supply that communities should implement widespread criminal justice testing programs, *as long as the testing can be enforced with immediate sanctions*. In 1994 the District of Columbia, through the DC Pretrial Services Agency, established a drug court demonstration project with an outside independent evaluation using an experimental design (Harrell *et al.* 2000). One of the three randomly assigned tracks of the demonstration project incorporated graduated sanctions. Treatment was available, but not required. The sanctions escalated as follows: first sanction – three days of courtroom observation; second sanction – three days in jail; third sanction – seven days in a residential drug detoxification program; and fourth sanction – seven days in jail. The program was structured in such a way that participants could be sanctioned within one day of a positive drug test result or missed appointment.

By tracking the test results and the sanctions of defendants who tested positive at arraignment, the following picture emerged. Of 100 defendants testing positive immediately after arrest and ordered into twice-weekly testing, 18 never tested positive again. The remainder (82) continued to be tested, but of those only 51 needed to be sanctioned. At each subsequent level, fewer defendants were using drugs and fewer needed to be sanctioned.[29] For some, the continuing pressure of testing and sanctions prompted them to seek treatment. Others evidently could not control their drug use, despite the pressure of testing and sanctions. In a sense, these more difficult drug users "selected themselves" for more criminal justice scrutiny. In other words, in an environment where the prevalence of drug use far outstrips available treatment resources, drug testing serves a triage function, quickly sorting out those who really need whatever treatment and supervision resources are available. Scarcity of treatment, rather than being an excuse *not* to implement testing, is one of the best reasons *for* testing.

The myth that coerced treatment does not work

Despite the growing evidence that coerced treatment is effective in keeping drug users in treatment longer, thus producing better outcomes, and despite the experience of drug courts, skepticism continues among treatment and criminal justice professionals alike. There is an enduring belief that addicts must voluntarily enter treatment. They must come to terms with their own need for treatment. They must get beyond the denial stage before they can hope to benefit from treatment. If they are only in treatment because a judge or a probation officer ordered it they will not be in the proper frame of mind to begin the recovery process.

This mindset affects the way all parts of the treatment and criminal justice systems interact with the drug offender. Some judges are reluctant to set a testing condition absent treatment, fearing that to do so simply sets the defendant up for failure. Treatment providers sometimes look for ways to reject court referrals on the grounds that they are not "amenable" to treatment. Supervising authorities (probation or parole officers) may be more interested in finding reasons to ask for warrants (thus trimming their caseloads) than in using their powers and their imaginations to pressure offenders into treatment participation.

The one exception to this widely held myth appears to be in drug courts. In the drug court judges, prosecutors, treatment specialists, and offenders see on a daily basis the important role of the court in creating incentives to remain in treatment. These incentives are created through frequent testing, frequent judicial reviews of progress, acknowledgment of progress through courtroom ceremonies, and swift, certain, and measured consequences for missteps on the long road to recovery. The best drug courts use clear and unambiguous contracts between the court and the drug user. These contracts are enforced through consistent and predictable responses to violations. In this way, drug court participants begin to learn that it is their own behavior, rather than – say – the judge's mood, that determines the outcome of the process.

While successful drug courts have long since dispelled the myth that coerced treatment does not work, it is worth remembering that drug courts handle only a tiny fraction of drug-involved individuals flowing through the criminal justice system every day. Outside of the drug court, the myths and the counterproductive practices live on.

The inability to fashion meaningful, short-term sanctions

Many jurisdictions find it difficult to develop the kinds of "smart punishments" necessary to change drug-using behaviors. A frequently heard reason for maintaining the status quo is that the jail is too crowded to support additional sanctioning capacity. The point has some validity. The long-term objective is to use scarce jail cells more intelligently. If supervision of probationers were more effective – that is, if the system could respond effectively with short sanctions at the first signs of relapse – *some* of the revocations would not be necessary. It is entirely conceivable that a fully developed system of community corrections with the ability to deliver immediate and brief punishments would ease the pressure on jails and prisons. The dilemma is finding the additional resources in the short run needed to change the system and the drug offenders' perception of the system for the long run.

Another reason for inaction is the fact that judges are already stretched to the limit. Most simply do not have the time to conduct hearings on each of the thousands of "technical violations" for positive drug tests. As with jail capacity, the demands on scarce judicial resources would be greatest during the early phases of implementation. Eventually, after the legal challenges had worked their way through to resolution and the system of contracts and consequences became the norm, there would undoubtedly be fewer challenges and less need for judicial involvement. Again, the dilemma is getting started.

Recognizing the practical and logistical difficulties in getting violations before a judge in a timely fashion, some supervision agencies have attempted to fashion a series of administrative sanctions to be used prior to invoking judicial sanctions. Though promising in theory, most leave much to be desired in practice. Virtually all supervision agencies have their own resource limitations, and tend to develop "sanctions" more with an eye on what they can do than on how the punishment affects the probationer. For example, one state probation and parole agency developed the following schedule of sanctions for positive drug tests: first infraction – reprimand; second infraction – another reprimand by a supervisor; third infraction – twice-weekly reporting to sign a log book; fourth infraction – administrative review to extend sign-in log and/or review for treatment; fifth infraction – request warrant.[30] While some of these activities may be useful for managing the case, they are sanctions in name only.

Public funding processes do not favor major new investments in criminal justice

The case for major public investment in community supervision of drug offenders is strong. As discussed earlier, spending public funds to reduce drug consumption is estimated to yield future savings at a rate of seven times the cost of the treatment (Gerstein *et al.* 1994). As a crime control strategy, spending funds to reduce drug consumption through treatment rather than incarceration would reduce serious crimes 15 times more effectively (Caulkins *et al.* 1997). Comprehensive drug testing, backed up with immediate sanctions for violations, provides the pressure to optimize treatment outcomes.

One reason it is difficult to implement a "good government" public policy such as the one proposed here is the magnitude of the initial investment and the way in which legislative bodies manage the appropriations process. Budgeting in most states is done annually. The initial investment required to implement such a strategy is significant. The "return on investment" will not be realized for a number of years, and even then only if there is continuity of strong leadership. Ironically, because of the high and relatively fixed costs of maintaining prison systems many states are severely limited in their ability to fund new initiatives. Compounding many legislators' skepticism about correctional programs is the fact that they simply don't have the money to make the kind of investment that would be needed to produce significant benefits. Strong political leadership will be required at the gubernatorial level. However, more than a few state governors have come to rue the day they embraced the need for better offender supervision programs. It only takes one heinous crime for political leaders to become defined by their opponents as "soft on crime."

The investment required is substantial. Although the per-test cost of urinalysis has continued to fall, the cost of implementing a high-quality, legally sufficient program of comprehensive drug testing is significant. Program integrity is a prerequisite. Once drug abusers begin to feel true pressure to provide "clean" tests, they become much more creative in probing for holes in the system. Without a high level of quality control, without numerous built-in protections, it is inevitable that some will find ways to corrupt the system. When these attempts come to light, as they generally do, program integrity is undermined, doubts are raised, and the legal system finds it almost impossible to enforce its orders. Agencies often try to conduct drug testing "on the cheap," with low-paid, poorly trained urine collectors, and without iron-clad chain-of-custody procedures or proper laboratory protocols. Poorly designed programs of drug testing create more problems than they solve. Drug users know immediately if a testing program is serious. If it is not, the denial that goes with addiction is reinforced.

Setting up a high-quality testing program with quick turnaround on results is only the beginning. Equally important is the sanctioning capacity. While there are effective sanctions that do not involve incarceration,[31] these sanctions work best as initial consequences. If drug users continue to use drugs or do not show up for their testing appointments there must be a mechanism in place to escalate the response to short stints in jail. This often requires a combination of system-wide commitment to the process, judicial time, and jail beds – resources that tend to be in short supply.

Drug users always test the limits of any program. Thus, at the beginning it is likely that most would violate the terms of their release and would require a sanction. However, to the extent that a system could actually back up its expectations with quick and predictable and real sanctions, the need for sanctioning capacity would eventually decline, as was demonstrated by the evaluation of the DC Drug Court Demonstration Project.[32] It is because so many systems operate without any meaningful or immediate consequences that so many drug offenders continue to use drugs in violation of explicit court orders.

Conclusion

Substance abuse and drug-related crime continue to be significant factors that rob communities of their security and their resources. Many of the popular strategies for combating drug use and lowering crime rates have been ill conceived, politically driven, and either ineffective or downright counterproductive.

The most promising strategy for achieving significant reductions in crime is to focus specifically on those individuals who are consuming drugs at a high rate. Conveniently, most of these high-rate drug users are already under criminal justice control and, at least in theory, subject to supervision. We now know that reductions in the rate of drug consumption translate directly into reductions in criminal behavior. We have considerable experience in the application of criminal justice leverage to create the environment of accountability necessary to overcome an addict's denial and encourage engagement in the long process of recovery. Effective leverage is best achieved through frequent drug testing, immediate sanctions, and availability of drug treatment. So far, this approach is seen only on a small scale, primarily in drug treatment courts. The challenge is to apply what works in specialized programs to the entire system of criminal justice supervision, from pretrial release to the completion of the sentence.

There are many obstacles to implementing such a strategy. Myths associated with drug testing and treatment will have to be overcome. Political vision and leadership will be required. Community corrections and treatment professionals must be willing to embrace performance management goals related to reductions in recidivism and to be held accountable for the achievement of those goals. Ultimately, adopting such a strategy will require a major shift in the allocation of correctional resources, with much greater funding for monitoring and assisting those already in our communities. The initial investment will be high, but the eventual return on investment is enormous.

Notes

1   According to the US General Accounting Office (2002), the number of drug court programs has more than tripled since 1997, to almost 800 in 2001.

2 For a succinct description of the pros and cons of different drug testing methodologies, see Robinson and Jones (2000).

3 For example, data from the District of Columbia collected as of November 1997 on probation violations showed that only 29 percent of the infractions reported to the court were handled within 60 days; 71 percent were either never reviewed by the sentencing judge, or were handled more than 60 days after the violation (Taxman and Kubu 1999).

4 For a carefully documented history of the origins of American drug control policy, see Musto 1987.

5 For an overview of the scientific literature on the relationships among drug use, drug selling, criminal activity and predatory criminality, see Chaiken and Chaiken 1990.

6 Every annual report of the Drug Use Forecasting System and the Arrestee Drug Abuse Monitoring Program (ADAM) has documented the pervasive extent of drug use among arrestees. The most recent report notes that in half of the 35 ADAM sites urinalysis indicated that 64 percent or more of adult male arrestees used at least one of five tested drugs (National Institute of Justice 2003).

7 California implemented the Civil Addict Program in 1961 as a compulsory drug treatment program for narcotics-dependent criminal offenders who were committed under court order. It was a highly structured program with strong justice system linkages. Douglas Anglin and W. H. McGlothlin have published numerous papers based on longitudinal studies of addicts in the program and comparable addicts eligible for the program but who did not enter, or others who were admitted but immediately discharged for reasons related to the commitment procedures. By following these groups for several decades, the research found that, although both groups had comparable levels of drug use and criminal behavior prior to the program, in the decade after the program the civil commitment group had committed fewer crimes, spent less time incarcerated, and were less likely to use drugs than those in the comparison group (McGlothlin *et al.* 1977; also see Anglin 1988).

8 The research is summarized in Nurco 1997: 47; original study published in Nurco 1981.

9 A "crime-day" is defined as a 24-hour period during which one or more crimes are committed by an individual while in the community.

10 The evaluation is summarized in Harrell *et al.* 2000. The full report can be found on the Urban Institute web site at www.urban.org.

11 For a discussion of the use of drug testing in the pretrial release process, see Carver 1991.

12 Convicted offenders do not have the same legal standing as pretrial defendants. However, pretrial release conditions requiring drug testing and treatment participation can be imposed and enforced.

13 There are confidentiality and disclosure issues presented by the Code of Federal Regulations and by various state laws. While a discussion of these issues is beyond the scope of this chapter, there are methods for sharing relevant information that are consistent with the regulations.

14 For a detailed description of the proposal and a discussion of the political context of the day, see DuPont and Wish 1992.

15 In their 1992 retrospective of that era, Dr. DuPont and Dr. Wish write that "the proposal itself was one of the factors that led to the request by the secretary of the Department of Health, Education and Welfare for the resignation of DuPont as NIDA director a few months later. The climate of the times was hostile to this proposal" (DuPont and Wish 1992: 92).

16 Anti-Drug Abuse Act of 1988, Pub. L. No. 100–690, 102 Stat. 4312 (1988).

17 The General Accounting Office reports that between fiscal years 1995 and 2000 the Department of Justice awarded 340 planning grants, 298 implementation grants for new drug court programs, and 167 enhancement grants to improve existing services (US General Accounting Office 2002).

18 Most diversion programs hold out the possibility of dismissed charges as the reward for successful completion of program requirements. As a matter of office policy, prosecutors

are understandably reluctant to offer diversion to individuals charged with serious offenses.

19 The federal law providing funding for drug courts specified that defendants admitted to drug court treatment must have no prior violent offenses. Thus were excluded some of the more troublesome defendants, who, from a public safety standpoint, should be a high priority for the most effective interventions.

20 A 1997 General Accounting Office report on the characteristics and effectiveness of drug courts concluded there was insufficient data and research to determine whether drug courts were effective in reducing recidivism and drug relapse. Among the concerns noted were the lack of comparison groups, inadequate follow-up data, short observation periods, and differences among programs in target populations and treatment services (US General Accounting Office 1997). An update of the General Accounting Office study was conducted by the National Center on Addiction and Substance Abuse a year later, which reviewed both published and unpublished evaluations. While noting the continuing methodological shortcomings of many evaluations, the review also synthesized promising findings emerging from 30 studies. (See Belenko 1998.)

21 Indeed, Justice Department survey data from 1997 indicate that fully 83.9 percent of expected releases by 1999 were involved in alcohol or drugs at the time of the offense, and 58.8 percent were using illegal drugs in the month before their offense. Data based on US Department of Justice (2000) and included in US Department of Justice (2001).

22 Drug courts transform the roles of everyone in the courtroom, establishing a collaborative (rather than an adversarial) approach aimed at inducing the addict to remain in treatment. For a thorough discussion of these unconventional roles, see Fulton Hora *et al.* 1999.

23 The Commission consisted of 28 members, including judges, prosecutors, defense attorneys, academics, court administrators, substance abuse experts, and other public- and private-sector representatives.

24 In New York City, according to the report, the average caseload is 240 probationers per officer. Given such high caseloads, which are not atypical of many large probation operations, it is not surprising that few probationers get the supervision or support consistent with their level of risk. Illustrative of this dilemma are the statistics regarding treatment referrals in New York City, which are made through a Central Placement Unit. According to the commission's report, 39 percent of those referred to treatment never went at all. Of those who did go as directed, approximately 69 percent were discharged or were otherwise non-compliant. Even when violations are detected and reported, the Probation Department estimated that it generally takes three months just to get the violation calendared, much less adjudicated. "These delays...are particularly troubling," notes the report, "in cases where offenders are supposed to be receiving supervised drug treatment, since...a swift and certain 'stick' is essential to such treatment" (New York State Commission on Drugs and the Courts 2000: n.p.).

25 The entire statement can be found at http://www.senate.gov/edwards/statements/20020612—parole.html.

26 In 1970, state and federal prisons housed approximately 200,000 individuals. By 1990 that figure had more than tripled, to 743,382. By 2001 the figure had doubled again, to 1,406,031. Needless to say, spending on prisons has absorbed an ever-greater proportion of state budgets (Harrison and Beck 2002).

27 A major study funded by the National Institute on Drug Abuse was the Treatment Outcome Prospective Study (TOPS). Published in 1983, this study compared criminal-justice-referred clients, clients under criminal justice coercion through TASC (Treatment Alternatives to Street Crimes), and voluntary treatment clients. The findings demonstrated that clients under legal coercion – that is, clients monitored and case managed by TASC programs – remained in treatment longer than persons simply referred for treatment. See Leukefeld and Tims 1988.

28 For a full description of the early implementation of this program, see Carver 1986.

29 The finding that fewer sanctions were required as the sanctions escalated was consistent throughout the study period of the program. The Urban Institute tracked 240 participants. Most (182) were sanctioned at the first level, which was three days in the jury box. At each subsequent level fewer needed to be sanctioned. The fourth-level sanction, seven days in jail, was imposed only 52 times (Harrell *et al.* 2000).

30 In actual practice, probation agents grouped multiple violations for application of the "sanction," further diluting any possible impact.

31 One highly successful sanction pioneered in the DC drug court and then adopted elsewhere is the requirement that the drug court participant spend three days in the jury box of the courtroom observing the interaction between the drug court team and the other participants. This three-day, non-jail punishment not only disrupts the defendant's daily routine (thus meeting the definition of "sanction") but has proven therapeutic as well. Observing the daily parade of drug users offering similar, usually unconvincing reasons for their relapses eventually causes the defendants in the jury box to begin to reflect on their own behavior. Some judges conduct informal wrap-up discussions at the end of the day with sanctioned defendants. This process appears to instill confidence in the drug court team and reinforce the point that one's own behavior determines the outcome.

32 See note 29.

References

Anglin, M. Douglas (1988) "The Efficacy of Civil Commitment in Treating Narcotic Addiction," in Carl G. Leukefeld and Frank M. Tims (eds.) *Compulsory Treatment of Drug Abuse: Research and Clinical Practice*, NIDA Research Monograph no. 86, Washington, D.C.: NIDA.

Ball, J. C., Shaffer, J. W., and Nurco, D. N. (1983) "The Day-to-Day Criminality of Heroin Addicts in Baltimore: A Study in the Continuity of Offense Rates," *Drug and Alcohol Dependence* 12: 119–42.

Belenko, Steven, Ph.D. (1998) "Research on Drug Courts: A Critical Review," *National Drug Court Institute Review* I(1): 10–55.

Bonczar, T. P. (1997) *Characteristics of Adults on Probation, 1995*, Washington, DC: US Department of Justice, Bureau of Justice Statistics.

Boyum, David and Kleiman, Mark A. R. (1995) "Alcohol and Other Drugs" in James Q. Wilson and Joan Petersilia (eds.) *Crime*, 303 ICS Press.

Carver, John A. (1986) *Drugs and Crime: Controlling Use and Reducing Risk Through Testing*, Washington, DC: National Institute of Justice Research in Action.

Carver, John A. "Pretrial Drug Testing: An Essential Step in Bail Reform," *BYU Journal of Public Law* 5(2): 000.

Caulkins, J. P., Rydell, C. P., Schwabe, W. and Chiesa, J. R. (1997) *Mandatory Minimum Sentences: Throwing Away the Key or the Taxpayers' Money?*, RAND publication MR-827-DPRC, Santa Monica, CA: RAND.

Center for Civic Innovation (1999) *"Broken Windows" Probation: The Next Step in Fighting Crime*, Civic Report no. 7, New York: Center for Civic Innovation at the Manhattan Institute.

Chaiken, Jan M. and Chaiken, Marcia R. (1990) "Drugs and Predatory Crime," in Michael Tonry and James Q. Wilson (eds.) *Drugs and Crime,* Chicago: University of Chicago Press.

DuPont, Robert L. and Wish, Eric D. (1992) "Operation Tripwire Revisited," Annals of the *American Academy of Political and Social Science* 521 (May): 91–111.

Fulton Hora, Hon. Peggy, Schma, Hon. William G., and Rosenthal, John T. A. (1999) "Therapeutic Jurisprudence and the Drug Court Treatment Court Movement: Revolutionizing the Criminal Justice System's Response to Drug Abuse and Crime in America," *Notre Dame Law Review* 74(2) (January): 439–538.

Gerstein, D. R., Johnson, R. A., Harwood, H. J., Fountain, D., Suter, N. and Malloy, K. (1994) *Evaluating Recovery Services: The California Drug and Alcohol Treatment Assessment (CALDATA)*, Sacramento, CA: California Department of Alcohol and Drug Programs.

Harrell, Adele, Cavanagh, Shannon, and Roman, John (2000) *Evaluation of the DC Superior Court Drug Intervention Programs*, National Institute of Justice, Research in Brief, April 2000, Washington, DC: National Institute of Justice.

Harrison, Paige M. and Beck, Allen J. (2002) *Prisoners in 2001*, Washington, DC: US Department of Justice, Bureau of Justice Statistics.

Inciardi, J.A. (1986) *The War on Drugs: Heroin, Cocaine, Crime, and Public Policy*, Palo Alto, CA: Mayfield.

Inciardi, James A., McBride, Duane C., and Rivers, James E. (1996) *Drug Control and the Courts*, Drugs Health, and Social Policy Series, Thousand Oaks, CA: Sage Publications.

Kleiman, Mark A. R. (1992) "Fight Crime, Seriously," *New York Times* op-ed, Saturday, July 25.

Kleiman, Mark A. R. (1997) "Coerced Abstinence: A Neo-Paternalistic Drug Policy Initiative," in L. A. Mead (ed.) *The New Paternalism*, Washington, DC: Brookings Institution Press.

Kleiman, Mark A. R. (2002) "Stop the Revolving Door," *Blueprint Magazine*, September 25; available online at http://www.ndol.org/ndol—ci.cfm?contentid=250880&kaid=119&subid=213.

Leshner, Alan I. (1999) "Science-based Views of Drug Addiction and Its Treatment," *Journal of the American Medical Association (JAMA)* 282 (October 13): 1,314–16.

Leukefeld, Carl G. and Tims, Frank M. (1988) *Compulsory Treatment of Drug Abuse: Research and Clinical Practice*, NIDA Research Monograph no. 86, Washington, DC: NIDA.

Lipton, Douglas, Martinson, Robert, and Wilks, Judith (1975) *The Effectiveness of Correctional Treatment* New York: Praeger.

McGlothlin, W. H., Anglin, M. D., and Wilson, B. D. (1977) *An Evaluation of the California Civil Addict Program*, NIDA Services Research Monograph Series, DHEW Publication no. ADM 78–558, Washington, DC: NIDA.

Musto, David F., M.D. (1987) *The American Disease*, 3rd edition, New York: Oxford University Press.

National Institute of Justice (2003) *2000 Arrestee Drug Abuse Monitoring: Annual Report. National Institute of Justice*, NCJ 193013, Washington, DC: National Institute of Justice.

New York State Commission on Drugs and the Courts (2000) "Confronting the Cycle of Addiction and Recidivism: A Report to Chief Judge Judith S. Kaye by the New York State Commission on Drugs and the Courts," unpublished report.

Nurco, David (1981) "The Criminality of Heroin Addicts: When Addicted and When Off Opiates," in James A. Inciardi (ed.) *The Drugs–Crime Connection*, Sage Annual Reviews of Drug and Alcohol Abuse, Vol. 5, Thousand Oaks, CA: Sage Publications.

Nurco, David N. (1997) "Narcotic Drugs and Crime: Addict Behavior While Addicted Versus Nonaddicted," in *Effective Medical Treatment of Opiate Addiction, NIH Consensus Statement Online 1997*, November 17–19.

Office of National Drug Control Policy (2001) *Drug Treatment in the Criminal Justice Population*, Drug Policy Information Clearinghouse Fact Sheet, Washington, DC: Office of National Drug Control Policy.

Petersilia, Joan (1997) "Probation in the United States," in M. Tonry (ed.) *Crime and Justice: A Review of Research*, Chicago: University of Chicago Press.

Robinson, Jerome J. and Jones, James W. (2000) *Drug Testing in a Drug Court Environment*, prepared by the Drug Court Clearinghouse and Technical Assistance Project, Washington, DC: American University.

Rydell, D. Peter and Everingham, Susan S. (1994) *Controlling Cocaine: Supply Versus Demand Programs*, Santa Monica, CA: RAND.

Solicitor General of Canada (1999) "Basic Facts About Federal Corrections," Published under the authority of the Solicitor General of Canada.

Taxman, Faye S. and Kubu, Bruce (1999) "Understanding Supervision in the District of Columbia: The Baseline Study," unpublished paper prepared for the Trustee of the Court Services and Offender Supervision Agency, College Park, MD: Bureau of Governmental Research, University of Maryland.

Trone, Jennifer and Young, Douglas (1996) *Bridging Treatment and Criminal Justice*, New York: Vera Institute of Justice.

US Department of Health and Human Services (2000) *2000 National Household Survey on Drug Use*, US Department of Health and Human Services, Substance Abuse and Mental Health Services Administration.

US Department of Justice (1997) *Defining Drug Courts: The Key Components*, Washington, DC: Drug Courts Program Office, US Department of Justice.

US Department of Justice (1999) *Substance Abuse and Treatment, State and Federal Prisoners, 1997*, Washington, DC: US Department of Justice, Bureau of Justice Statistics.

US Department of Justice (2000) *Drug Use, Testing, and Treatment in Jails*, Bureau of Justice Statistics Special Report, Washington, DC: US Department of Justice.

US Department of Justice (2000) *Survey of Inmates in State Adult Correctional Facilities, 1997*, Washington, DC: Bureau of Justice Statistics, US Department of Justice.

US Department of Justice (2001) *Trends in State Parole, 1990–2000*, Washington, DC: Bureau of Justice Statistics, US Department of Justice.

US General Accounting Office (1997) *Drug Courts; Overview of Growth, Characteristics, and Results*, Washington, DC: US General Accounting Office.

US General Accounting Office (2002) *Drug Courts: Better DOJ Data Collection and Evaluation Efforts Needed to Measure Impact of Drug Court Programs*, GAO-02–434, Washington, DC: US General Accounting Office.

White House (1989) *National Drug Control Strategy*, Washington, DC: White House.

White House (1990) *National Drug Control Strategy*, Washington, DC: White House.

9 Therapeutic addicts

Their treatment and control

Philip Bean and Andrew Ravenscroft

Background

The term 'therapeutic addict' was used in the Annual Reports of the Home Office to the United Nations. A distinction was made between non-therapeutic and therapeutic addicts; the former were said to have become addicted for non-medical reasons, the latter as a result of being prescribed addictive drugs for their medical condition, including relief of medical symptoms. Table 9.1 gives details for the years 1959 to 1970.

Table 9.1: Therapeutic and non-therapeutic addicts, 1959–70

Year	Therapeutic	Non-therapeutic	Not known	Total
1958	349	68	25	442
1959	344	98	12	454
1960	309	122	6	437
1961	293	153	18	470
1962	312	212	8	532
1963	355	270	10	635
1964	368	378	13	753
1965	344	580	3	927
1966	351	982	16	1,349
1967	313	1,385	31	1,729
1968	306	2,420	56	2,782
1969	289	2,533	59	2,881
1970	295	2,321	45	2,661

Source: Bean (1974).

The data from Table 9.1 come from the Home Office Addicts Index, which was based largely on data from all addicts, therapeutic and otherwise, who informed the Home Office of their addiction. The addicts were then were placed on a register, hence the term 'registered addict'. The Home Office and others made no claims that these were other than a self-selected group, probably unrepresentative of addicts generally.

Table 9.1 shows that up to 1964 the therapeutic addicts outnumbered the non-therapeutic addicts; in 1959 just under 76 per cent of all known addicts were therapeutic. The numbers of therapeutic addicts remained fairly constant, with the lowest in 1961 (293) and the highest in 1964 (368), giving a range of 75. In contrast, the number of non-therapeutic addicts increased alarmingly from 1964 onward: the lowest was in 1958 (68) and the highest was in 1969 (2,533), giving a range of 2,465. There are no details of any socio-demographic features of the therapeutic group. The Annual Reports said of 1959: 'detailed information about age grouping is not available, the majority of addicts are over 30 years of age' (quoted in Bean 1974: 104).

The genesis of the therapeutic addict was recognised by the Rolleston Committee in 1926 (Ministry of Health 1926). The report of this Departmental Committee, which formed the basis of the British system of drug control, listed what it called four specific events which led to addiction. It said the first and the most important was through the use of morphine or heroin in the course of medical treatment; some witnesses thought more than half of all addicts were created in this way. The second was when morphine or heroin was taken as a form of self-treatment for the relief of pain or emotional distress, usually by those whose occupation gave them access to drugs, i.e. physicians, but curiously enough not pharmacists. Third, drugs were taken as a result of the influence of others. And, finally, they were taken out of curiosity or indulgence. The first two 'events' covered the therapeutic addicts; the others covered the non-therapeutic group, although here we are concerned only with those addicted 'in the course of medical treatment' (see Bean 1974: 61–2.)

The term 'therapeutic addict' is rarely used nowadays – a recent Medline search gave no listings for the term. This is regrettable as it has considerable heuristic value. It suggests what it says: an addiction created as a result of some therapeutic endeavour through the treatment of an illness. The term was earlier used to cover those addicted to opiates, but can be expanded to include the opioids, i.e. synthetic narcotics such as pethidine, palfium, etc. No data are collected on this group, but defined in this way the numbers are probably huge. If addiction to benzodiazepines is included, then it is likely that the numbers of therapeutic addicts again greatly exceed the non-therapeutic group, and do so massively for the over-40 age group. The numbers and range of addicted drugs have also increased since Rolleston, as have the numbers and range of proprietary medicines. No data were ever collected by the Home Office on those addicted to proprietary medicines, nor is much known of them today, but again their numbers may well be large.

All general practitioners (GPs) will have some therapeutic addicts on their caseload, at a rough guess probably between 10 and 15; only a small number will be referred to specialist centres for treatment, and these are likely to be the extreme and out of control ones. The remainder will be on relatively controlled doses of drugs, nonetheless taking huge quantities, and may have been on them for years.

These modern-day 'therapeutic addicts' are not likely to differ greatly from those described by Rolleston in that they will have began taking addictive substances for much the same reasons. That they are addicted (in the classical sense of that term) may not of itself be of overriding importance as long as the drug prescribed deals successfully with the underlying disease condition. Addiction *per se* is not the problem. A person might be addicted to morphine or heroin as a terminal patient, but with the type of drugs and the amount of drugs being prescribed as entirely appropriate. It is the patient who is inappropriately prescribed, whether too much or too little – although the latter is not of concern here – who fits this definition of a therapeutic addict. Inappropriate prescribing means receiving more than is required, whether the wrong type of drugs or the wrong amount. Where prescribing is inappropriate it is often out of control.

Problems arise when the patients' behaviour becomes drug seeking and they over-report symptoms in order to obtain a larger prescription than is considered necessary. If they do so they are likely to resist all attempts at reducing their dose. Sometimes the problem is exacerbated when the symptoms of their addiction are couched in terms of their illness. Benzodiazepines are the best example of this; the drugs are prescribed for anxiety, but the withdrawal symptoms from benzodiazepines are anxiety. Accordingly, patients claim they need the drugs: without them they feel ill, therefore it was right to prescribe and continue to prescribe. They will rarely accept the alternative view, that they feel ill because of withdrawal symptoms rather than an underlying disease condition.

It is not the intention here to see the problem as single faceted, i.e. as a problem created by over-prescribing, though often this may be so. In spite of Rolleston, the aetiology of the therapeutic addict is rather more complicated and may arise from many different sources. The aim is to examine the nature of this group of patients in more detail. It is suggested that whilst the problem is complex it is useful to see it as arising out of a contradiction inherent in medical practice. This is exemplified by Brendtsen *et al.*, who talk of a breakdown in the 'therapeutic alliance' so that the doctor–patient relationship becomes increasingly strained. The oft-suggested solution is to exercise controls over patient and physician, so that prescribing is more under the physician's control (Brendtsen *et al.* 1999: 90). Clearly this is important, but, as will be shown below, it is difficult to achieve, and to talk solely of controlling the patient or physician is an oversimplification of a difficult task.

A description of some therapeutic addicts

It is suggested that the types of patients listed below represent many to be found on almost all GPs' lists. They are composites, approximating more to a set of ideal types but likely to be recognised by many physicians as corresponding to many of those patients now called 'therapeutic addicts'. All are being inappropriately prescribed, as are those whose case histories are provided later. Of course, there can be no agreed definition as to what constitutes 'appropriate' prescribing; the decision to prescribe must be a clinical one which defies scientific information, or, as Turk says, it is based on 'idiosyncratic philosophical beliefs created by prior education...and cultural norms interacting with regulatory pressures' (Turk 1996: 218)

First, probably the most common type of therapeutic addict would be the classic benzodiazepine patient who seeks medical assistance because of personal problems, perhaps because he or she is unable to sleep or feels depressed. From relatively small amounts of benzodiazepines, the patient is soon taking large amounts and being sustained on repeat prescriptions. Thus the typical therapeutic addict is produced. There was never any disease condition in the first place, unless one calls being unable to sleep a disease, yet prescriptions were provided, and like it or not the patient then finishes up with an addiction. This is also a classic case of an iatrogenic condition.

Second, there is the patient suffering from an illness, perhaps arthritis, or with a severe back problem, or someone who recently had major surgery. It might be an elderly lady or a man in middle age, or indeed anyone with an acute condition. The first point of contact could be the GP, but equally it could be a hospital consultant, and the first prescription is likely to be a painkiller. The natural history of the condition would then be as follows: the patient takes the prescribed drugs; they offer some relief (whether this is a placebo effect or not does not matter) and the patient asks for a repeat prescription. This is given as a matter of course, as are other repeat prescriptions. However, other problems appear. The patient then says he or she is unhappy and unable to sleep. The solution: the patient is prescribed another substance, perhaps amitriptyline or something similar. Inevitably, tolerance develops, as do withdrawal symptoms when the drugs are reduced or not available. However, the patient still remains in pain; the arthritis or back pain has not gone away in spite of the physician's prescribing, and soon it becomes impossible to determine which is which – i.e. is the increase in pain the result of the physical condition or the result of withdrawal of the drug? And what should the doctor do about it? So, from small beginnings, medically speaking, the patient has turned into someone with a serious addiction. Moreover, there is no certainty that the pain from the arthritis or whatever has been or will be reduced.

Another type of patient seeks medical help after an accident, often an industrial accident, but it could as easily be an accident in the home or in the car. These patients are usually male, in middle age, have worked hard all their lives and never or rarely had to call on the health services. Typically he – it is usually a male – has hitherto led a blameless hard working life, but is now at a point in life where he cannot easily find another job. To make matters worse, the accident may not have been his fault. Yet he is in considerable discomfort, often in pain. The physician responds immediately with the typical resounding comment of 'we'll soon have you back on your feet, old chap', for this patient is a worthy cause. The physician probably prescribes palfium and morphine. However, the patient finds the amount prescribed is not enough; he is still in pain and the prescription is increased. Very soon the patient is taking large quantities, perhaps 800 mg of morphine per day and up to 15 doses per day at 5 mg of palfium per hour. There is another problem: the pain has not gone away. The patient continues to demand more to get rid of the pain. And then another problem arises which has only just come to light – the drugs had a euphoric effect which the patient may have enjoyed initially, which did little for pain relief but was pleasant nonetheless. As so often happens, it then becomes impossible to determine whether the patient is taking the medication for the relief of pain or because of the euphoric effect of the drugs. And how to tell the difference?

The other problem for the physician is that this patient, once defined as wholly worthy and therefore a good patient, has now turned into an addict, making increasing demands on the physician so that treating him becomes a burden. Prescribing is now out of control. The patient is now a demanding patient resisting all attempts to reduce the dose. In fact he is behaving like other 'junkies': he is demanding more and more of the drug of his choice. The relationship with the physician becomes increasingly difficult, with the patient and physician blaming each other.

Fourth, there is the patient whose medical condition is his or her life's work. These patients regard a meeting with their physician as of supreme importance, particularly if they can get the physician to recognise their complaint. Their condition may not be easy to diagnose – one patient claimed a physician had said he had been born with a defect, but currently no one has been able to identify the nature of that deformity – but their complaints are continuous, most saying they are in constant pain. These patients are time-consuming for the health services and costly too. If discharged by one specialist they will instantly find another. They will also be taking huge quantities of drugs. They will be taking painkillers to relieve the pain – sometimes but not always it will be back pain – and because they are unhappy will invariably be taking antidepressants. They don't sleep, so they will take sleeping pills, and so it goes on. But all the time they will be seeking meetings with one or more physicians explaining and complaining about their physical ailments. Every GP practice has a small number of such patients, probably addicted to one – perhaps more than one – prescribed drug. Their life's work is to seek and obtain medical attention.

Fifth, there is the patient who began by taking proprietary medicines such as Gees linctus or Nightnurse, purchased through the local chemist, or indeed any other drug with an opiate base. This patient is almost certainly someone with an obsession about health and eager to purchase proprietary medicines whenever there is a hint of illness. The medicine cupboard at home is likely to be filled with boxes of pills and potions which all convey the same message about the paramount importance of health to the patient and to members of the family. As these proprietary medicines contain opiate derivatives, albeit in small quantities, taking them over a long period produces the same addiction as to other opiates. Local chemists may identify this patient as an 'addict' and refuse to sell these proprietary drugs. The patient will then try to seek alternative chemists, sometimes having to travel long distances to obtain supplies.

Finally, there is the predatory dealer who may be a persistent user but has learned to take advantage of the lax prescribing found elsewhere. This is a different sort of therapeutic addict, less addicted herself but entrepreneurial enough to take advantage of the weakness of prescribing for others. She – it is invariably a woman – has found how easy it is to get her physician to increase the number of tablets on her prescription, valium usually, and finds she has tablets to spare – what in the 1960s was called 'spillage', i.e. surplus from the prescription sold to other users. She also knows there is a market for these, particularly amongst the street junkies. She knows too that other patients have similar surpluses. She finds it easy to act as a local entrepreneur organising buying and selling of the surpluses. She requires repeat prescriptions for her own habit but, more importantly, encourages other patients living nearby to receive repeat prescriptions to maintain her illicit business. She may use the profits to buy illicit drugs such as cocaine. In a study of drug taking in Nottingham (Bean and Pearson 1992) we found just such an example. A woman on a housing estate sent her 15-year-old daughter each Thursday evening to buy surplus valium from other residents. She would buy about 500 each week at £1 per tablet and sell them to the illicit market for £2 per tablet. She was a regular user of valium and had been for the last decade. Her position supported the oft-quoted comment that 'the largest pusher of drugs in Britain is the National Health Service' (NHS), which may be an overstatement but contains a germ of truth.

There is no suggestion, of course, that these composite case histories provide anything more than vignettes, nor any suggestion that they provide a typology of therapeutic addicts. For example, there may be patients who having had an industrial accident also receive benzodiazepines after telling their GP they are unhappy, or not able to sleep, and the patient taking proprietary medicines might supplement purchases with prescriptions from the GP or other physician. Other variations might occur; so, instead of being prescribed palfium, the patient is prescribed pethidine or morphine – this would change the nature of the problem. The aim here is to provide something of a flavour of this type of patient.

Pain relief and the nature of pain

The first case history presented below raises questions about the nature of pain.

There are many psychological physiological and pharmacological factors which can create difficulties when managing pain. It is clear that pain is a subjective experience and there are no tests that can prove, disprove or measure it. Personal factors, cultural, ethnic and linguistic patterns influence both how the pain is expressed and how it is interpreted. When two patients seek treatment and both say they are in severe pain it is impossible

> A woman aged 50 has a medullary sponge kidney which leads to the formation of multiple stones and episodes of renal colic. She was seen by an urologist, who suggested she be prescribed pain relief when she gets colic. The patient, however, says she is in pain all the time. The GP prescribed pethidine, and soon the patient was taking huge quantities, 30–40 amps and by injection. She was also taking huge amounts of valium (she said she is anxious). She has become toxic on the pethidine and 'stoned' on the valium but is still complaining of pain. The GP said he knows she is taking too much but he cannot say no to her and cannot reduce the dose. Last time he tried to reduce the dose the patient fell on the floor of his surgery and started screaming.

to decide which patient is in a more painful state than the other. The physician is almost entirely reliant on the patient history in formulating treatment strategies. Furthermore, clinicians are classically trained in the biomedical model, in which pain is believed to be due to a clearly identifiable point of tissue injury. In chronic pain this may no longer be the case. A shift must occur to a biopsychosocial model in which the complaint of pain is viewed in a more global holistic framework. For example, if the patient says the drugs thought to produce pain relief do not relieve pain, then what is the physician to do? Dispute the claim or continue to prescribe? Physicians know that prescribing pethidine will not completely alleviate a patient's, pain but at best it will reduce it to a manageable level. Should the physician continue to increase the dose of painkiller until the patient says the pain is manageable, irrespective of other consequences? It is difficult to say.

The International Association for the Study of Pain (IASP) defines pain as 'an unpleasant sensory and emotional experience associated with actual or potential tissue damage or described in terms of such damage' (Merskey and Bogduk 1994: 209). From the above definition, pain can be seen to have both a physiological component and an emotional (psychological) one. Pain is therefore a sensation and a reaction to that sensation, both of which contribute to the suffering of the individual. In some patients there may be an exaggerated emotional component to pain, sometimes termed psychological overlay, and this may affect both their pain tolerance and how they respond to painkillers. Other patients may exhibit somatisation, a personality trait characterised by psychological distress manifesting itself as unexplained medical symptoms, including pain. These hypochondriachal patients may go from one hospital clinic to another complaining of pain for which no cause can be found and are likely to end up in the pain clinic.

Further problems arise when we consider that pain can be classified into different types depending on what is thought to be the underlying cause. For example, pain may be described as nociceptive (e.g. cancer, postoperative fractured bone) when the nervous system is deemed to be intact and sensory nerve fibres are responding to chemical, thermal or mechanical tissue damage appropriately. This type of pain is likely to respond to opiate medications. On the other hand, in neuropathic pain syndromes (neuralgias) pain is not caused by tissue damage but by aberrant processing in a dysfunctional/damaged nervous system. Neuropathic pain often fails to respond to opiate drugs even at high doses, and neuropathic pain is often difficult to distinguish from opiate-responsive nociceptive pain. Given this, we can see how a patient may receive rapidly escalating doses of opiates based on a misdiagnosis.

Accordingly, in the absence of any reliable objective severity scale, assessment and treatment will always be difficult. Sometimes it is no more than trial and error, described by one physician as 'suck it and see' (McQuay 2001: 1,134). A physician, however, probably a GP, is exposed to the obvious contradiction that on the one hand pain relief is, if not an absolute, then a key rationale of medical practice, and on the other it is one of the areas of medicine where knowledge is sparse. As McQuay says, 'There is no evidence base on which we can rely other than common sense, experience and that of others. Patients wishes are simple but hard to fulfil', and he asks what he calls 'the common clinical question', which is 'What is an adequate dose?' (2001: 1,135). As one GP said, the aim is to establish a decent prescribing regime, but what that should be remains a mystery.

In the case histories listed above the prescriptions for pain relief did not always make the pain go away. The patient with renal colic said she was in severe pain, and of course renal colic is a painful condition. However, she said she was in pain all the time. Clearly for the physician the obvious solution is to secure pain relief, and given the severity of that condition the solution is to prescribe a drug likely to produce the required effect. In this case there was probably little dispute that a drug capable of relieving severe pain was needed. At one level, relief of pain must be a basic *sine qua non* of medical practice, and faced with demands for this type of pain relief few physicians would resist them. Yet for the less severe conditions, what then?

How much relief should we expect? And should we always be entitled to pain relief all the time? More importantly, is pain relief an absolute, i.e. to be given preference over all else in medicine? As far as this patient was concerned she clearly thought that was her entitlement. (We recently heard of a case where a heroin addict receiving 500 mg of heroin daily fell over and hurt his shoulder. He complained of pain and his GP gave a small prescription of five tabs of dihydrocodeine for pain relief. As a direct measure of pain relief, rather than as a placebo, this will do little good; the patient's opiate receptors are already blocked. Nonetheless, it shows that the demand for pain relief is not easily resisted.)

Management and control

Whereas the first case history raised questions about the nature of pain, the second raises questions about the nature of control, whether of patient or physician.

To some extent, the problem of management is reflected in both case histories, as of course is the problem of pain, for in the first the woman aged 50 with a medullary sponge kidney threatened to disrupt the surgery. This may not be an everyday occurrence but it is perhaps not wholly uncommon. In the first case history the patient has been able to assert a measure of control over future prescribing through threats about being disruptive in the surgery. In the second the physician had almost given up, and the patient has resisted all attempts at controlling the prescribing.

Regaining control is likely to be difficult as key points on the care pathway have been missed, i.e. that escalating doses in the absence of disease progression are, or should have been, a red flag in the management of chronic non-malignant pain (McQuay 2001: 1,134). The second case history shows how the patient was able to secure drugs on demand. This 28-year-old patient with Crohn's disease has already developed the traditional 'junkie' mentality, which expects to receive the drug of choice on demand. In that qualitative sense she is no different from the traditional street 'junkie'. Something has clearly gone wrong in the patient's management and control, for the patient has been able to assert her control over the GP. It is likely that two key indicators were missed: first, there was a failure to recognise that many of the drugs producing pain relief are also pleasant to take – they give the patient a 'buzz'; and, second, the patient's potential for aberrant drug-related behaviours was ignored.

> A woman aged 28 years had an ileostomy because of Crohn's disease. She claimed to have pain. She was prescribed morphine. The patient was resistant to any attempt to modify and control the amount of morphine being prescribed, and the GP referred the patient to a consultant for advice on management and control. The GP was advised to reduce prescribing and gain control of the patient. The latest report from the GP was that the patient was receiving the same amounts and type of drugs as before and in fact was virtually receiving morphine on demand.

In the first, the initial reactions to a drug such as heroin is to produce the 'honeymoon high', that euphoric and soporific phase which occurs only in the first stages of drug use and can never be repeated. Not everyone taking opiates or synthetic opiates experiences anything as sensational as this, but many might experience something approximating to it. Where patients seek pain relief alongside forms of psychological assistance, drugs such as pethidine, palfium, or dihydrocodeine will help should they provide that all-important 'buzz'.

In the second case history there were warning signs which suggested prescribing was almost out of control. Portenoy has identified a number of behaviours which are regarded as predictive of aberrant drug-related behaviour (Portenoy 1996: 209). These include multiple episodes of prescription 'loss', repeatedly seeking prescriptions from other clinicians or from emergency rooms without informing the prescriber, and repeated resistance to changes in therapy despite clear evidence of adverse physical or psychological effects from the drug. Less predictive are those which involve aggressively complaining about the need for more drugs, drug hoarding, and occasional non-compliance with therapy. In this case the major problem was a resistance to any form of prescribing control which might lead to a reduction in the amounts of morphine prescribed, or, in Portenoy's terms, 'repeated resistance to changes in therapy despite clear evidence of adverse physical or psychological effects from the drug' (1996: 209).

It is possible, of course, that patients with chronic non-malignant pain are able to achieve sustained pain relief from opioid drugs without substantial toxicity, functional deterioration or the development of aberrant drug-related behaviours (Portenoy 1996: 206). The examples given here are different; they are of patients who have not found relief, have developed drug-related behaviour and consequently are a problem to their physicians, themselves and presumably numerous others with whom they are in contact. It is this group who require additional attention – alongside, of course, their physicians, who must continue to treat them.

Conflicts and dilemmas

There is little data on the prescribing practices of physicians in respect of this group – as opposed to, say, the total number of prescriptions provided and the types of drugs being prescribed. (These can be obtained from the Annual Reports of the Prescription Pricing Authority.) Nor are there any longitudinal studies on the effects of opioid prescribing or similar prescribing for therapeutic addicts (Savage 1996). There is, however, an increasing debate on some of the issues. Recently there has been renewed interest in the prescribing of opioids for non-malignant pain (McQuay 2001), but this subject remains a minority interest.

Unfortunately, political questions often cloud the discussion; mostly these relate to the prescribing of opiates and their use in pain control. These matters are particularly relevant to physicians in the USA. Clarke and Sees (1993) point out that the 'War on Drugs' has made it additionally important that American physicians who prescribe opioids for the purpose of pain control must recognise that legal issues are an important part of the prescription process. In Britain there are no *additional* restrictions imposed on physicians if they wish to prescribe opiates or opioids for pain relief. There are additional restrictions involved in prescribing selected drugs such as diamorphine for non-therapeutic reasons.

A feature of the existing literature centres on the two aspects highlighted above, i.e. pain relief and the management and control of the patient and physician. Brendtsen *et al.* examine the major dilemmas confronting the physician and say: 'Faced with the risk of prescription abuse and the need for adequate pain treatment the physicians are faced with conflicting interests' (1999: 90). In their study of 86 physicians in Sweden, Brendtsen *et al.* found that the suggestions offered to resolve those conflicts fell into three main groups:

- There should be unified management plans with precise conditions, clarified prescription responsibility, and improved communication between hospital and primary care. For example, 'all doctors should try to have the same policy to stop patients getting supplies from another doctor'.
- Sufficient consulting time should be made available. The implication here is that doctors who are rushed fail to provide an adequate service.
- There should be increased education in pain management, with improved pharmacological knowledge.

Brendtsen *et al.* 1999: 93)

Brendtsen *et al.* imply that the dilemmas, such as they are, can be found in the physician's moral world. Relief of pain – sometimes including 'emotional pain' – is the driving force behind many initial consultations. Physicians are rarely able to resist demands to relieve pain – that, after all, was a major reason for entering medicine – and faced with constant demands for pain relief may find those demands particularly difficult to refuse. The problem soon becomes apparent when the physician is turned into an addiction-treating physician. The treatment model, or the model required to treat pain, is not the same as that required to treat addiction: the first is permissive; the second is restrictive. The permissive model involves prescribing according to the agreement of the patient, tacit or otherwise. The restrictive model means acting against the wishes of the patient by reducing the use of the addictive substance in order to reduce harm. Managing a restrictive model does not fit easily into most physicians' practice, and nor does saying no when the patient demands ever-increasing amounts.

Yet the choice of drug and the manner in which it is to be used (e.g. dose and duration of therapy) are factors under the control of the prescriber (Rochon and Gurwitz 1995). Rochon and Gurwitz emphasise the importance of sticking to a patient regime in therapeutic decision-making, which has to be established through a partnership between physician and patient. But what happens if this goes wrong? Presumably, it remains the responsibility of the physician to put it right. Critics such as Friedman (1990) say that many health care professionals do not understand what addiction really is. The less critical would say it is understandable that the physicians may not deal with matters and let things slide. It is easier to avoid dealing with the inevitable awkward confrontations. Perhaps, too, it was not recognised that the drugs themselves, whether pethidine, morphine, dihydrocodeine (or DF118), etc., produce their own pleasant euphoric effects over and above any pain relief they offer. Nor may the fear of addiction be as ever-present as it should be.

In part, the solution must lie in the control of physician and patient – that is, both have to be subject to control. Control of the physician can operate at two levels. The most obvious is to help obtain agreement with the patient to reduce prescribing to acceptable levels. It may also be necessary to find ways to support the physician in 'how to say no' if the patient will not co-operate, whilst at the same time preserving the integrity of the doctor–patient relationship. Control at this level means getting the patient involved through the usual motivational techniques. Where prescribing is out of control, it can easily lead to what Brendtsen *et al.* have called a resulting loss of self-esteem, which includes recognising that there has been a failure in the doctor-patient relationship (1999: 95).

The second level of control involves the patient more directly. It means referring the patient to a colleague, perhaps someone specialising in the treatment of addiction, but taking away responsibility for prescribing from the GP. The physician taking on the referral should not expect to find the process an easy one, and is likely to be met with a hostile comment questioning why a referral was necessary – 'I am not an addict. I am a cancer patient. I do not commit crime. I do not rob' – this being the standard opening response when patients are confronted with their addiction. They do not see themselves as addicts, and to some extent they are correct in the sense that they rarely have an otherwise deviant lifestyle. Yet demanding a drug of choice and resisting all attempts to reduce the level of prescribing approximates to the typical 'junkie'.

The aim of treatment is to reduce prescribing to the point where it controls the underlying condition yet allows the patients to reassert control over their own life. Treatment involves a programme of quantity reduction not necessarily aimed at abstinence but operating under a strict regime. Physicians who have acted as referral doctors almost always say that initially various attempts are made to subvert the controls, whether by way of registering with a second GP, getting admitted to the local hospital in the hope of receiving extra supplies, or playing off the existing GP against the referral doctor. Brendtsen *et al.* (1999) describe this as drug-seeking behaviour, i.e. apparent loss of prescription or pills, strong preference for a particular drug, or physician shopping. The patient's aim is to return to the *status quo ante*; that of the physician is to impose a new regime aimed at avoiding earlier pitfalls. The other common feature is that all concerned must work in harmony. Once there are differences of approach the patient is likely to exploit them to advantage. The key is to work together but to do so in a way that does not involve the GP in matters which are likely to damage his or her future relationship with the patient.

Future research

There is little or no research conducted on this group of therapeutic addicts. The literature, such as there is, tends to concentrate on the role and position of the prescribing physician, examining matters from that standpoint. The most obvious starting point for any research programme is to determine the extent of the problem. In other words, what is needed is a straightforward epidemiological study using an established and workable definition. If our calculations are correct and each GP in Britain has about 10–15 such patients, the problem is massive and the cost equally so. Other research questions need to be asked, such as what type of referral agents are the most appropriate? Drug addiction units? Pain clinics? Or whatever. Moreover, we need to be clear about the circumstances in which a cocktail of addictive drugs should be prescribed. And, finally, what are the demands these patients make on the NHS in time resources etc.? The outcome of such research might help pave the way for a more considered approach to a problem which has remained hidden, or if not, then rarely discussed, and of which questions have rarely been asked.

References

Bean, P. T. (1974) *The Social Control of Drugs*, Oxford: Martin Robertson.

Bean, P. T. and Pearson, Y. (1992) 'Crack Cocaine in Nottingham. Report to the Home Office', mimeo.

Brendtsen, P., Hensing, G., Ebeling, C. and Schedin, A. (1999) 'What Are the Qualities of Dilemmas Experienced When Prescribing Opioids in General Practice', *Pain* 82: 89–96.

Clarke, H. W. and Sees, K. L. (1993) 'Opioids, Chronic Pain and the Law', *Journal of Pain and Symptom Management* 8(5): 297–305.

Friedman, D. P. (1990) 'Perspectives on the Medical Use of Drugs of Abuse', *Journal of Pain Symptom Management*. 5: 82–5.

McQuay, H. (1999) 'Opioids in Pain Management', *Lancet* 353 (June 26): 2,229–32.

McQuay, H. (2001) 'Opioids in Chronic Non-malignant Pain', *British Medical Journal* 322 (12 May): 1,134–5.

Merskey, H. and Bogduk, N. (eds)(1994) *Classification of Chronic Pain. Task Force on Taxonomy*, 2nd edition, Seattle: IASP Press.

Ministry of Health (1926) *Departmental Committee on Morphine and Heroin Addiction* [the Rolleston Report], London: HMSO.

Portenoy, R. K. (1996) 'Opioid Therapy for Chronic Nonmalignant Pain: A Review of the Critical Issues', *Journal of Pain Symptom Management*. 11(4) (April): 203–17.

Rochon, P. A. and Gurwitz, J. H. (1995) 'Drug Therapy', *Lancet* 346(8,966) (1 July): 32–6.

Savage, S. R. (1996) 'Long Term Opioid Therapy: Assessment of Consequences and Risks', *Journal of Pain Symptom Management*. 11(5) (May): 274–86.

Turk, D. C. (1996) 'Clinicians Attitudes about Prolonged Use of Opioids and the Issue of Patient Heterogeneity', *Journal of Pain Symptom Management* 11(4): 218–230.

10 Therapeutic community drug treatment in the US criminal justice system[1]

Tammy L. Anderson and Lana Harrison

Introduction

The considerable growth of the criminal justice population in the United States due to War on Drugs policies provides an opportunity for interventions for drug offenders while they are under the jurisdiction of the criminal justice system. Take, for example, incarceration, an intervention increasingly used to address substance abuse problems in the United States. Various drug problems (e.g. illicit drug sales and drug use) are temporarily halted with imprisonment because access to drugs is seriously limited and withdrawal from drugs is often accomplished among abusers. However, release from prison often features a return to drug use and the criminal lifestyles that accompany it. Research shows that many offenders with substance abuse problems before incarceration resume drug use and a criminal lifestyle when they are returned to the community (see Petersilia and Travis 2001 for a review). It is estimated that over 500,000 offenders were released from correctional institutions in the US in 1999 and 2000 (Travis *et al.* 2002). Programs that promote effective re-entry are, consequently, critically important for 21st-century justice policy in the United States and elsewhere. Without intervention, drug offenders may repeat the same types of behaviors that led to their incarceration. Implementing effective interventions is, therefore, critically important to the future social and economic welfare of US society.

Findings like these underscore the importance of additional interventions specific to drug offenders during the incarceration stage. At least four efforts have emerged recently to cultivate improved outcomes among drug offenders. They include arrestee drug testing, drug courts, HIV and infectious disease testing of offenders and/or inmates, and drug treatment in prison. Correctional therapeutic communities (TCs) are one of the most critical and promising of these efforts. This chapter argues that correctional-based TCs are perhaps the most effective intervention for drug offenders and are better equipped to meet the re-entry challenge than other initiatives. We begin with a justification for the TC approach, followed by an explanation of how such programs operate and why they are so successful in promoting individual outcomes and, ultimately, societal well-being.

Prevalence and nature of substance abuse problems among inmates

Perhaps the best argument for drug treatment in correctional facilities is that the criminal justice population is heavily involved in drugs and, consequently, needs a relevant intervention that will remove future motivations and behaviors that lead to continued drug use and the criminal activities required to finance it. The relationship between drug use and crime is evident at every juncture in the criminal justice system (Harrison 2001). Data in the United States show that arrests for drug abuse violations increased 57.5 percent between 1989 to nearly 1.6 million in 2001. By 1996 drug offenders comprised one-third of all persons convicted of a felony in State courts (BJS/Brown and Langan 1999). The 1984 Sentencing Reform Act resulted in the proportion of drug offenders in the Federal system increasing from 79 percent in 1988 to 92 percent in 1998. Over the same time period the proportion of all Federal defendants sentenced to prison increased from 54 percent to 71 percent (BJS/Brown and Langan 1999). Currently, more than 2 million people are incarcerated in the United States and research shows many, if not the majority, have problems with substance abuse (Belenko 1998).

While those arrested on drug charges are frequently drug abusers, a large proportion of arrestees and inmates charged and convicted of other crimes (e.g. property crime) are as well. Among the incarcerated population in 1997, over 80 percent of State and 70 percent of Federal prisoners reported past drug use (BJS/Mumola 1999). The 1997 Survey of Inmates in State and Federal Correctional Facilities found that half (52 percent) of State prison inmates and one-third (34 percent) of Federal prison inmates indicated they were under the influence of alcohol or drugs while committing the offense that led to their incarceration (BJS/Mumola 1999). The same study found that one in five (19 percent) State prisoners reported committing their offense in order to purchase drugs; 16 percent of Federal prisoners in 1997 and 16 percent of jail inmates in 1996 admitted the same (BJS/Mumola 1999). Because the criminal justice system contains a large proportion of drug abusers, it is an ideal place to organize and provide drug treatment. The criminal justice system has become the largest source of mandated drug treatment in the United States (National Institute on Drug Abuse 1992). These findings document the extent of illicit drug and alcohol abuse among the correctional population in the United States and demonstrate the need for substance abuse treatment during incarceration.

Reintegration

Research shows that drug treatment significantly reduces crime, drug use and healthcare expenses (Gerstein *et al.* 1994). A recent study estimated that for every $1 spent on treatment approximately $7 in State funds could be saved in the future (Gerstein *et al.* 1994). Corrections-based drug treatment programs like the TC foster reintegration goals by helping inmates become productive members of society who desist in drug use and criminal activity. Research in New York (Wexler *et al.* 1988), California (Wexler *et al.* 1999) and Delaware (e.g. Butzin *et al.* 2002) has consistently shown that TCs help produce outcomes congruent with reintegration. The Stay'N Out prison TC in New York was the first large-scale study of in-prison drug treatment to show reductions in recidivism (Wexler *et al.* 1988). A study of the Amity TC in California replicated the Stay'N Out findings, and showed that even more positive outcomes were produced by adding aftercare TC treatment in the community (Wexler *et al.* 1999).

The combined TC treatment and work-release programs established in Delaware may be even more valuable in helping to enhance social and economic welfare by promoting offender re-entry. Delaware employs a TC continuum of treatment, which includes 12 months of in-prison TC treatment, followed by six months of combined TC treatment and then work release and six months of aftercare. The Center for Drug and Alcohol Studies (CDAS) at the University of Delaware, under the direction of Dr. James A. Inciardi, has been conducting treatment effectiveness research with offenders since 1991. Much of the work at CDAS has found that the integrated continuum of corrections-based treatment just described significantly improves outcomes for seriously drug-involved offenders. Numerous studies on the TC continuum demonstrate considerable success, i.e. desistence from crime and abstinence from drug use, at the 12-month, 18-month, 36-month and 42-month follow-ups (Butzin *et al.* 2002; Inciardi *et al.* 2001; Butzin *et al.* 1999; Martin *et al.* 1999). Other benefits consistent with promoting economic and social welfare include significant reductions in the use of injection drugs and in the amount of income from crime, fewer returns to correctional facilities for new sentences, fewer hospital stays for drug and alcohol problems, and an increased likelihood of having health insurance when working (Inciardi *et al.* 1997).

Healthcare cost containment

Drug treatment programs in correctional settings can also assist in reducing health-related complications among offenders. The growing literature on health problems associated with drug use has revealed a disproportionate prevalence of physical and mental health problems among substance abusers, especially those under criminal justice jurisdiction (see Anderson 2003 for a review). Drug-involved inmates often report high rates of infectious disease (HIV and Hepatitis; see Hammett *et al.* 2002), asthma, poor nutrition and dental care, diabetes, hypertension, and reproductive health problems (Hammett *et al.* 2001).

Corrections-based drug treatment programs like the TC, help contain healthcare expenditures for the government by teaching inmates how to take better care of themselves mentally, emotionally, and physically. In addition, many correctional TCs include HIV and infectious disease testing and reduction awareness that assists in disease prevention, containment, and management. Because of the length of the TC program, other chronic and acute health problems common to drug-related lifestyles and the physiological-biochemical effects of drugs can be diagnosed and referred for appropriate treatment.

Social welfare dependency

Today, we know that drug offenders are disproportionately from poor families and single-headed households (e.g. Harrison 2001). Over half of State prison inmates (56 percent) indicated in the 1997 Survey of Inmates in State and Correctional Facilities they did not grow up with both parents, as did 46 percent of Federal inmates (BJS/Mumola). Among jail inmates in 1996, 43 percent lived primarily with their mother only while growing up. Nearly one-quarter (22 percent) reported that their family received welfare during childhood. About one-third of State prison and jail inmates had a parent or guardian who abused alcohol or drugs while they were growing up. The figure among Federal inmates was 20 percent. About 40 percent of State prisoners and 26 percent of Federal prisoners had not graduated from high school or finished an equivalency program. About one-third of State prison (31 percent) and jail inmates (36 percent) and one-quarter of Federal prisoners (27 percent) were not working before their arrest. Among jail inmates, almost half reported incomes of $600 or less in the month before their arrest, which amounts to an annual income of less than $7,200. About one-quarter (22 percent) received one or more kinds of financial support from government agencies in the month before arrest (BJS/Harlow 1998).

Perhaps one of the greatest insights of drug treatment is that drug abuse is a disorder of the whole person (De Leon 2001). Drug abusers oftentimes have considerable underlying problems that must be treated in order for them to terminate drug use. The TC modality adopts a holistic approach to treatment, making it especially useful for this group. Because most correctional TCs attempt to instill pro-social values and provide educational programming and work opportunities, they also help equip the drug offender to become independent after release. Research shows that drug treatment can reduce social welfare expenditures among substance abusers by helping them to remain drug and alcohol free and remove them from drug lifestyles (Gerstein et al. 1994; Belenko 1998). It increases their ability to obtain and maintain employment after release, which promotes their independence.

Active drug abusers often have difficulty meeting basic sustenance needs due to financial and social consequences of participating in drug lifestyles. Their independence suffers and they become increasingly dependent on social welfare programs. As such, many have histories of receiving financial assistance from various federally and state-funded social welfare programs for things such as housing, food, medical care, and transportation (Anderson *et al.* 2002; Hammett *et al.* 2001). Social welfare programs (e.g. Temporary Assistance to Needy Families, public housing, and food stamps) offer assistance to those with the fewest resources or the economically underprivileged. Drug abusers often fall within this group. Without effective drug treatment like that provided by the TC many drug offenders would return to communities unable to function independently without considerable help from social welfare programs.

Investment in the future generation

If drug treatment in correctional institutions can promote offender reintegration by reducing future crime and drug use and foster attachment to conventional activities (e.g. employment), it may also help produce individuals better equipped to effectively parent the next generation. In 1999 more than 1.5 million minors in the US had an incarcerated parent and many more reported having a parent incarcerated at some point in their lives (Beck 2000). Incarceration of a parent is a significant threat to an often vulnerable family unit. When fathers are incarcerated about 90 percent of their children remain in the custody of their mothers, while less than one-third remain with their fathers when their mothers are incarcerated (Beck 2000).

The incarceration of parents places children at greater risk of being neglected and of not getting their basic needs met. Numerous negative social outcomes may result, including health problems and increased illness, an increased risk of delinquency, drug use, unemployment, and lack of educational attainment due to the absence of parents to and provide a role model and guidance. Correctional TCs often feature parenting seminars in addition to other educational and therapeutic groups that teach and foster pro-parenting skills.

Therapeutic community treatment in the correctional setting

While there are several treatment modalities in use in US correctional facilities, the TC is the most often used intensive program and is most widely endorsed. Brown (1992) documented five separate types of programs available for drug abusers in correctional settings. The first is incarceration without specialized services. However, institutions like this offer no anti-drug-specific programming; they often provide some programming (e.g. educational classes, release planning, and vocational counseling) that may promote abstinence and is consistent with reintegration. They are most common in correctional settings today.

The second most commonly used program is incarceration with drug education and/or drug abuse counseling. Prison staff offer HIV educational classes and individual counseling within the daily operations and existing structure of the facility. A third type of program features incarceration with specialized services initiated or maintained by the inmates or clients themselves, such as self-help groups like Alcoholics Anonymous. A fourth program type is incarceration with specialized services for issues other than drug abuse but which are primarily provided to drug abusers. Again, educational training and vocation services comprise current examples. The fifth and final program type is incarceration with residential units dedicated to drug treatment.

History of correctional TCs

TCs entered the United States correctional arena in the late 1960s in the Federal prison system (Wexler and Love 1994). The Aesklepieon program at the Marion, Illinois, maximum-security prison was perhaps one of the first prison-based TCs in the United States. After a promising start, it was closed in the early 1970s due to management problems between staff and inmates. Other Federal correctional programs emerged during the time the Marion, Illinois, program was in operation, but they too closed because of similar problems with management and corruption. By the late 1970s prison-based TCs were pretty much extinct.

State-level correctional TCs at the time suffered the same problems as did the Federal programs. Distrust between staff and inmates and mismanagement of the program led to closures of most, with one major exception: the Stay'N Out program in New York. Founded in the late 1970s, the Stay'N Out program stayed open while other State and Federal prison TC programs were closing, because of research (Wexler et al. 1988) showing the program had positive results for inmate/participants after release. Later, similar results were found at programs such as the Cornerstone program in Oregon and the Wharton program in New Jersey (Wexler and Love 1994). The discovery of positive findings across programs like these led to the re-emergence of TCs as an effective drug-specific intervention for drug-involved inmates in the 1990s.

Since that time, the structure of the correctional TC has changed significantly in a fashion that has produced even more beneficial outcomes. Take, for example, the experience of corrections-based TCs in Delaware. The Delaware TC was established in a maximum-security prison for men in 1988. A year later, a treatment demonstration grant from the National Institute on Drug Abuse (NIDA) was used to create a TC in a correctional work-release facility. Very few offenders are paroled "to the streets" in Delaware, but, rather, spend the last six months of their sentence in a work-release facility. There they search for and secure employment while spending nights incarcerated. The TC work-release program follows a five-phase model designed to facilitate re-entry to the community, while inmates are undergoing intensive TC treatment. Inmates are given increasing time away from the work-release TC as they successfully work through the phase system. An aftercare component was added in 1994, although it did not become fully functional until 1997. The *aftercare* component entails an additional six months, and requires total abstinence from drug and alcohol use, a two-hour group session per week, monthly individual counseling, and urine monitoring. Graduates must return once a month to serve as role models for current work-release TC clients.

As inmates completed the in-prison TC, they were ideally released to the work-release TC. However, due to the shortage of treatment beds in the state, judges started sentencing offenders directly to the work-release TC independently of whether they had completed the prison TC. Some inmates also requested that they be placed in the work-release TC. This created a natural experiment allowing the research team to examine the efficacy of different doses and types of transitional treatment. A TC was also initiated in a women's prison, and a small proportion of the beds at the work-release TC were designated for women. A comparison group generated from an adjacent work-release program without a treatment component is also being followed over time.

Figure 10.1 demonstrates the effectiveness of the continuum of treatment at the 18-month follow-up. Logistic regression models controlling for possible intervening variables (gender, age, race, criminal history, previous drug use, and prior treatment) and correcting self-report with urinalysis results found that 16 percent of the comparison group, 22 percent of the in-prison TC group, 31 percent of the work-release TC group, and 47 percent of those receiving both in-prison and work-release TC treatment were drug free at the 18-month follow-up. This suggests a pattern of increasing effectiveness through in-prison and work-release TC treatment. This pattern is even more impressive for arrest-free status.

Figure 10.2 shows 46 percent of the comparison group, 43 percent of the in-prison TC group, 57 percent of the work-release TC group, and 77 percent of those receiving both in-prison and work-release TC treatment arrest free at 18 months (Inciardi *et al.* 1997). The outcome data support the improvement of a work-release TC relative to an in-prison TC, but suggest the strongest and most consistent pattern of success comes from the group who received TC treatment in-prison and in work release. The gains of prison TC treatment were generally non-significant compared to the control group. However, the size of the in-prison TC group is relatively small, and is destined to remain so, since most offenders graduating from an in-prison TC get preference for a work-release TC in the state of Delaware.

The gains made in treatment are impressive, although some will point out that even among those who got the full continuum of treatment in both the prison and work-release TCs half (53 percent) had relapsed by the 18-month follow-up. But relapse is a high standard, in which a single incident of drug use results in permanent failure. In a groundbreaking article on treatment myths, O'Brien and McClelland (1996) compare drug addiction to other chronic diseases such as asthma, diabetes, and hypertension, in

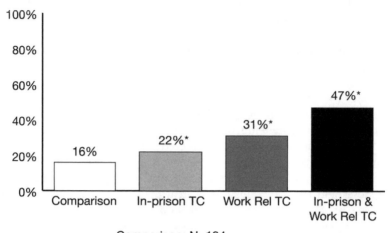

Comparison: N=184
In-prison TC: N=38
Work Release TC: N=183
In-prison & Work Release TC: N=43

Figure 10.1: Delaware corrections-based therapeutic community (TC) treatment continuum, drug free since release by self-report and urine test at 18-month follow-up

Note Adjusted percentages from logistic regression controlling for gender, race, age, criminal history, previous drug use, and prior treatment.

*   Significantly different from comparison group at $p<0.05$

which relapse may occur despite considerable improvement. They contend that treatment should be considered successful if considerable improvement occurs, even though complete remission or cure is not achieved.

With this in mind, the 18-month outcomes were re-examined in logistic regression models controlling for the same intervening variables but using a dependent variable of frequency of illicit drug use where 0=no use, 1=less than once a month, 2=1–3 times a month, 3=weekly, 4=several times a week, 5=once a day, and 6=several times a day. Figure 10.3 shows that the same stair-step pattern of results is achieved as shown in Figures 10.1 and 10.2. The mean frequency of illegal drug use for the comparison group was 3.29, compared to 2.45 for the in-prison TC group, 2.16 for the work-release TC group, and 1.12 for those participating in both the in-prison and work-release TC. A similar pattern was evident for alcohol use, with the mean frequency of use for the comparison group 3.24, 2.26 for the in-prison TC group, 1.9 for the work-release TC group, and 0.7 for those participating in both the in-prison and work-release TC. These results demonstrate that the continuum of treatment was strongly related to reductions in the frequency of illicit drug and alcohol use. There are obvious gains from the in-prison TC group, to the work-release TC, to those participating in both.

More recent analyses have been conducted examining the added value of

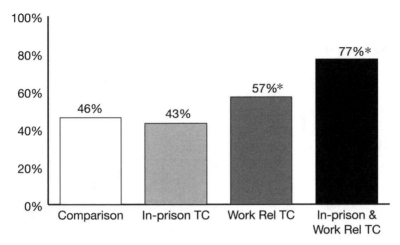

Figure 10.2: Delaware corrections-based therapeutic community (TC) treatment continuum, arrest free since release at 18-month follow-up

Note Adjusted percentages from logistic regression controlling for gender, race, age, criminal history, previous drug use, and prior treatment.
*   Significantly different from comparison group at $p<0.05$

aftercare. However, the treatment groups had to be organized differently. Due to the small numbers who received in-prison TC treatment only, they were omitted from the analysis. Figure 10.4 compares work-release TC dropouts with completers, and with those who completed both the work-release TC and the six-month aftercare program. It also compares these three groups with a comparison group that did not receive treatment. The comparison group includes those with identified drug problems attending a work-release facility without a TC. Figure 19.4 shows the drug-free status of offenders three years after release from the work-release TC. Figure 10.5 shows the arrest-free status. It is worth noting that even among the comparison group many sought treatment of their own accord, although their mean frequency of treatment sessions/contacts was much lower than for those in the treatment groups.

With these groupings, using logistic regression models that control for possible intervening variables, the same stair-step pattern of positive results related to treatment involvement was achieved three years following treatment. The number completely drug free among the comparison group was 5 percent; 22 percent among the work-release TC dropouts; 24 percent among the work-release program graduates; and 34 percent among those who

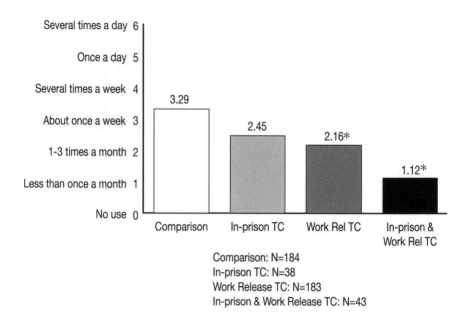

Figure 10.3: Delaware corrections-based therapeutic community (TC) treatment continuum, maximum frequency of drug use during any period since release at 18-month follow-up

Note Adjusted means from logistic regression controlling for gender, race, age, criminal history, previous drug use, and prior treatment.
*   Significantly different from comparison group at $p<0.05$

completed both the work-release TC and aftercare. The arrest-free statistics show 27 percent of the comparison group arrest-free at the three-year follow-up, compared to 33 percent of the work-release TC dropouts, 49 percent of the work-release graduates, and fully 57 percent of those completing both the work-release and aftercare program (Martin and Beard 2001). The arrest-free statistics are more impressive than the drug-free ones, but, again, the drug-free statistics hold the user to total abstinence for three years.

The analyses were repeated with the three-year follow-up data, controlling for the same variables, to examine the impact of the work-release TC treatment with and without aftercare on drug use in the past 30 days. Figure 10.6 shows the anticipated stair-step pattern of results found in earlier analyses, with drug use in the past 30 days prior to the three-year follow-up strongly correlated with the continuum of treatment. The percent drug free in the past 30 days is significantly higher than the percent completely drug free at the three-year follow-up, showing the gains from treatment.

The research program by Inciardi and colleagues in Delaware demonstrates the importance of treatment continuing during the transition stage to work and the free community. Remember, the comparison group was in work release, so the gains are the result of the TC treatment program and six-month aftercare services. The gains made in the TC work-release program even without aftercare show the value of inmates receiving treatment as they are reintegrating into the community, finding a job and housing, and spending increasing amounts of time with family and friends. Aftercare provided when TC work-release graduates begin living in the community helps to further reduce relapse and recidivism. Those inmates who graduated from the six-month aftercare programs have the greatest chances for success. This research program generally demonstrates a linear relationship between length of time in treatment and both relapse and recidivism. These findings obviate the need for transitional drug treatment services, including aftercare in the community for drug-involved offenders as they exit correctional institutions.

As previously stated, Inciardi and colleagues' longitudinal research within the Delaware criminal justice system supports the efficacy of TCs, and, additionally, makes a strong case for the use of TCs in correctional settings to combat substance abuse problems, crime, and other obstacles to reintegration (Inciardi *et al.* 1997; Martin and Inciardi 1993a, 1993b; Martin *et al.* 1999). Today, TCs are probably the most popular treatment approach for offenders (Belenko 1998). Their goal is to effect a global change in lifestyle (De Leon 1999).

TC structure and approach

The correctional TC is typically an isolated unit within a facility. Inmates generally receive three forms of therapy: behavioral, cognitive, and emotional. Behavioral therapy fosters positive demeanor and conduct by not accepting antisocial actions. Cognitive therapy helps individuals recognize errors and fallacies in their thinking. Emotional therapy deals with unresolved conflicts associated with interactions with others and the resulting feelings and behaviors. All three forms focus on getting the individual to change. The underlying philosophy is that these individual-based therapies produce an individual who is better equipped to solve everyday life problems because his or her values are more pro-social, he or she has learned how to resolve interpersonal problems without confrontation, anger, or frustration, and has been exposed to routine activities associated with conventional life.

TC participants (what inmates are often called in correctional TCs) progress through a system where they participate in various roles and positions to help run the TC, all while gaining increased responsibility. Residents are involved in all aspects of governing the TC and its operations, and take responsibility for their own and others treatment. Groups and meetings provide positive persuasion to change attitudes and behaviors, and confrontation by peers when values or rules are violated. Through participation

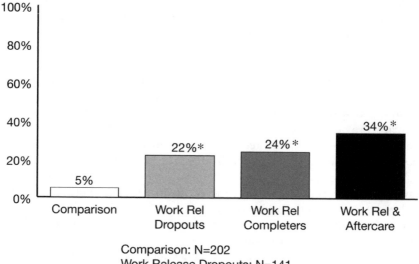

Comparison: N=202
Work Release Dropouts: N=141
Work Release Completers: N=133
Work Release & Aftercare: N=144

Figure 10.4: Delaware corrections-based therapeutic community (TC) treatment continuum, arrest free since release at three-year follow-up

Note: Adjusted percentages from logistic regression controlling for gender, race, age, criminal history, previous drug use, and prior treatment.
*   Significantly different from comparison group at $p<0.05$

in the TC process, individuals hopefully achieve a more positive and pro-social sense of self (De Leon 1995a; Simpson *et al.* 1995). Ultimately, participants come to see themselves, others, and even the world differently. This program structure allows for the acquisition of values and experience that are congruent with the reintegration goals of criminal desistence, drug abstinence, and commitment to conventional pursuits (e.g. employment). The other modalities mentioned above, e.g. drug education, do not directly attempt to provide these experiences or achieve these goals.

The typical TC is six to 12 months in duration, and time in treatment has long been recognized as critical to treatment success. It is generally staffed by a mixture of recovering addicts and treatment and mental health professionals. Because of this, TCs are often less expensive than other residential treatment modalities since they are less reliant on paid professional staff.

What distinguishes the TC from other treatment approaches and other communities is the deliberate use of the peer community to facilitate social and psychological change in individuals (De Leon *et al.* 1997). TCs are marked by significant "client" participation in all aspects of the treatment program. In the development of community, their role is equal to that of

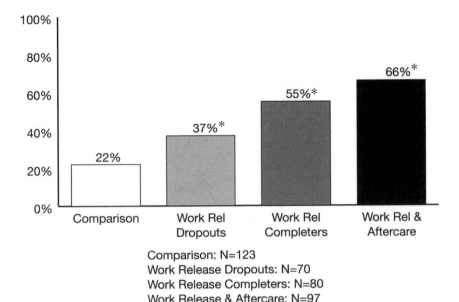

Figure 10.5: Delaware corrections-based therapeutic community (TC) treatment continuum, drug free in last 30 days by self-report and urine test at three-year follow-up

Note: Adjusted percentages from logistic regression controlling for gender, race, age, criminal history, previous drug use, and prior treatment.

*   Significantly different from comparison group at $p<0.05$

staff. Much of the attention given to TCs has focused on the participant role in the treatment process. This role is unique; however, staff is the other half the community component. In De Leon's words, "Regardless of professional discipline or function, the generic role of all staff is that of community member who, rather than providers and treaters are rational authorities, role models, facilitators, and guides in the self help community method" (1995b: 10). Traditionally, TC clinical staff is comprised primarily of former substance abusers who were participants in a TC (Melnick and De Leon 1999). However, staffing compositions have changed, and in some cases drastically (De Leon 1995a, 1995b; Inciardi and Lockwood 1994). Modified TCs, those serving specific populations such as offenders, tend to rely more heavily on professional staff.

In the prison setting, TC staff composition must also include, at a minimum, correctional officers (Lockwood and Inciardi 1993). Integration of correctional staff requires extensive and ongoing training and monitoring (Lockwood *et al.* 1998; Inciardi and Lockwood 1994). Due to security requirements and hiring policies, many prison TC graduates cannot be hired in the prison setting (Lockwood and Inciardi 1993), even though they would be ideal staff members. Furthermore, recent trends in managed care have also affected staffing patterns in TCs (De Leon 1995a). Managed care increasingly is requiring staff to be licensed and/or certified, thus focusing on academic achievement rather than personal experience with addiction.

Inner TC processes: the "community" concept

The "community-as-method" (CAM) approach was originally articulated by George De Leon (De Leon 2000, 1995a, 1995b; De Leon *et al.* 1994) and it remains the foundation of TCs in the US today. CAM contains eight essential elements (De Leon 1995a) to guide staff and participant interaction toward positive treatment outcomes. A review of these elements further illustrates the TC modality as a relevant and effective intervention for drug offenders and a mechanism for improved social and economic societal well-being.

The first element is called "member roles." It refers to how the TC provides opportunities to inmate/participants to assume conventional social roles, such as worker, leader, tutor, friend, etc. Performance of these roles purportedly translates into improved behaviors, attitudes, values, and emotional management that are consistent with abstinence and reintegration. The second element, membership feedback, refers to the communication style that characterizes the TC. Inmate/participants are encouraged to actively take part in providing direct feedback, both positive and negative, on other inmate/participants' behaviors, values, and attitudes. The assumption here is that providing such feedback gives the inmate important occasions to see positive and negative behaviors and attitudes in others and to take responsibility in helping them (and, therefore, him- or herself) toward recognition and change. Closely related to this is a third element called "membership as role models," where the TC encourages the inmate/participant to become a positive and responsible role model for individual change. In other words, through this element the inmate/participant secures the possibility to perform the tasks of a responsible citizen on a trial-and-error basis without real-world consequences. Such experience is believed to build up the individual's self-efficacy so that similar tasks can be effectively achieved when he or she is released into the community. He or she will also serve as an important role model to other participant/inmates (De Leon 2001).

The therapeutic community places a strong emphasis on the development of relationships in order to foster personal recovery and promote personal growth. The operational environment of the TC and its activities are geared toward getting the inmate/participant to build relationships that will be sustained after release, so that he or she will not fall back into destructive relationships focused on drug use and criminal activity (De Leon 2001). This fourth community element is critically important for both abstinence and crime-desistence goals since research has found that relationships with others engaged in negative activities comprise a significant obstacle to effective reintegration (Petersilia and Travis 2001).

TC participants obtain exposure to these four essential community elements through certain collective learning formats that are provided by the TC. Educational, training, recreational, employment, and counseling seminars and groups comprise some of the program components that allow TC participants to excel in new roles and behaviors and acquire more pro-social values and skills. As such, the collective learning activities are a vital fifth component in the TC's community concept. Along these lines, a sixth community element, i.e. culture and language, focuses on the use of argot, norms, and values that reflect assimilation into the TC and progress toward lasting identity change after release (De Leon 2001). Acquisition of language, values, and norms of behavior that are consistent with those of the TC, and contrary to more antisocial versions common in street drug subcultures, will assist the TC participant in more pro-social identity development that will guard against a return to drugs and crime.

Participating in various job functions, chores, and procedures required in the daily operations of the TC helps to buttress self-help and development. This structure and systems operational strategy ensures the order and safety of the TC community and facilitates individual change. It is a sixth element of the TC community concept. The public sharing of personal feelings and information and other open communications is a seventh community element that goes to the heart of the therapeutic approach. Getting participant/inmates to open up about their experience and feelings (traumatic and stressful), within the confines of a supportive and protected environment, helps them resolve often deep-seated emotional issues that can drive the abuse of drugs and alcohol. Finally, the development of positive and healthy relationships with peers and staff is an eighth element that further promotes effective reintegration by allowing the participant/inmate to learn how to work effectively with people from diverse backgrounds and who occupy different positions in society. This framework has become the foundation of most TC programs, particularly those in correctional settings (Lipton 1998).

As community members, participants demonstrate an understanding of the TC philosophy; they develop an affiliation with the community. As well, participants demonstrate behaviorally their community membership by role modeling. Socialization is evident in the acquisition of pro-social skills, attitude and values. Developmental change refers to the behaviors that indicate advances in maturity and responsibility, such as delayed gratification, self-control, and dependability. Finally, psychological change refers to the expected cognitive and emotional skill development that results from the TC process, including awareness, decision-making, communication, and emotional regulation.

In summary, the correctional TC provides a comprehensive and effective type of treatment that is unparalleled in other correctional treatment programs. The TC not only produces an individual less likely to resume drug use and criminal activity; it also cultivates an effective re-entry into society. The TC accomplishes this by taking a holistic approach to the treatment of drug abuse – anchoring program components in both abstinence from substance abuse and competence in basic life skills and experience. For example, TC programs in Delaware correctional facilities offer the group counseling for chemical dependency and relapse prevention, alterations in criminal thinking, life skills attainment, HIV/STD (sexually transmitted disease) and health education, and family and employment counseling. They also routinely feature 12-Step meetings and provide individual counseling. Programming like this helps reduce crime and promote reintegration.

Managing policy challenges with TC implementation

If correctional TCs are the most effective intervention with offenders involved in drugs and related crime, what would be the obstacles to their widespread implementation in correctional settings? We can attempt to answer this question at the ideological, economic, and social levels.

To begin, ideology about crime control policy in the United States grew increasingly punitive during the last quarter of the 20th century and remains so today. For most of that time, public opinion and beliefs about how to handle the country's drug problems were also punitive. As Federal and State governments adopted a zero-tolerance approach to drug use, massive anti-drug educational campaigns were launched alongside an all-out War on Drugs. The public was bombarded with rhetoric and images that equated drug users with serious criminality. It wasn't surprising to subsequently find that punitive crime control and zero-tolerance policies produced negative perceptions of drug offenders among the general public. Advocating for intensive drug treatment, like the TC, would face considerable challenge from the average citizen and the politician dependent on his or her vote. The question became who would possibly support programming, at the taxpayer's expense, that would help the "evil-doing" drug offender?

Ironically, by the early 2000s public sentiment and governmental political activity began showing such support. Pessimism about the effectiveness of the War on Drugs is now prevalent and exists alongside growing support for various harm reduction initiatives (e.g. medical marijuana) that define the drug problem in a more human and medical fashion. More importantly, the public wants as much as possible from its crime control tax dollars. There is an increased interest in having correctional institutions achieve multiple functions, balancing crime control, retribution, and effective reintegration. Support for correctional drug treatment programs like the TC is growing.

Economically, the United States faces considerable challenge in providing enough drug treatment beds given the outlandish costs of incarcerating more than 2 million offenders. TC treatment may simply be a luxury the government cannot afford. Consider that recent reports find wide gaps between treatment need and availability in correctional facilities. In 1997 about one-quarter of State and Federal prison inmates reported that they had participated in either professional substance abuse treatment or other treatment programs since they were incarcerated. However, only about 1 in 10 State inmates reported doing so in 1997, compared to 1 in 4 in 1991 (BJS 1997). About 1 in 5 State and Federal prison inmates report participation in self-help or drug education programs in 1997, which is up from 1 in 10 Federal prisoners and 1 in 6 State prisoners in 1991. Beck (2000) indicates that, among those State prisoners due to be released in the next 12 months, only about 1 in 5 drug and/or alcohol abusers received treatment. About 1 in 3 participated in self-help, peer counseling, or other education/awareness programs.

Although the amount of treatment available in the criminal justice system generally increased in the 1990s, treatment need far outstrips treatment availability. There are obviously more inmates requiring treatment than receive it, and much treatment is either short term or not intensive enough to address inmates' needs. Treatment programs in correctional institutions, particularly more intensive programs, oftentimes have waiting lists. Considering the depth of the typical inmate's addiction, self-help or drug education programs are unlikely to effect long-lasting change. Nor is prison time, since 77 percent of State and 62 percent of Federal inmates in 1997 had served prior sentences (General Accounting Office 2000). Therefore, it is imperative to the social and economic welfare of U.S. society to endorse and fund corrections-based TC programs for drug offenders.

Notes

1   Support for this paper was provided by grant #5R37-DA06124–12 from the National Institute on Drug Abuse.

References

Anderson, T. L. (2003) "Issues in the Availability of Healthcare for Women in Prison," in S. Sharp (ed.) *Female Prisoners in the United States: Programming Needs, Availability, and Efficacy*, Englewood Cliffs, NJ: Prentice Hall.

Anderson, T. L., Shannon, C., Schyb, I., and Goldstein, P. (2002) "Welfare Reform and Housing: Assessing the Impact to Substance Abusers," *Journal of Drug Issues* 2(1): 265–96.

Beck, A. J. (2000) *Prison and Jail Inmates at Mid-Year 1999*, Bureau of Justice Statistics Bulletin, US Department of Justice Publication no. NCJ 181643, Washington, DC: US Department of Justice, Bureau of Justice Statistics.

Belenko, S. (1998) *Behind Bars: Substance Abuse and America's Prison Population*, New York: National Center on Addiction and Substance Abuse at Columbia University.

Brown, B. S. (1992) "Program Models," in *Drug Abuse Treatment in Prisons and Jails*, NIDA Research Monograph no. 118, Washington, DC: US Department of Health and Human Services.

Butzin, C. A., Scarpitti, F. R., Nielsen, A. L., Martin, S. S., and Inciardi, J. A. (1999) "Measuring the Impact of Drug Treatment: Beyond Relapse and Recidivism," *Corrections Management Quarterly* 3(4): 1–7.

Butzin, C. A., Martin, S. S., and Inciardi, J. A. (2002) "Evaluating Component Effects of a Prison Based Treatment Continuum," *Journal of Substance Abuse Treatment* 1: 1–7.

Bureau of Justice Statistics (BJS) (1997) *Correctional Populations in the US, 1995*, Washington, DC: DOJ, OJP, BJS.

Bureau of Justice Statistics (BJS) (1998) *Substance Abuse and Treatment of Adults on Probation, 1995*, Washington, DC: Department of Justice, Office of Justice Programs, BJS.

Bureau of Justice Statistics (BJS) (1999) *Felony Criminal Case Processing, 1998*, Washington, DC: Department of Justice, Office of Justice Programs, BJS.

Bureau of Justice Statistics (BJS)/Bonczar, T. P. (1997) *Characteristics of Adults on Probation, 1995*, Washington, DC: DOJ, OJP, BJS.

Bureau of Justice Statistics (BJS)/Harlow, C. W. (1998) *Profile of Jail Inmates, 1996*, Washington, DC: Department of Justice, Office of Justice Programs, BJS.

Bureau of Justice Statistics (BJS)/Mumola, C. J. (1999) *Substance Abuse and Treatment, State and Federal Prisoners, 1997*, Washington, DC: Department of Justice, Office of Justice Programs, BJS.

Bureau of Justice Statistics (BJS)/Brown, J. M. and Langan, P. A. (1999) *Felony Sentences in State Courts, 1996*, Washington, DC: Department of Justice, Office of Justice Programs, BJS.

De Leon, G. (1995a) "Therapeutic Communities for Addictions: A Theoretical Framework," *International Journal of the Addictions* 30(12): 1,603–45.

De Leon, G. (1995b) "Residential Therapeutic Communities in the Mainstream: Diversity and Issues," *Journal of Psychoactive Drugs* 27(1): 3–15.

De Leon, G. (1999) "Therapeutic Communities," in P. J. Ott and R. E. Tarter (eds.) *Sourcebook on Substance Abuse: Etiology, Epidemiology, Assessment, and Treatment*, Needham Heights, MA: Allyn and Bacon.

De Leon, G. (2000) *The Therapeutic Community: Theory, Model, and Method*, New York: Springer Publishing Co., Inc.

De Leon, G. (2001) "Therapeutic Communities for Substance Abuse: Developments in North America," in B. Rawlings and R. Yates (eds.) *Therapeutic Communities for the Treatment of Drug Users*, London: Jessica Kingsley Publishers.

De Leon, G., Melnick, G., Kressel, D., and Jainchill, N. (1994) "Circumstances, Motivation, Readiness and Suitability (the CMRS Scale): Predicting Retention in Therapeutic Community Treatment," *American Journal of Drug and Alcohol Abuse* 20(4): 495–515.

De Leon, G., Melnick, G., and Kressel, D. (1997) "Motivation and Readiness for Therapeutic Community Treatment among Cocaine and Other Drug Abusers," *American Journal of Drug and Alcohol Abuse* 23(2): 169–87.

Federal Bureau of Investigation (2001) *Crime in the United States: 1990–2000*, Washington, DC: Department of Justice.

General Accounting Office (GAO) (2000) *State and Federal Prisoners: Profiles of Inmate Characteristics in 1991 and 1997*, Washington, DC: General Accounting Office.

Gerstein, D. R., Johnson, R. A., Harwood, H. J., Fountain, D., Suter, N., and Malloy, K. (1994) *Evaluating Recovery Services: The California Drug and Alcohol Treatment Assessment (CALDATA)*, Sacramento, CA: California Department of Alcohol and Drug Programs.

Hammett, T. M., Roberts, C., and Kennedy, S. (2001) "Health-related Issues in Prisoner Reentry," *Crime and Delinquency* 47(3): 390–409.

Hammett, T. M., Harmon, M. P., and Rhodes, W. (2002) "The Burden of Infectious Disease among Inmates of and Releasees from US Correctional Facilities, 1997," *American Journal of Public Health* 92(11): 1,789–94.

Harrison, L. (2001) "The Revolving Prison Door for Drug-involved Offenders: Challenges and Opportunities," *Crime and Delinquency* 47(3): 462–84.

Inciardi, J. A. and Lockwood, D. (1994) "When Worlds Collide: Establishing CREST Outreach Center," in B. W. Fletcher, J. A. Inciardi, and A. M. Horton (eds.) *Drug Abuse Treatment: The Implementation of Innovative Approaches*, Westport, CT: Greenwood Press.

Inciardi, J. A., Martin, S. S., Butzin, C. A., Hooper, R. M., and Harrison, L. D. (1997) "An Effective Model of Prison-based treatment for Drug-involved Offenders," *Journal of Drug Issues* 27(2): 261–78.

Inciardi, J. A., Martin, S. S., and Surratt, H. L. (2001) "Therapeutic Communities in Prison and Work Release: Effective Modalities for Drug Involved offenders," in B. Rawlings and R. Yates (eds.) *Therapeutic Communities for Drug Users*, London: Jessica Kingsley Publishers.

Lipton, D. S. (1998) "Therapeutic Community Treatment Programming in Corrections," *Psychology, Crime and Law* 4(3): 213–63.

Lockwood, D. and Inciardi, J. A. (1993) "CREST Outreach Center: A Work Release Iteration of the TC Model," in F. M. Tims, B. W. Fletcher, and J. A. Inciardi (eds.) *Innovative Approaches in the Treatment of Drug Abuse: Program Models and Strategies*, Westport, CT: Greenwood Press.

Lockwood, D., McCorkel, J., and Inciardi, J. A. (1998) "Developing Comprehensive Prison-based Therapeutic Community Treatment for Women," *Drugs & Society* 13(1/2): 193–212.

Leukefeld, C. G. and Tims, F. M. (eds.) (1992) *Drug Abuse Treatment in Prisons and Jails*, NIDA Research Monograph no. 118, Washington, DC: US Department of Health and Human Services.

Martin, S. S. and Beard, R. A. (2001) "Drug Treatment and Minority Populations in Prison and Work Release," paper presented at the Bridging Science and Culture to Improve Drug Abuse Research in Minority Communities Conference, September 25, 2001.

Martin, S. S. and Inciardi, J. A. (1993a) "Case Management Approaches for Criminal Justice Clients," in J. A. Inciardi (ed.) *Drug Treatment and Criminal Justice*, Newbury Park, CA: Sage Publications.

Martin, S. S. and Inciardi, J. A. (1993b) "A Case Management Treatment Program for Drug Involved Prison Releasees," *Prison Journal* 73(3/4): 319–31.

Martin, S. S., Butzin, C. A., Saum, C. A., and Inciardi, J. A. (1999) "Three-year Outcomes of Therapeutic Community Treatment for Drug-involved Offenders in Delaware: From Prison to Work Release to Aftercare," *Prison Journal* 79(3): 294–320.

Melnick, G. and De Leon, G. (1999) "Clarifying the Nature of Therapeutic Community Treatment: The Survey of Essential Elements Questionnaire (SEEQ)," *Journal of Substance Abuse Treatment* 16(4): 307–13.

National Institute on Drug Abuse (1992) *Extent and Adequacy of Insurance Coverage for Substance Abuse Services*, Institute of Medicine Report: Treating Drug Problems, Drug Abuse Services Research Series, no. 2, vol. 1, Rockville, MD: National Institute on Drug Abuse.

O'Brien, C. P. and McClelland, T. A. (1996) "Myths about the Treatment of Addiction," *Lancet* 347: 237–40.

Petersilia, J. and Travis, J. (2001) *From Prison to Society: Managing the Challenges of Prisoner Re-entry*, special issue of *Crime and Delinquency* 47–3: 291–484.

Rawlings, B. and Yates, R. (2001a) *Therapeutic Communities for the Treatment of Drug Users*, London: Jessica Kingsley Publishers.

Rawlings, B. and Yates, R. (2001b) "Introduction," in B. Rawlings and R. Yates (eds.) *Therapeutic Communities for the Treatment of Drug Users*, London: Jessica Kingsley Publishers.

Simpson, D. D., Joe, G. W., Rowan-Szal, G., and Greener, J. (1995) "Client Engagement and Change during Drug Abuse Treatment," *Journal of Substance Abuse* 7: 117–34.

Travis, J., Robinson, L., and Solomon, A. (2002) "Prisoner Re-entry: Issues for Practice and Policy," *Criminal Justice* 17(1): 12–18.

Wexler, H. K. and Love, C. T. (1994) "Therapeutic Communities in Prison," in F. R. Tims, G. De Leon, and N. Jainchill (eds.) *Therapeutic Community: Advances in Research and Application*, NIDA Research Monograph Series no. 114, Washington, DC: US Department of Health and Human Services.

Wexler, H. K., Falkin, G. P., and Lipton, D. S. (1988) *A Model Prison Rehabilitation Program: An Evaluation of the Stay' N Out Therapeutic Community*, New York: Narcotic and Drug Research, Inc.

Wexler, H. K., De Leon, G., Thomas, G., Kressel, D., and Peters, J. (1999) "The Amity Prison TC Evaluation: Reincarceration Outcomes," *Criminal Justice and Behavior* 26(2): 147–67.

White House (2001) *National Drug Control Strategy 2000*, Washington, DC: US Government Printing Office.

11 Treating drug users
The role of the National Treatment Agency for Substance Misuse

Paul Hayes

Introduction

Established in 2001, the National Treatment Agency for Substance Misuse (NTA) is a special health authority within the National Health Service (NHS). The Agency is responsible for improving the availability, capacity and effectiveness of treatment for drug misuse in England.

This chapter sets out the background, role and progress of the Agency as at March 2004.

Background to the NTA

The UK's national strategy for tackling drug misuse, established in 1998 and updated in December 2002, places a strong emphasis on the value of treatment. The delivery of high-quality, effective treatment is fundamental to the success of the strategy. It recognises that

> getting drug misusers into treatment is the best way of improving their health and increasing their ability to lead fulfilling lives. Treatment breaks the cycle of drug misuse and crime, and investing in treatment reduces the overall cost of drug misuse to society.
>
> (HM Government 2002: 50)

This approach is supported by a growing body of research evidence indicating that appropriately delivered treatment works.

The drug treatment sector in the UK has developed in an ad hoc manner over the last 30 years. Although this fostered innovation, it also led to wide variations in coverage, methodologies and quality. There has also been a significant gap between the number of people requiring treatment and the number of places available, so many areas of the country have had lengthy waiting lists.

Faced with this situation, the government took two significant decisions. The first was to pool and increase central government funding for drug treatment. This will increase from £140 million in 2001/2 to £300 million in 2005/6, and does not include additional locally allocated resources. Second, the decision was made to create an independent body to oversee the spending of that money, and to lead a drive to improve the coverage and quality of treatment services. Consequently, the NTA was created as a special health authority to perform this role in April 2001.

Role of the NTA

The NTA's specific targets are to double the number of people in effective, well-management treatment from 100,000 in 1998 to 200,000 in 2008; and to increase the proportion of people completing or appropriately continuing treatment, year on year. This is in line with the national drugs strategy targets. Furthermore, the NTA is committed to ensuring equal access to relevant and appropriate drug treatment services for England's diverse populations, the eradication of unlawful discrimination and the promotion of equal opportunities. Its first guiding principle is that the Agency exists to serve the needs of services users, their carers and the communities in which they live.

In order to meet its targets, and given the complex range of issues linked to drug misuse, the NTA works in partnership with health, social care, drug user, training and education agencies. The NTA also works closely with criminal justice agencies to ensure that offenders can access treatment at all points in the criminal justice system. Although it is not directly responsible for the management of treatment in prisons, it works with the prison services to ensure that the quality of treatment in prisons equals that available in the community.

The NTA focuses on:

- improving the commissioning of drug treatment services;
- promoting evidence-based and co-ordinated practice;
- improving the performance of drug action teams and treatment providers.

Improving the commissioning of drug treatment services

Drug treatment services are commissioned by locally based drug action teams (DATs). DATs are the consortiums responsible for local delivery of the national drugs strategy – including the planning and commissioning of drug treatment. Organised along local authority boundaries, the 149 DATs in England comprise senior representatives from health, local authority and criminal justice agencies. As such, the DAT analyses local treatment needs; plans and monitors expenditure of central and local funding allocations; and commissions services from a wide range of treatment agencies, including specialist NHS services, general practitioners (GPs), and national and local voluntary organisations.

Improving the quality of commissioning will be one of the keys to the NTA's success. The Agency's network of regional teams, based in the government offices for the regions, provides guidance and support to DATs and their joint commissioning groups (JCGs) on all aspects of the commissioning process, from needs assessment to contract monitoring. DATs' draft treatment plans are subject to scrutiny by the NTA regional manager, supported by colleagues from the government offices for the regions, strategic health authorities and relevant inspectorates. Regional teams also assess whether or not the plan meets the needs of diverse local populations, including women, young people and those from black and ethnic minority backgrounds, and look for evidence of service user and carer involvement in planning. An agreed version of the treatment plan is then used by NTA's regional teams to review the performance of each DAT on a quarterly basis.

Promoting evidence-based and co-ordinated practice

The NTA promotes practice that is evidence based, appropriately delivered, outcome focused, and integrated into a system of co-ordinated drug treatment and care. To equip DATs and service providers to meet this agenda the NTA does the following:

- *Distils and disseminates best practice drawn from research:* as well as commissioning new research, the Agency's briefing series, *Research into Practice*, brings together research from the UK and abroad, analyses the evidence of what works best and presents the implications to drug treatment providers and commissioners of services. The Agency works with clinicians, service users and relevant agencies to develop guidance on the provision of services (e.g. heroin prescribing).
- *Is working in partnership with the Healthcare Commission to create an inspection capacity able to hold DATs and providers accountable for the effective use of public money.*
- *Is implementing a human resources strategy to attract, retain and train high-quality staff in the drug treatment sector:* in order to meet the drugs strategy target of doubling the numbers in treatment, the capacity of the sector must be expanded. In addition, existing staff need to be retained and given opportunities to expand their skills. This will require a major cultural shift towards the prioritisation of career development. In some areas drug treatment services have under-invested in human resource management, yet without this development the national drugs strategy cannot be fully implemented. The NTA's workforce strategy aims to reverse this trend and promote adequate investment in professional development, offering workers the opportunity to develop a specialist career in drug treatment.
- *Promotes the involvement of services users:* the NHS Plan outlines the important contribution that service users, and their unpaid carers, make to the

planning of services. The NTA advocates this patient-centred approach and believes that drug treatment service users should contribute to the planning of their own individual care, and to the development of treatment services generally.

Improving performance

NTA's regional teams work with DATs, JCGs and service providers locally to improve the quality and effectiveness of treatment available to their communities. Working closely with the government offices for the regions and other regional structures, particularly strategic health authorities and other NHS performance management, the NTA's regional teams provide:

- an authoritative drug treatment lead in each region;
- a clear line of communication and accountability between the NTA as the manager of the pooled treatment budget and DATs/JCGs as the bodies with local responsibility for ensuring that the budget is spent to best effect;
- a conduit through which the NTA and others will hold the agencies represented within the DAT to account for poor performance.

As part of this performance management process, the NTA works with others (e.g. District Audit) to monitor local drug treatment spending. The NTA also works with DATs/JCGs to develop management information systems on which reliable judgements about performance can be based.

Progress to date

Improvements in commissioning

In its first year of operation NTA regional teams have been able to help DATs refine their treatment plans, overcome blockages to service developments, identify and reverse disinvestment by other local partners, and refocus on key NTA priorities such as driving down waiting times.

Guidance on commissioning has been published and systems have been improved. The majority of DATs now have a dedicated commissioning manager in place.

The NTA aims to ensure that all DATs commission a comprehensive range of services that meet the diverse range of local needs. Furthermore, services should not be commissioned in isolation. Instead, a comprehensive drug treatment *system* should be developed, focused on the needs of clients and co-ordinated in such a way as to enable a client to move through the system rather than becoming inappropriately blocked in one service.

Models of Care, the NTA's new service framework for the commissioning and development of treatment services, establishes the system of services to be provided to clients across the country. Models of Care groups services into four broad tiers:

1   Non-substance misuse specific services that interface with drug treatment, including primary care services, non-substance misuse social services, housing, probation, sexual health, accident and emergency, general psychiatric services, etc.
2   Open access drug misuse services, including advice and information services, drop-in services, needle exchanges, outreach services, etc.
3   Structured community-based specialist drug misuse services, including structured counselling and therapy; structured day programmes; community-based detoxification, prescribing and treatment for offenders; and structured aftercare programmes following discharge from residential care or prison.
4   Residential services for drug and alcohol misusers, including residential substance misuse specific services (e.g. inpatient drug detoxification services, drug and alcohol residential rehabilitation services, etc.) and highly specialist non-substance misuse services (e.g. young people's hospital and residential services, specialist liver disease units, specialist psychiatric units, HIV specialist units, etc).

Since April 2003 DATs have been responsible for ensuring that this full range of services is available to their local residents.

The first fully developed integrated care pathway for a specific client group within the Models of Care framework has been developed by the NTA in partnership with the Home Office. Focusing on offenders who misuse drugs, the pathway is being rolled out progressively over the next three years, in DAT areas with the highest concentrations of drug-related offending as part of the criminal justice interventions programme (CJIP).

Building on existing criminal justice interventions designed to enable offenders to access treatment as they move through the criminal justice system, dedicated integrated criminal justice teams are being established. These will deal with offenders who are referred from police stations following positive testing for classified drugs, from court on bail or for Drug Treatment and Testing Order (DTTO) assessment, and following discharge from prison. Offenders will be assessed, referred to appropriate services, or their needs met within the dedicated team. All offenders will be case managed through the process, enabling them to be referred to and tracked through the treatment systems that are most appropriate for their needs, and maintaining motivation whilst they are assessed.

This approach not only makes best use of current interventions such as arrest referrals, but also plugs the significant gap in the otherwise comprehensive range of criminal justice interventions, by responding to the needs of prisoners on return to their communities.

Promotion of evidence-based and co-ordinated practice

Reflecting historic patterns of use, most treatment services remain focused on the needs of opiate misusers to the detriment of the growing numbers of poly drug misusers who use both opiates and stimulants, and frequently alcohol. To promote the growth of stimulant treatment, particularly for crack cocaine misuse, the NTA has undertaken a study of services for crack misusers. The crack research, combined with a review of published research from the UK and USA, has formed the evidence base for a new approach to crack treatment. The evidence, which showed that cognitive behavioural therapies were particularly effective in treating crack/cocaine misuse, was published as part of the Agency's regular *Research into Practice* briefing series. The new approaches are being tried out in some of the country's high crack areas and are being supported by additional training and resource material for staff.

The Agency has also worked with the Department of Health, Home Office, clinicians and service users to provide guidance on when it is appropriate to consider the prescription of heroin/diamorphine to opiate users. The evidence-based guidance concludes that, while oral methadone will remain the most appropriate and effective form of treatment for the majority of heroin users, there may be a case for an increase in the use of heroin prescribing for entrenched injectors who have not responded to other forms of treatment. Such treatment would only be provided by competent, appropriately skilled and authorised practitioners.

The NTA provides an ongoing programme of briefings, visits and workshops designed to support providers in understanding and implementing existing standards such as QuADS (Quality in Alcohol and Drugs Services) and residential care standards. The Agency is also developing standards criteria in partnership with the Healthcare Commission.

The first phase of the NTA's workforce strategy has moved into action and the target of having 9,000 workers in the sector by 2008 has already been met, ahead of schedule. For the first time, there is now a set of Drug and Alcohol National Occupational Standards (DANOS) which establishes the levels of competency required of drug treatment staff in order to carry out particular duties. The Agency has examined the training needs of the workforce and is developing training to support drug workers in meeting the DANOS standards.

The NTA has also delivered a leadership programme for commissioners and managers, the first of its kind to be introduced into the entire drug treatment service on a national basis. A partnership including DrugScope and Alcohol Concern, the Community Justice National Training Organisation (CJNTO) has been developed competency-based training modules. These too have been designed to meet DANOS criteria. The CJNTO is also involved in the Agency's apprenticeship pilots to recruit and develop young black and minority ethnic trainees. In residential drug treatment services managers now have to ensure that standards set by the

National Care Standards Commission (NCSC) are met, and the NTA has provided guidance to help them do so.

There is a national drive to get more GPs recruited into providing drug treatment. This, one of the issues highlighted in a Home Affairs Select Committee report in 2002, attracted a further £1.2 million in funding from the Department of Health. The Royal College of General Practitioners (RCGP) manages the programme to provide training in substance misuse for GPs, and is working with the NTA and the Substance Misuse in General Practice group (SMMGP) to develop shared care arrangements between GPs and specialist services throughout the country. The NTA is also liaising with the RCGP on a long-term strategy to include expertise in drug and alcohol treatment in basic training programmes for GPs.

The NTA has established user and carer advisory groups and appointed user and carer representatives to the Agency's Board. At local level regional teams have established regular meetings with user and carer representatives. The Agency is currently establishing formal mechanisms for regional and national user and carer involvement with DATs and the NTA.

Improved performance

Crucially, more people are able to access treatment, more services are being developed and waiting times are falling.

There has been a significant increase in the number of people able to access drug treatment services – from 100,000 in 1998 to 141,000 in 2002/3 (Department of Health 2002). This means that the system is currently on track to meet the national target of 200,000 people in treatment by 2008.

A recent survey by DrugScope indicated that since 1997 there has been a one-third increase in the number of treatment services operating in the country. This is backed up by the experience of NTA regional teams, who have reported an expansion in existing services and the creation of new services on an ongoing basis.

In its first months of operation, the NTA established benchmarks for and provided guidance on waiting times for all forms of treatment (see Table 11.1). No one should wait for more than two or three weeks, depending on the type of service, by December 2004. A joint programme of support, via the NHS Modernisation Agency, has realised significant results. Many DATs have been performing well ahead of targets. Some have cut waiting times to zero; for example, in the Wirral 82 per cent of GPs are involved in shared care programmes and waiting times for community prescribing are virtually non-existent. In West Sussex a triage system was brought in to make sure clients were referred to the most appropriate service; waiting times came down from five months to two weeks.

Table 11.1: Waiting times targets and progress, average waiting times in weeks

Treatment	December 2001	December 2003	% change	NTA target 2003	NTA target 2004
Inpatient treatment	12.0	3.7	69	4	2
Residential rehab	9.1	4.1	55	4	3
Specialist prescribing	14.1	4.4	69	6	3
GP prescribing	5.7	2.3	60	4	2
Day services	6.0	2.1	65	4	3
Structured counselling	7.6	2.7	64	4	2
Overall	9.1	3.2	65	4.3	2.5

Note:
1 week 5 working days.
Waiting times are measured from the time of referral to the time of entry into structured treatment.

It has been recognised within government that the information systems to track the effectiveness of the drug treatment system are inadequate. The NTA is working closely with the Department of Health and the Home Office to rationalise and redevelop National Drug Treatment Monitoring System (NDTMS). Central to this will be the need to meet local, regional and central performance and business information needs without unnecessary duplication of effort. This will enable a flow of regular, real-time information to treatment agencies to enable them to manage their business; to DATs as commissioners of services to enable them to ensure value for money; and to the NTA to enable it to account to ministers and the public for the achievement of drug strategy targets.

In conclusion, the NTA works in partnership with local and national agencies to identify and share best practice, ensure value for money and develop the drug treatment sector workforce. The end result should be more effective treatment available to those who need it, when they need it and where they need it.

References

Department of Health (2002) *National Drug Treatment Monitoring System*, London: Department of Health.

HM Government (2002) *Updated Drug Strategy*, London: HMSO.

House of Commons Home Affairs Committee (2002) *The Government's Drug Policy: Is It Working?*, London: The Stationery Office Limited.

12 Linking treatment services to the criminal justice system

Philip Bean

The aim in this chapter is to provide a model for the treatment of drug offenders – defined as those offenders who take drugs irrespective of whether drug taking and offending are causally linked. It is not about those non-offenders who may seek treatment voluntarily; it is about those who come within the ambit of the criminal justice system – itself defined to include law enforcement. A major assumption underlying this model is that the treatment services must work with and alongside law enforcement, and not, as at present, operate in ways where the two systems at best talk past each other and at worst are plainly hostile. A second assumption is that successful treatment outcomes require the input of the treatment services working with and using the controls afforded by the criminal justice system. A third strand of the model concerns research; this is to inform and provide data as well as help formulate hypotheses. A clearly formulated research strategy is as important as co-operation between treatment and criminal justice. Research is there to help evaluate the programmes, help conceptualise thinking and direct attention at new developments. Mandatory drug testing is also a key feature; it will not be discussed here as it is dealt with elsewhere in this volume (see Chapter 6), except, that is, to emphasise that mandatory drug testing provides the most valid and reliable data on the progress of offenders in treatment and is an essential prerequisite of all treatment programmes.

Treatment within criminal justice: an overview

The Government's Ten Year Strategy *Tackling Drugs to Build a Better Britain* (Cabinet Office 2000) includes treatment as one of the four major targets. The aim is to improve services so that '*all* problem drug mis-users irrespective of age, gender, and race, have proper access to support for appropriate sources including primary care when needed' (Cabinet Office 2000: 26; emphasis in original). The key performance target is 'to increase the participation of problem drug users including prisoners in drug treatment programmes which have a positive impact on health and crime' (Cabinet Office 2000: 26) Clearly, the government recognises the importance of treatment for offender populations but the question is how is it meeting these objectives? There is no doubt the task is daunting. Notwithstanding the number of offenders who are drug users, the number of drug users in treatment as a ratio of new problem drug use is estimated at only about 1 in 7 (Cabinet Office 2000: 26).

The other target areas are prevention, enforcement and interdiction – the latter sometimes called upstream enforcement, i.e. preventing drugs coming into the country. Again, there is recognition that enforcement (including interdiction) has a part to play, but what sort of a part, and what are the links with other strategies? Rarely is law integrated with enforcement and treatment – publicly made comments from the police that more offenders should be in treatment are welcome, but just sending them off to an arrest referral scheme will not achieve much if there is no treatment available. Moreover, enforcement and treatment sometimes interact, not always in a positive manner, or in ways fully intended. For example, an increase in the effectiveness of law enforcement may well increase the numbers seeking treatment, thereby overloading the treatment services. Or increasing the effectiveness of treatment may equally increase the recruitment of new users by removing the most influential, albeit negative, role models of other users. Alternatively, an increase in certain methods of law enforcement may drive users into higher levels of crime to secure their money for drugs. None of these is a reason for reducing the strategies, least of all failing to provide treatment; they merely point to the difficulties of seeing any target in a one-dimensional degree of goodness (McCoun and Reuter 1998: 217). For these purposes, however, the aim is to leave aside any effects, detrimental or otherwise, that may arise.

The major ideological thrust behind the government's Strategy is the claim that 'Treatment Works'. The empirical basis to support this proposition, especially that which says treatment reduces crime, is, however, less certain than is often supposed (for a full discussion, see Bean 2001). For example, many drug users are offenders in their own right. This makes it difficult to disaggregate offences directly attributable to drug use and those that would be committed anyway. Nonetheless, large numbers of offenders report drug use at arrest: 61 per cent in the Trevor Bennett study (1998), and whilst many had taken the less addictive drugs 10 per cent reported dependency on heroin, 18 per cent tested positive for opiates and a further 10 per cent had taken crack cocaine. About 20 per cent expressed an interest in receiving treatment. Other studies report similar findings, some suggesting a strong causal connection between drugs and crime, and others content to show that drugs and crime were but co-morbidities in the offender's deviant lifestyle (Hough 1996).[1]

No one knows how many offenders would benefit from treatment, or what the effectiveness of different treatment modalities is. The data sets are simply not available. One major stumbling block has been methodological. For example, one problem when assessing the impact of treatment is to control for the impact of other treatment variables; we cannot assume that other inputs do not exist, or that family, friends and other drug users do not offer their own forms of therapy. Or, when assessing the impact of sentences, the difficulty is to compare like with like; for example, the opportunities to commit offences whilst on probation are greater than for offenders in prison. In my research study aimed at assessing the latter we found insurmountable problems (Bean 1995). Tentative results showed that the probation order with a condition of treatment had a slight advantage over the other sentences in terms of outcome, but even then this result should be treated with caution. The sampling frame was defective in that we used the probation report as a means of identifying the drug users, but the probation officers did not always know whether the offender was a drug user, or if they did they did not always record it. Then we were able to follow up only about 66 per cent of the sample. Accordingly, determining the impact of any variable was a hit-or-miss affair; these offenders led such chaotic lives that they were likely to have received other sentences during the 12-month follow up period, making it impossible to attribute effects to any particular sentence.

In terms of treatment within the criminal justice system the range of treatment services and the qualifications and experience of the staff are not likely to differ greatly from those outside it. There will, however, be significant differences in the type of patients; those in the criminal justice system, especially in prison, are likely to have many previous convictions, have poor educational attainment, a poor employment record (in some cases a nonexistent employment record) and few social skills. Nonetheless, the government is correct to assert that major social benefits can come from a reduction in the crimes of this population group (McCoun and Reuter 1998: 222). Generally speaking, offenders in treatment tend to commit fewer offences than when not. Street heroin users, who tend to be the most criminal, reduce their criminality to the order of something like 70 per cent when in treatment (Chaiken and Chaiken 1990: 233–4). This in spite of the fact that repeated cycles of success and failure have to be built into every programme before lasting behavioural change takes place. Offenders remaining in the programme for 60 days or more seem to have the best prognosis; anything less and relapse rates are higher.

Looking at the sentencing patterns for drug offenders, i.e. those convicted of a drug offence, about 10 per cent are sentenced to immediate custody, with about the same proportion being fined or placed on probation. Most are cautioned, itself strictly speaking not a sentence but included as such for these purposes. In spite of an increase in the numbers of drug offenders entering the criminal justice system, the proportion of drug offenders going to prison has not changed in the last decade. Proportionate changes, where they have occurred, have been in the increase in the use of cautions and a decrease in the use of fines (Corkery 2000). Drug offenders sentenced to a probation order have retained the same proportionate rate. It is these noncustodial sentences, which successive governments have seen as 'too soft' on

offenders, drug offenders or otherwise, which have been the target of government criticism. Toughening up community penalties, albeit with treatment
attached, has been a major feature of Government strategy.

There are, of course, many other offenders in the criminal justice system
who are not classified as drug offenders, whose Index offence is invariably a
property offence but who require treatment. Paradoxically, those drug
offenders who do not require treatment are themselves drug offenders, but
usually high-level suppliers. These are rarely users, and the longest sentences
are reserved for this group (Corkery 2000). Those using drugs will have been
sentenced for a range of offences, some having previous convictions for drug
offences, others not. There is no single pattern; there are no offences which
are unique to drug users; nor is it possible to identify current drug users or
predict future use from their previous convictions.

Figure 12.1 gives the data on sentenced drug offenders, i.e. whose Index
offence was a drug offence. This table shows how the fine has been replaced
by the caution – incidentally showing too how the percentage sentenced to
immediate custody remains steady. The caution in this case means a formal
caution, used predominantly, though not exclusively, for young offenders.

Our knowledge of the use and effects of treatment among offender populations is limited – the research evidence is simply not available – but in
general terms the position seems to be as follows. Drug offenders who are

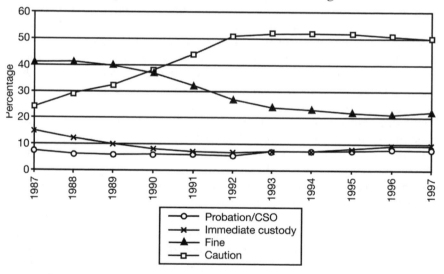

Figure 12.1: Sentences given to drug offenders, 1987–97

Note:
CSO   Community Service Order.

Source Home Office Seizures and Offenders Bulletin, in Corkery (2000). (I am grateful to John
Corkery for granting permission to reproduce this table.)

cautioned are usually thought to be casual users, with few criminal convictions who would not otherwise be in the criminal justice system – or at least that is the general view. There is, however, little research evidence to support it. The Metropolitan Police are able to show that those cautioned for, say, cannabis possession have multiple convictions; they are not the criminally naïve that they are largely supposed to be (G. Monaghan, personal communication, 2001). That apart, Figure 12.1 has at least two other implications for treatment programmes within criminal justice. First, it seems axiomatic that the criminal justice system must play a major part in any programme concerned with treatment of drug abuse, if only because of the large numbers of users within that system. For that reason alone it is easy to see why the Government is concerned to reduce drug abuse, and why it sees drug users as responsible for a large number of crimes, especially property crimes. Second, about 10 per cent of those convicted of drug offences are sentenced to immediate imprisonment, together with an indeterminate number of others whose Index offence is invariably a property offence; the evidence suggests that many will continue to use whilst in prison. That is why Nina Cope talks of a drug continuum, by which she means that many inmates are at as great, if not greater risk, of using drugs in prison as they are of using them outside (Cope 2000).

Taking first those offenders in custody, there are three main reasons why treatment should be made available to prisoners. First, on humanitarian/medical grounds: prisoners may want it, the opportunity is there to provide it, and if successful it will improve their health and well-being. Second, treatment helps reduce drug use in prison, the extent of which is not known but is thought to be extensive, and can have a positive effect on the prison regime. Third, treatment can help prepare offenders for release – most relapses occur soon after discharge. Treatment is therefore part of the philosophy of rehabilitation, a point to be returned to later.

The research evidence shows that offender populations have high levels of drug use – especially among prison populations. Burrows *et al.* (2000) found that in the 12 months prior to sentence it was as high as 70 per cent, and many continued to use whilst in custody. Most offenders were polyusers, with heroin or crack/cocaine as the favoured drug. Dealing with this high-using offender population requires patience and skill. Recently, considerable advances have been made by the prison service in the development of treatment services, with the latest review aimed at providing 'an equitable provision of basic and enhanced specialist services to meet low level moderate and severe drug problems' (HM Prison Service 1998: 4). This is to be achieved through the development of an integrated counselling assessment referral advice and through-care service (known as CARATS) (Duke 2000). Determining the effects of this and earlier programmes is impossible with current data sets; there are no measures of the numbers of drug users in prison generally, so it is not possible to estimate the impact of the programmes, let alone compare one with another. Karen Duke, in her review of prison drug policy since 1980, says the basic punitive framework for delivering the drug strategy remains intact (Duke 2000: 403), i.e. a mixture of control, order and punishment alongside a policy of strengthening supply-side programmes, which mean restricting the entry of drugs into the prison. (It is odd that she should refer to this as a 'punitive framework'; what else is prison for if not punishment?)

Nor is it clear what should be the criteria used to measure that impact, or whether it is possible to determine the extent to which incarceration itself had any overall effect. Reconviction rates and continuing drug use are the most favoured indicators, but these are not always valid, or reliable. The lack of an appropriate comparison group remains a severe constraint. In the absence of a control group it is difficult to determine whether unanticipated bias occurs in selecting the subjects for treatment (Anglin and Hser 1990: 407–8). Furthermore, without comparison groups behavioural changes during and after treatment that result from the passage of time may be wrongly attributed to programme activities.

The range of programmes for prisoners must of necessity be limited, whether due to available facilities, length of stay or the demands of the prison regime. John Burrows *et al.* (2000) reported that the provision of treatment services throughout prison establishments in Britain was uneven, with prisoners reporting that treatment often depended on what was available rather than on treatment needs. A similar picture was painted for through-care facilities. Burrows *et al.* say that drug through-care is characterised by structural impediments where delivery is restricted by disputes over professional boundaries, areas of responsibility and fragile funding. They go on to say that successful schemes are typically the product of one or two charismatic individuals and unusually strong inter-agency partnerships.

Turning now to offenders in the community, we can begin with the most common sanction: the caution. Like the fine, the caution carries no treatment requirement. That means a large number of drug users entering the criminal justice system are not offered treatment, unless, that is, they are offered treatment through arrest referral schemes, which typically provide the names, addresses and contact numbers of drug services either routinely or on request (Hough 1996: 21–2). The take-up rates for these schemes have not been high. Dorn (quoted in Hough 1996: 22) says that one problem is that arrestees may be led to believe, intentionally or otherwise, that they can receive a caution if they attend a treatment programme. He is also concerned that drug workers are a poor substitute for legal advice. Nonetheless, where arrest referral schemes are successful and take offenders out of the criminal justice system into treatment, they are to be welcomed, although Dorn wants a different type of arrest referral scheme which will include dealing with other problems as well as drug abuse.

It is not known how many problem drug users are dealt with by means of a probation order, but it would be reasonable to suppose that would be high – perhaps 30–40 per cent, depending on the geographical area. Nor is there information on the impact of probation on drug offenders generally. A study by Ian Hearnden (2000) involving interviews with a group of 15 Inner London probation officers and 278 drug users reported that there were large reductions in drug use and crime during the period of probation, especially where the probation order included a condition of treatment. Yet although the results give comfort the author cautions against reading too much into them, as the study suffered from sampling and interview bias. The probation officers were largely responsible for generating the samples, whilst the comparison group was drawn from the probation officers' pre-sentence reports. Moreover, the extent of drug use was based on self-report, which is not the most accurate way of determining the impact of supervision. As this study was one of the few trying to determine the impact of a sentence, in this case the probation order, it shows how much further we need to go in any research programme.

Recently (in 1998), the Government introduced the Drug Treatment and Testing Order (DTTO). Community provisions centre around the probation service, with the DTTO, the Government's flagship, derived from the model of American drug courts, but nowhere is there an acknowledgement that this is so. The DTTO adds to the facilities provided by the probation order, with or without a condition of treatment – and, as its name suggests, involves a mixture of treatment and drug testing, backed by periodic reviews by the court. The DTTO is provided for under Sections 61–64 of the Crime and Disorder Act 1998. (Drug testing in prison is carried out under Section 16A of the Prison Act 1952.) It links the treatment services with the criminal justice system in a way that requires the treatment services to work according to criminal justice requirements. It was introduced for a number of reasons, one of which was an attempt to formalise a more controlled approach to drug offenders. Earlier attempts have not always worked. For example, the 1991 Criminal Justice Act gave courts powers to impose treatment as part of a sentence. They were rarely used. The Home Office Probation Inspectorate said this for the following reasons:

- the Home Office and Probation Service adopted a neutral stance, declining to issue guidance;
- probation officers did not believe coerced treatment would work, so were reluctant to recommend it in their pre-sentence reports;
- sentencers lacked information on the treatments available;
- within the criminal justice system treatment providers were unenthusiastic about operating coercive systems.

The DTTO requires an offender to undergo treatment either as part of or in association with an existing community sentence. It will be targeted at serious offenders. The Government says the crucial difference between the DTTO and earlier provisions is that the DTTO provides mandatory drug testing accompanied by a review of the offender's progress in the courts

(Home Office 1998). DTTOs were piloted in three areas in England and Wales, but the Government decided, inexplicably, to introduce them nationally before the evaluation was completed. Had it waited it might have learned things to its advantage, for the results were far from convincing and the defects in procedures enormous. There was no comparison group to test out the impact of the DTTO, and the results, such as existed, were provided through self-report. The urine testing procedures lacked care and rigour, where only one of the sites observed routinely examined the urine samples provided. (American drug testing services start with the slogan 'if you don't see the sample being given, don't bother to give the test'.) Inter-agency working was poorly developed and the three sites had widely different approaches to warnings, breaches and revocation (Turnbull *et al.* 2000).

The probation order and the DTTO remain the main sentences through which offenders in the community can obtain treatment. Little research has been conducted on the use of probation, so that our knowledge base is slim, whether of the service as a referring agency or as an agency undertaking its own treatment. Unless there are radical changes to the way the DTTO operates we should expect little that is positive from that quarter. There remain other possibilities, one of which is to introduce drug courts into England and Wales and thereby follow the example of Scotland.[2]

This brief overview shows the extent of the problem and the range of services available within the criminal justice system. I want now to turn to the main features of the model, which are to link treatment services to criminal justice, supported by a coherent research strategy.

Linking treatment to the criminal justice framework: a model

Research results suggest the following links between drug abuse and crime, all of which have an impact on treatment programmes, whether in or outside the custodial services:

* drug use is both a direct and indirect consequence of crime;
* drug-dependent offenders are specifically responsible for an extraordinary proportion of crime;
* those using heroin or cocaine have the highest rates of all;
* as the severity of drug use increases so does the severity of offending;
* multiple drug users or heroin and cocaine users are at the highest risk of reconviction when leaving prison.

This means that policies for dealing with substance abuse assign a primary responsibility for controlling drug abuse and its behavioural consequences to the criminal justice system. In Britain we have tended to assign treatment services to the criminal justice system along the lines of the Second National Plan (Cabinet Office 2001) – that is, to develop services to deal with an expected rise in the numbers entering treatment who have been referred from the criminal justice system. Presumably the Probation Service will be responsible for making those referrals, the basis of which remains unclear, and presumably on the recommendation of the court – or perhaps referred by someone or from somewhere else. The assumption seems to be that referrals will be made according to some assessed need. Yet without some formal structure it is doubtful whether referrals are likely to be made in any rational way, or, if they are, it is doubtful whether the treatment services are sufficiently tied into the criminal justice system to ensure that the demands of criminal justice are met.

We have a National Treatment Agency, one of whose objectives is to 'ensure an effective interface between treatment settings (e.g. the community, prisons, youth justice) so that clients' needs are not compromised by moving between settings' (Department of Health/Home Office 2001: para. 9.iv). The Drug Action Team (DAT) is to be the conduit through which local treatments are provided, DATs being made up of representatives of the police, probation, social services, etc. Treatment providers are largely ignored in the Consultation Document. That apart, it is difficult to believe that these proposals will produce the appropriate results; more likely, DATs will become another talking shop.

Why should this be so, or why is it likely that the DAT approach will fail? Or, again, why is it that law enforcement and the criminal justice system have a limited success in dealing with drug offenders, most going back to drug abuse on release from prison or continuing abuse whilst on probation? The suggestion by the police for more offenders to be diverted to treatment is entirely laudable, but why will that also fail? The answer is that the schemes suggested do not take into account the basic requirements of a successful model. Those are simply this: that successful treatment depends on treatment services and law enforcement being integrated, and supported by a well-thought-out research programme. That level of integration does not exist in Britain; what is needed is integration at the political level, at the ideological level where each side appreciates what the other is doing, and at the structural level where both sides work together. Nor do we have a research programme that informs treatment services or law enforcement; in fact there is no centrally directed research programme at all.

Why is integration necessary? The answer is that treatment without control and control without treatment will not work. All have to be linked with the programme delivered in such a manner as to demonstrate to all – patients and treatment providers alike – that integration is complete. Each feature is important but of itself cannot produce satisfactory results. It is no good having a treatment programme unless satisfactory supervision is available to back up the programme, and no good having supervision without providing the necessary treatment – and no good having them without a research programme to inform. And to repeat the point, integration must take place at the political, ideological and structural level if it is to work.

There are tried and tested models available, albeit not in the form proposed above, but worth examining nonetheless. For example, there is TASC (Treatment Accountability for Safer Communities) in the USA. TASC began operations in Wilmington, Delaware, in 1972.[3] At its peak in 1981, before Federal funding was withdrawn, there were 130 TASC programmes in 39 states. It has continued under State and local auspices, described by many commentators as the largest and most widely respected organisation of its kind. Its purpose was and still is to serve as a link between the traditional functions of criminal justice and the treatment community. The objective is to provide an effective bridge between two groups with differing philosophies: the justice system and community treatment providers. Whereas the justice system's sanctions reflect community concerns for public safety and punishment, the treatment community recommends therapeutic intervention to change behaviour and reduce the suffering associated with substance abuse and related problems. The basic goal of TASC is to identify offenders in need of drug treatment from within the criminal justice system, and under close supervision to provide community-based treatment as an alternative or supplement to more traditional criminal justice sanctions. TASC is in part a diversion programme, yet also a supervisory programme, for it not only refers drug users from the courts to the appropriate treatment programmes but undertakes supervision, monitors progress whilst in treatment, and links the programmes to the courts. Some TASC programmes undertake the treatment themselves, but that is not a critical element of the standard TASC model. TASC takes offenders sentenced to deferred prosecutions, community sentences, probation and pre-trial services as well as taking those on parole.

TASC programmes make the links, place the offenders, undertake the supervision and monitor progress, whilst acting as a bridge between the courts and treatment. The bridge is required because of the philosophical differences between the two systems. Presumably, in Britain the probation service already acts as a sort of TASC, able to operate in the same manner; but could it, or would it, behave like TASC if required to do so? If so, there is no doubt that community-based treatment services could be linked to the courts, arrest referrals, probation, parole, etc. – i.e. operate in one large all-purpose treatment centre – and be monitored accordingly. The fear is that the probation service does not see the value of enforced treatment, and would not monitor the progress of offenders as vigorously or effectively as required, or conduct supervision as rigorously as required. If this is so, a new TASC like organisation would need to be set up, and that might well be the answer.

I am not saying we in Britain should copy the TASC programme, but even if we did that would be an advance over the present system. The absence of a research strategy is no less worrying; two or three research centres should have been introduced, aimed at providing information about existing programmes and data on various projects. It is hard to see why drug research has been given such a low priority, but it has, and it will be difficult to make up the lost ground.

Some implications of the proposed model

Introducing a model of the type suggested here would involve major changes in the way we treat and deal with drug offenders in Britain. Here I wish to mention two, the first involving giving up some cherished beliefs and the second about the impact of these proposed changes on the criminal justice system itself. These are by no means the only changes; they have been selected to show that introducing this model requires mores than making the decision that the two systems work more closely together.

One of the cherished beliefs that would have to go is that which asserts that treatment will only be provided if the patient seeks it voluntarily. This view, which has been held with little or no research evidence to support it, is one of the shibboleths of the treatment world. It is based on a view of addiction that suggests that unless the patient gives of him- or herself to a treatment programme it will not be successful. In fact the research evidence, albeit American, points to a different conclusion; it is almost the opposite, so that how an individual becomes exposed to treatment is irrelevant in terms of outcome. The important variable is how the drug user is brought into an environment where intervention occurs; the more routes into this environment the better, but some will be coercive routes. The point is that treatment outcomes are not based on the reasons for entering treatment but the length of time one remains in treatment, and the longer the period in treatment the better the outcome. In practice that means the longer a person spends in treatment the greater the number of options there will be, implying too that there will be a greater possibility that one option will be that offenders choose to be abstinent.

Much confusion centres on the term 'coercion', as if there was something sinister about offenders being coerced into treatment (see Chapter 6). The distinction needs to be made between civil commitment as occurs in the USA, where commitment is made by a civil court on the basis that a person is a drug user, without there having been an offence. The point here is concerned only with judicial commitment, i.e. after an offence has been committed. Coercion is a *sine qua non* of the criminal justice system. Yet in a different form it occurs also outside the criminal justice system, for rarely do offenders enter treatment free of all forms of coercion, whether from friends, relatives or others. To talk, therefore, of 'coercion' and compare this unfavourably with 'voluntary' decisions to enter treatment is to be too optimistic about the nature of many drug users' lives.

Treatment retention is an important contributor to treatment effectiveness. If an individual leaves treatment within a few days it is unlikely that treatment has permanently changed the characteristics or conditions that are related to his or her drug problem (Hubbard *et al.* 1988). The rule of thumb is that 60 days is the optimum time; anything less and the chances of success are greatly reduced. Court orders which coerce patients into treatment will not of themselves guarantee success; the skills of the treatment personnel, which hold the patient's interest and attention, are as, if not more, important. Debates about coercion are out of place in their way; coercion may be appropriate at the stage when the offender enters treatment but of less importance when it comes to keeping him or her there. (Women, incidentally, are much less likely to enter treatment through the courts, but on the recommendation of the personal social services. Coercion for women is a less significant matter than for men.) The insistence that offenders enter treatment as volunteers undermines the whole notion of treatment within the criminal justice system and provides a barrier to more effective communication between the two systems.

A closer working partnership with the courts will inevitably involve a loss of independence for the treatment agencies, and with it a more strait-jacketed theoretical approach to treatment. (Hitherto treatment services have provided a fertile ground for ideologies, not always to their advantage. For example, when discussing the DARE (Drug Abuse Resistance Education) programme we found DARE attracted considerable hostility, even though many who were most hostile had not read the evaluations of DARE or did not know a great deal about the methodological strengths and weaknesses of the various evaluations.) Treatment agencies could well finish up subcontracted to the criminal justice system in ways which are already happening but are likely to increase in the short and long term. Independent agencies will be increasingly dependent on criminal justice contracts for their survival – again, a process already in its early stages. Yet there are advantages, not least an increase in contracts, which many voluntary agencies will be able to exploit.

Also, there are advantages to working within criminal justice; in drug courts, for example, treatment providers talk of working in a more exhilarating environment where the standards of work are higher than hitherto.

The treatment of drug users within criminal justice reintroduces rehabilitation into the criminal justice system in new forms and with renewed energy. Traditional forms of rehabilitation were practised extensively up to the late 1970s but lost much of their appeal. They were replaced by a 'just deserts' model more akin to the times. Rehabilitation was criticised for two main reasons: first, the research results were poor, leading to the view that 'nothing works'; second, rehabilitation contained within it some less than palatable matters. One of its most potent critics was the American Friends Service Committee, which said 'there was compelling evidence that the individualised treatment model, the ideal to which reformers have been urging us for at least a century, is theoretically faulty, systematically discriminatory in practice and inconsistent with some of our basic concepts of justice' (1971: 12). It was theoretically faulty because crime was based on a medical model of disease; it was systematically discriminatory because it was directed more at those from poorer backgrounds; and it was inconsistent with justice because the offence was only a symptom, so that the length of the sentence was based on the offenders 'needs', an imprecise and subjective concept.

This is not the place to enter a full critique of the Rehabilitative Ideal, for that has been done elsewhere (Bean 1976; Allen 1964). As part of the accusation that rehabilitation was theoretically faulty, rehabilitation – or reform (the terms can be used interchangeably) – was criticised, *inter alia*, because of the extensive and unbridled powers given to those providing treatment. It was they who decided when treatment was complete and, accordingly, when the offender was to be released or discharged. Also it used language which allowed it to merge treatment with punishment in ways that deceived those who were being punished. So, 'punishments' became 'adjustments' or 'forms of assistance', where, if the aim was not intentionally to deceive, it came close to it.

With the emphasis on treatment, rehabilitation has re-emerged, albeit in different circumstances, but with the same potential to be criticised as before. Its current prominence is entirely a result of the demand to do something about the large numbers of drug users who appear before the courts, many of whom are incarcerated. It is also driven by the recent belief that 'treatment works', and more positive research findings than hitherto that reveal the effectiveness of drug abuse treatment (Lipton 1995). There remain the same dangers, or rather the same lessons to be learned from that earlier period. The most important is that whenever treatment and criminal justice systems work in harmony the tendency is for them to overreach themselves and intrude too closely into the offenders' personal lives. Treatment and criminal justice produce a heady mixture, so that where treatment services and criminal justice work together the result has not always been to the benefit of those receiving treatment. Civil rights tend to be trampled upon in the eagerness to extend treatment.

Already the danger signs are there; directing attention at the novice drug user may be justified on the basis that it will save resources later on, but the danger of net-widening is also present. Reducing the parole opportunities for drug users is discriminatory. As treatment services develop we should expect more and more power to be given to the treatment providers, and a corresponding loss of interest in procedural rules and legal rights. We should expect, too, that the 'thank-you' theory of psychiatry will be increasingly invoked; this theory operates on the basis that when the patient is cured he or she will thank the therapist even though the patient was an unwilling participant in the programme at the time. We should also guard against attempts to subvert the language. Prison remains a prison; it is not a therapeutic institution. Treatment accompanies punishment; treatment does not operate independently of punishment; nor does it replace punishment. Moreover, we should guard against any belief that decisions are made on the basis of treatment, not on the basis of justice. In that way it may then be possible for treatment and criminal justice to work together.

Conclusion

This latter point is important, as it highlights a key feature of treatment programmes within criminal justice. What is known about success in treatment is that it is related to the control exercised over the offender during the programme, so that, paradoxically, the treatment itself becomes less important than the treatment regime. Weaknesses occur when patients perceive inconsistency or discover that treatment programmes fail to implement their philosophy adequately. Most of all, failure occurs when the offender (patient) does not experience appropriate pressure to maintain compliance. Positive controls are essential when the offender is in treatment. On this basis it is not surprising that DTTOs received such a poor evaluation, and unless these matters are resolved, which seem unlikely given some anecdotal reports of the way DTTOs operate nationwide, they will fail. If the control system is unclear there is every reason to suspect that the offenders (patients) will exploit this to their advantage.

Hence the value of the model proposed here.

Notes

1   The new Criminal Justice and Court Services Bill currently before the House of Lords extends government thinking on treatment, insofar as it relies on detection and control of those who take drugs. It says,

> Identifying drug misusing offenders at every stage in the criminal justice system is now a prime objective of the crime reduction strategy and will make an important contribution to the overall drug strategy.
> (House of Commons, para. 28, Explanatory Notes, Criminal Justice and Court Services Bill, HMSO)

Under Clauses 40–42, 48, 49, 51 and 52 additional powers are given to require offenders and alleged offenders to be drug tested at various points in their contact with the criminal justice system. These are at a cost of national implementation of £45. 5 million, of which £20 million will be police costs (paras 133 and 134). In other words, a sizeable proportion of the budget for drug abuse goes on reducing the supply side. There will also be the Drug Abstinence Order, requiring the offender to refrain from misusing class A drugs and to undertake a drug test on instruction. Pre-sentence drug testing will also be introduced.

2   Drug courts were introduced into the USA in 1989 in Florida. A decade or so later there were drug courts in every state in the USA and they had been introduced into Australia, Eire and Canada. Numerous other countries, including Malta, Bermuda and Brazil, want to introduce them shortly. The drug court in Scotland started in November 2001 in Glasgow as a pilot scheme with the possibility that the scheme will be extended if proved successful. There are no immediate plans to introduce them into England and Wales; the DTTO is the Government's favoured option, but presumably when that is seen not to be working successfully the Government will finally accept the inevitable and drug courts will be introduced throughout the UK.

Briefly, drug courts can be defined as a slow-track court-based treatment programme which involves placing eligible offenders under the jurisdiction of the court for up to 12 months or two years (Bean 1996). Unlike the controls for the DTTO, in drug court control of the offender is exercised directly through the court, which also controls the treatment programme. There are likely to be a wide range of programmes offering a wide range of treatments, which often are subject to frequent drug tests, involving daily contact with the treatment agencies. The treatment programmes offer educational, vocational, medical and other support services, including acupuncture. Unlike the DTTO, sanctions are clear, swift and certain; drug courts operate on the basis that treatment must be supported by controls, and that those controls are best exercised through the court. I have argued elsewhere (Bean 1996) that, whilst drug courts may not be the panacea for all the problems that flesh is heir to, at least they should be tried and evaluated. It would be best if they were to be tested out in two or three city courts, preferably with stipendiary magistrates, and then evaluated. This is what is happening in Scotland. Drug courts are able to take those difficult repeat offenders who are not acceptable for probation or the DTTO. The task of drug court is to treat the untreatable; that is their strength (Bean 2001).

3   The Associate Director of TASC puts it this way:

> TASC provides a bridge between the criminal justice system which employs legal sanctions that reflect community concerns for public safety which emphasises therapeutic relationships as a means for changing individual behaviour and reducing substance abuse and other problems.
>
> (Cook and Weinman 1988)

There have been several evaluations of TASC programmes over the past 15 years, all showing that they are generally effective in reducing drug abuse and criminal activity, and establishing useful links between criminal justice and the treatment systems. These evaluations show that TASC successfully identifies and assesses substance abusers within the criminal justice system. There is a move to extend the TASC model and make TASC responsible for identifying the multiple treatment needs of criminal justice clients. It would then make and monitor the appropriate referrals to drug treatment, or other services able to provide comprehensive care – this in response to a greater awareness of the multiple problems presented by many long-term drug users. The earlier TASC approach, which simply treated the addiction, is now seen as too simple. Contemporary drug users typically have poor employment records, low educational attainment, poor social skills, etc., and these need attention alongside the substance abuse.

References

Allen, F. A. (1964) *The Borderland of Criminal Justice*, Chicago: University of Chicago Press.

American Friends Service Committee (1971) *Struggle for Justice*, New York: Hill and Wang.

Anglin, M. D. and Hser, Y.-I. (1990) 'Treatment of Drug Abuse', in M. Tonry and J. Q. Wilson (eds) *Drugs and Crime*, Chicago: University of Chicago Press.

Bean, P. T. (1976) *Rehabilitation and Deviance*, London: Routledge and Kegan Paul

Bean, P. T. (1995) 'The Effectiveness in Sentencing Drug Misusers', mimeo.

Bean, P. T. (1996) 'America's Drug Courts: A New Development in Criminal Justice', *Criminal Law Review* (October): 718–21.

Bean, P. T. (2001) *Drugs and Crime*, Cullompton, Devon: Willan Publishing

234 *Philip Bean*

Bennett, T. (1998) *Drugs and Crime: The Results of Research on Drug Testing and Interviewing Arrestees*, Home Office Research Study no. 183, London: Home Office.

Burrows, J., Clarke, A., Davison, T., Tarling, R. and Webb, S. (2000) *The Nature and Effectiveness of Drugs Throughcare for Released Prisoners*, Home Office Research Findings no. 109, London: Home Office.

Cabinet Office (2000) *Tackling Drugs to Build a Better Britain*, London: Cabinet Office.

Cabinet Office (2001) *Tackling Drugs to Build a Better Britain*, Second National Plan, London: Cabinet Office.

Chaiken, J. M. and Chaiken, M. R. (1990) 'Drugs and Predatory Crime', in M. Tonry and J. Q. Wilson (eds) *Drugs and Crime*, Chicago: University of Chicago Press.

Cook, L. F. and Weinman, B. A. (1988) 'Treatment Alternatives to Street Crime', in C. G. Leukefeld and F. M. Tims (eds) *Compulsory Treatment of Drug Abuse: Research and Clinical Practice*, Washington, DC: NIDA.

Cope, N. (2000) 'Drug Use in Prison: The Experience of Young Offenders', *Drugs Education Prevention and Policy* 7(4): 355–66.

Corkery, J. M. (1998) *Statistics of Drug Seizures and Offenders Dealt With*, UK Statistical Bulletin Issue 10/1998, London: Home Office Research and Statistics Directorate.

Corkery, J. M. (2000) 'The Nature and Extent of Drug Misuse in the United Kingdom – Official Statistics Surveys and Studies', mimeo.

Department of Health (1999) *Drug Misuse and Dependence – Guidelines on Clinical Management*, London: HMSO.

Department of Health/Home Office (2001) *The National Treatment Agency for Substance Misuse. A Consultation Document*, London: Department of Health/Home Office.

Drug Prevention and Advisory Service (DPAS) (1999) *Drug Intervention in the Criminal Justice System. A Guidance Manual*, London: Home Office.

Duke, K. (2000) 'Prison Drugs Policy since 1980', *Drugs Education Prevention and Policy* 7(4): 393–407.

Gebelein, R. S. (2000) *The Rebirth of Rehabilitation: Promises and Perils of Drug Courts*, Washington, DC: National Institute of Justice.

Hearnden, I. (2000) 'Problem Drug Use and Probation in London', *Drugs Education Prevention and Policy* 7(4): 367–80.

HM Government (1995) *Tackling Drugs Together. A Strategy for England* (Lord President of the Council and Leader of the House of Commons, the Secretary of State for the Home Department, the Secretary of State for Health, the Secretary of State for Education and the Paymaster General), London: HMSO.

HM Government (1998) *Tackling Drugs Together to Build a Better Britain: The Government's Ten Year Strategy for Tackling Drug Misuse*, London: HMSO.

HM Prison Service (1998) *The Review of the Prison Service Drug Strategy. Drug Misuse in Prison*, London: HM Prison Service.

Home Office (1998) *Drug Treatment and Testing Order: Background and Issues for Consultation*, London: Home Office

Hough, M. (1996) *Drug Misuse and the Criminal Justice System: A Review of the Literature*, Home Office DPI Paper 15, London: Home Office.

House of Commons (2000) *Criminal Justice and Court Services Bill. Explanatory Notes*, London: HMSO.

Hubbard, R. L., Collins, J. J., Valley Rachel, J. and Cavanaugh, E. R. (1988) 'The Criminal Justice Client in Drug Abuse Treatment', in C. G. Leukefeld and F. M. Tims (eds) *Compulsory Treatment of Drug Abuse; Research and Clinical Practice*, London: NIDA.

Lipton, D. S. (1995) *The Effectiveness of Treatment for Drug Abusers under Criminal Justice Supervision*, Washington, DC: National Institute of Justice, US Department of Justice.

MacCoun, R. and Reuter, P. (1998) 'Drug Control', in M. Tonry (ed.) *The Handbook of Crime and Punishment*, Oxford: Oxford University Press.

Ministerial Drugs Task Force (1995) *Drugs in Scotland: Meeting the Challenge*, Edinburgh: Scottish Home and Health Department.

National Institute on Drug Abuse (n.d.) *Principles of Drug Addiction Treatment. A Research based Guide*, Washington, DC: NIDA.

Royal College of Psychiatrists (2000) *Drugs. Dilemmas and Choices*, London: Gaskell.

Task Force to Review Services for Drug Misusers (1996) *Report of an Independent Review of Drug Treatment Services in England*, London: Department of Health.

Turnbull, P. J., McSweeney, T., Webster, R., Edmunds, M. and Hough, M. (2000) *Drug Treatment and Testing Orders: Final Evaluation Report*, Research Study 212, London: Home Office.

Welsh Office (1998) *Forward Together. A Strategy to Combat Drug and Alcohol Misuse in Wales*, Cardiff: Welsh Office.

13 Motivation enhancement in clients referred from the criminal justice system

Joris Casselman

Introduction

In January 2001 the Belgium government published a comprehensive Note on Federal Drug Policy (Belgian Federal Government 2001). The matter which caught most attention, nationally and internationally, was the government's attitude towards cannabis. It is proposed that in Belgium the possession of cannabis by adults for their own use will no longer be prosecuted.

This, however, is only one of a number of items in that policy note. Another is aimed at improving co-operation between the criminal justice system and the drug treatment services. We were asked by the Minister of public health to produce with co-workers a report on that issue. It has 25 recommendations and was finalised early in 2002 (Casselman *et al.* 2002). One of three major areas of concern examined in the report was the limited motivation of clients referred from the criminal justice system. The three main topics discussed were as follows:

1 It was stressed that the criminal justice system and the drug treatment system came from two different worlds with different objectives. They do not know each other's work, they speak different languages, and do not trust each other. The interface between the two systems is a grey area (Casselman 1998).

2 There is the delicate matter of confidentiality, especially where it involves circulating information between one system and the other. Many professionals have not been trained to handle such matters in their daily practice.

3 When clients are sent to the drug treatment system their motivation is often poor, and they risk falling between two stools. Traditional therapists consider these types of clients as being coerced into therapy by external pressures, therefore lacking the necessary motivation. The message here, however, is that if clients are not motivated to treatment the first task of the treatment professional is not to send them away because they do not fit, but to enhance their motivation towards more realistic objectives. This is called a pre-treatment strategy. Motivation

enhancement is a low-level treatment approach often better adapted to the real needs of drug clients referred for treatment.

The aim here is to ask two questions; what is motivation for treatment; and what are the possible directions of motivation enhancement in the context of drug users referred from the criminal justice system.

First, motivation for treatment. This is often considered in a rather narrow perspective (Marlatt and Gordon 1985; Miller and Rollnick 1991; Casselman 1996, 2002). Motivation for treatment exists on a continuum. It is not a black and white phenomenon as if, like a lamp, it is either on or off. The continuum ranges from full internal to full external motivation, with all possible nuances in between. It is more like a dimmer lamp that can be adjusted to give many different intensities of light from dark to bright.

There are many factors which influence motivation. It is a complex process, as one would expect for any kind of change, even that which has very limited goals such as in harm reduction. An important, albeit neglected factor, is the style of the treatment professional, which can greatly influence the client's motivation. Many professionals also need to be motivated to work with poorly motivated clients. Motivation is also a dynamic process rather than a once and forever fixed individual characteristic. It is not like a rigid personality trait but found in the client's readiness for change. It can fluctuate and, most important, it can be influenced.

Motivation enhancement is not only important as a starter – that is, before engaging in the treatment process – but should be considered of permanent concern throughout. Moreover, it should be considered a complementary strategy to relapse prevention, which is also a basic strategy. Accordingly, motivation enhancement and relapse prevention must go hand in hand. Motivation enhancement becomes a fascinating experience. In a recent publication we described how to combine motivation enhancement and relapse prevention; we see it like a risky but fascinating trip to a tropical island. In our experience introducing this combined strategy in a treatment programme not only produces a better client approach but also helps avoid burnout among the drug treatment professionals (Casselman 1996).

The second question is what are the possible directions of motivation enhancement in the context of those drug users referred from the criminal justice system. This is motivation enhancement as applied to daily practice. Numerous intervention strategies are available. The best known is the motivational interviewing strategy as applied by Miller and co-workers to clients with alcohol-related problems (Miller and Rollnick 1991). Later it was extended to other target groups (Baker and Dixon 1991; Garland and Dougher 1991; Saunders et al 1991; Van Bilsen 1991). This motivational interviewing approach was found to be useful in stimulating motivation for change for those clients referred from the criminal justice system. It was found also that it was relatively easy to integrate this special kind of counselling style into a more comprehensive treatment programme.

Another form of the same approach involves prisoners taking a written course whilst awaiting conditional release. It was first introduced in the pre-treatment of sexual deviants, who often had very persistent cognitive distortions. The programme involved a course of 10 exercises with written feedback from the supervisors (Vanhoeck and Van Daele 1999). This method has also been applied in the pre-treatment of drug users.

If we limit ourselves to some of the basic issues in motivational inter-viewing strategy, we refer to what has been called the wheel of change or the revolving door. This was developed by James Prochaska and Carlo DiClemente in their study of a large number of smokers (Prochaska and DiClemente 1986; Prochaska *et al.* 1992). This model helps us understand why people change either as a result of assistance by a counsellor or through their own efforts. Here people pass through a series of stages in the course of change. This is called the wheel of change or the revolving door, as they go around several times before achieving stability. At every moment relapse is possible. The client must be placed in one of the stages as the type of approach adopted depends on where the client is situated. There are six stages:

1   *The pre-contemplation or vestibule stage:* in fact this stage lies outside the revolving door, where clients stay in a kind of vestibule before entering the real motivation process. They are not yet able to consider change. Others, such as family, friends, general practitioners, the police, judges or their boss, will be convinced something drastic needs to be done to avoid disaster. When clients are referred under coercion they will be defensive at first and refuse to acknowledge that they have a problem. Others might accept that they have to face their problems but not accept that they are related to drug use.

2   *The contemplation stage, or stage of doubt:* in this second stage clients consider and reject change. They go back and forth between finding reasons for concern and providing justifications for not being concerned. They adopt these extreme positions simultaneously or in rapid alterna-tion.

3   *Determination or decision:* at a certain point in time some clients will suddenly decide they have to change, but this does not mean they take appropriate action there and then. Some take months or years before doing so. It is a window of opportunity that stays open for a limited period of time, and if during this period the client takes action the process of change continues. If not, the client is stuck in stage three for a long time or relapse occurs.

4   *Action:* in this stage the client engages in particular actions to bring about change. Some do not need professional assistance; they do it on their own. Most, however, need specific counselling.

5   *Maintenance:* the main challenge in this stage is to sustain any change and prevent relapse.

6 *Relapse:* this is what can be expected in each stage during a process of change. It can be a limited lapse hopefully neutralised by a quick relapse intervention. But even if it is a full relapse it should not be seen as wholly negative, as a great deal can be learned to prevent future relapses. A relapse does not mean only a relapse into drugs, but also relapse into injecting or using dirty injection materials.

General principles

The most original aspect of Miller's motivational interviewing is a sophisticated combination of mainly non-directive and some directive elements in the interactions with clients (Miller and Rollnick 1991). It is often necessary to divide up the main goal into a set of more realistic limited goals and to try to make step-by-step progress, sometimes with very small steps. It is essential to help the client decide if change is wanted and what kind, and to tackle that first, and then help the client reach a very limited goal. The five general principles are as follows:

1 *To Express sympathy:* a style of empathic warmth and reflective listening as described by Carl Rogers is employed from the very beginning and lasts throughout. The counsellor seeks to understand the client's perspectives and feelings without judging or blaming. Acceptance is not the same thing as agreement or approval. It is obvious that an attitude of unconditional acceptance and respect facilitates change.

2 *Increase discrepancy:* this involves creating and amplifying a discrepancy between where the client is and where the client wants to be. When behaviour conflicts with important personal goals (such as health, success, family happiness or self-image) change is likely to occur. But clients in this stage of treatment are ambivalent. If the client is in doubt it is important not to try to convince him or her with objective arguments but set out both sides of the argument. If this is successful it is not the client but the counsellor who expresses concern.

3 *Avoid argumentation:* the least productive situation is one in which the counsellor is arguing that the client has a problem and needs to change, with the client defending the opposite viewpoint. When resistance is encountered the counsellor should use another approach. For example, trying to force a client to accept the stigmatising label of addict can be counterproductive. Too often counsellors fight clients rather than trying to make them more prone to change.

4 *Roll with resistance:* some commentators call this 'psychological judo'. An attack by the opponent is not met with direct opposition (as in boxing); rather, the attacker tries to turn the movement to his or her own benefit. It is not a matter of winning or losing. The analogy of 'rolling with resistance' is useful; it is not a passive strategy but an active one.

5   *Stimulate self-efficacy:* self-efficacy is the client's belief in his or her ability to carry out and succeed in a specific task. A general goal must be to increase the client's perception of his or her ability to cope with obstacles and to succeed in change. No one else can do it. The client is responsible for choosing and carrying out personal change.

Some stage-specific aspects

For each stage some specific interventions can be made. Here are some examples:

1   *The pre-contemplation or vestibule stage:* what can you do if the client is convinced there is no problem? The message is: keep in contact! Ask the client to agree to at least three more sessions in order to collect more information. It can be introduced as a kind of check-up in order to provide a final evaluation at the end of the last session. And what if the link with substance abuse is not clear? Then ask the client to do some homework, such as recording each time he or she used substances in the last seven days, or note when were they used, and what were the costs? In this way the results can be examined at the next meeting. The aim is to raise doubts, to increase the client's perception of risks and problems associated with the use of drugs. This type of information could be used help raise the client's awareness.
2   *Contemplation or doubt:* it is useful and stimulating to make up a cost–benefit analysis of positive and negative motives about whether to change or not to change. The pros and cons can be considered over a short or long period of time. Good things and not so good things are put together in this way, which can be very helpful in discovering subtle factors influencing resistance to change.
3   *Determination or decision:* in this stage it is recommended that to help the client it is necessary to find a strategy that is acceptable, appropriate and effective – in other words, help the client to determine the best course of action in seeking change.
4   *Action:* here it is a matter of helping the client to take concrete steps towards producing change in the problem area.
5   *Maintenance:* the challenge here is to sustain that change and help the client identify and use strategies to prevent relapse.
6   *Relapse:* in this stage discouragement and demoralisation are to be avoided. It is important to avoid going round that revolving door again and also to avoid being stuck in the relapse stage.

Conclusion

If clients referred from the criminal justice system to the treatment system are not sufficiently well motivated for treatment, it is the task of the drug treatment professional to produce a step-by-step process of 'motivation enhancement'.

References

Baker, A. and Dixon, J. (1991) 'Motivational Interviewing for HIV Risk Reduction', in W. R. Miller and S. Rollnick (eds) *Motivational Interviewing: Preparing People to Change Addictive Behaviour*, New York and London: Guilford Press.

Belgian Federal Government (2001) *Beleidsnota van de Federale Regering in verband met de drugproblematiek can 19 januari 2001/Note politique du Gouvernement fédéral relative à la problématique de la drogue du 19 janvier 2001*, Brussels: Belgian Federal Government.

Casselman, J. (1996) *Met vallen en opstaan. Motivatiebevordering en terugvalpreventie bij alcohol- en andere drugproblemen* [Motivation enhancement and relapse prevention in alcohol- and other drug-related problems], Leuven: Apeldoorn, Garant.

Casselman, J. (1998) 'Grey Area between the Criminal Justice System and the Drug Treatment System in Belgium', paper read at European Harm Reduction Conference, Utrecht, the Netherlands, 3–5 June.

Casselman, J. (2002) 'Motivation Enhancement in Clients Referred from the Criminal Justice System to the Drug Treatment System', paper read at Caecere Misure e Cure Alternative Comunità, Milan, 14–16 March.

Casselman, J., Noirfalise, A., Meuwissen, K. and Maisse, L. (2002) *Justitie-Hulpverlening: duidelijke afsprakan/Justice-Assistence: des accords clairs* [Justice assistance: clear agreements], Brussels: Ministerie van Consumentenzaken, Volksgezondheid en Leefmilieu/Ministère de la Protection de la Consommation, de la Santé Publique et de l'Environnement; available at minsoc.fgov.be.

Garland, R. J. and Dougher, M. (1991) 'Motivational Intervention in the Treatment of Sex Offenders', in W. R. Miller and S. Rollnick (eds) *Motivational Interviewing: Preparing People to Change Addictive Behaviour*, New York and London: Guilford Press.

Marlatt, G. A. and Gordon, J. R. (eds) (1985) *Relapse Prevention. Maintenance Strategies in the Treatment of Addictive Behaviours*, New York: Guilford Press.

Miller, W. R. and Rollnick, S. (eds) (1991) *Motivational Interviewing: Preparing People to Change Addictive Behaviour*, New York and London: Guilford Press.

Prochaska, J. O. and DiClemente, C. C. (1986) 'Towards a Comprehensive Model of Change', in W. R. Miller and N. Heather (eds) *Treating Addictive Behaviour: Process of Change*, New York: Plenum Press.

Prochaska, J. O., DiClemente, C. C. and Norcross, J. C. (1992) 'In Search of How People Change: Applications to Addictive Disorders', *American Psychologist* 47: 1,102–14.

Saunders, B., Wilkinson, C. and Allsop, S. (1991) 'Motivational Intervention with Heroin Users Attending a Methodone Clinic', in W. R. Miller and S. Rollnick (eds) *Motivational Interviewing: Preparing People to Change Addictive Behaviour*, New York and London: Guilford Press.

Van Bilsen, H. P. J. G. (1991) 'Motivational Interviewing: Perspectives from the Netherlands, with Particular Emphasis on Heroin-dependent Clients', in W. R. Miller and S. Rollnick (eds) *Motivational Interviewing: Preparing People to Change Addictive Behaviour*, New York and London: Guilford Press.

Vanhoeck, C. and Van Daele, E. (1999) *Werkboek daderhulp. Therapie bij seksueek misbruik* [Help for offenders workbook. Treatment in sexual abuse], Leuven: Amersfoort, Acco.

Index